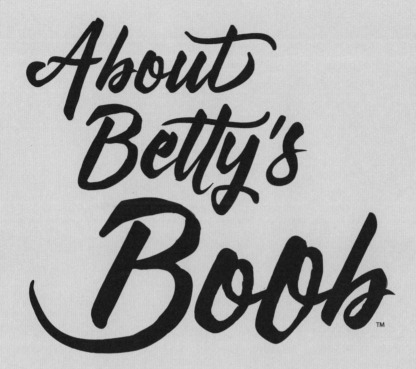

About Betty's Boob

Published by
ARCHAIA™

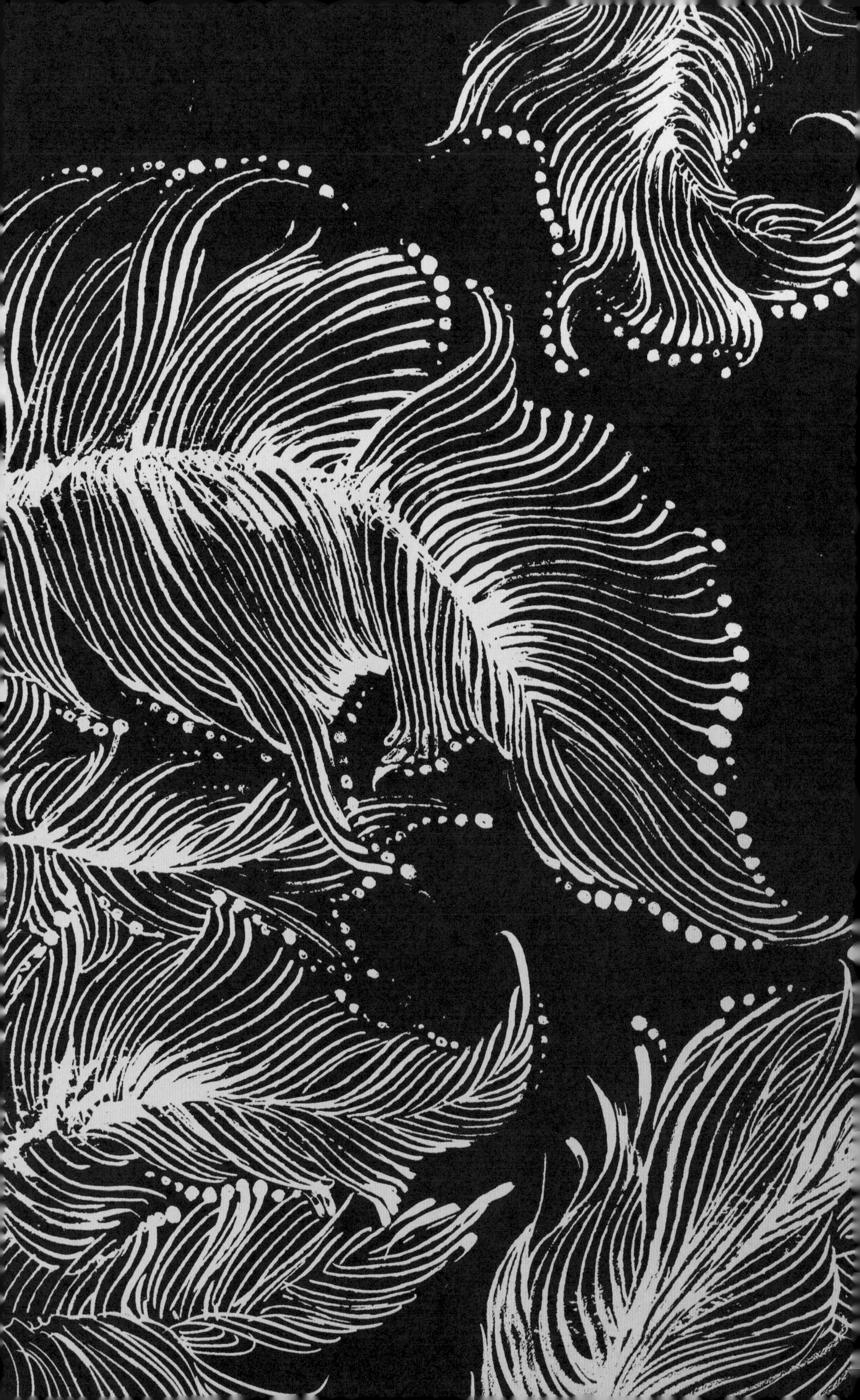

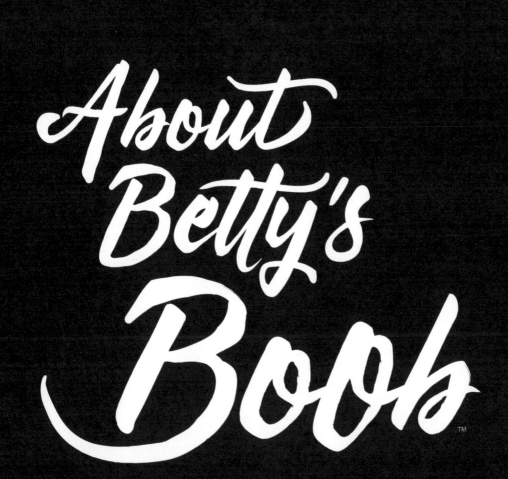

About Betty's Boob ™

Written by
VERO CAZOT

Illustrated by
JULIE ROCHELEAU

Translated by
EDWARD GAUVIN

Lettered by
DERON BENNETT

ARCHAIA
LOS ANGELES, CALIFORNIA

Cover by **JULIE ROCHELEAU**

ENGLISH EDITION
Designer **JILLIAN CRAB**
Assistant Editor **AMANDA LaFRANCO**
Editor **SIERRA HAHN**

ARCHAIA™

ABOUT BETTY'S BOOB, June 2018. Published by Archaia, a division of Boom Entertainment, Inc. About Betty's Boob is ™ and © 2017 Casterman. Originally published in France by Casterman as Betty Boob. ™ and © 2017 Casterman.

BOOM! Studios, 5670 Wilshire Boulevard, Suite 400, Los Angeles, CA 90036-5679. Printed in China. First Printing.

ISBN 978-1-68415-164-6, eISBN 978-1-61398-949-4

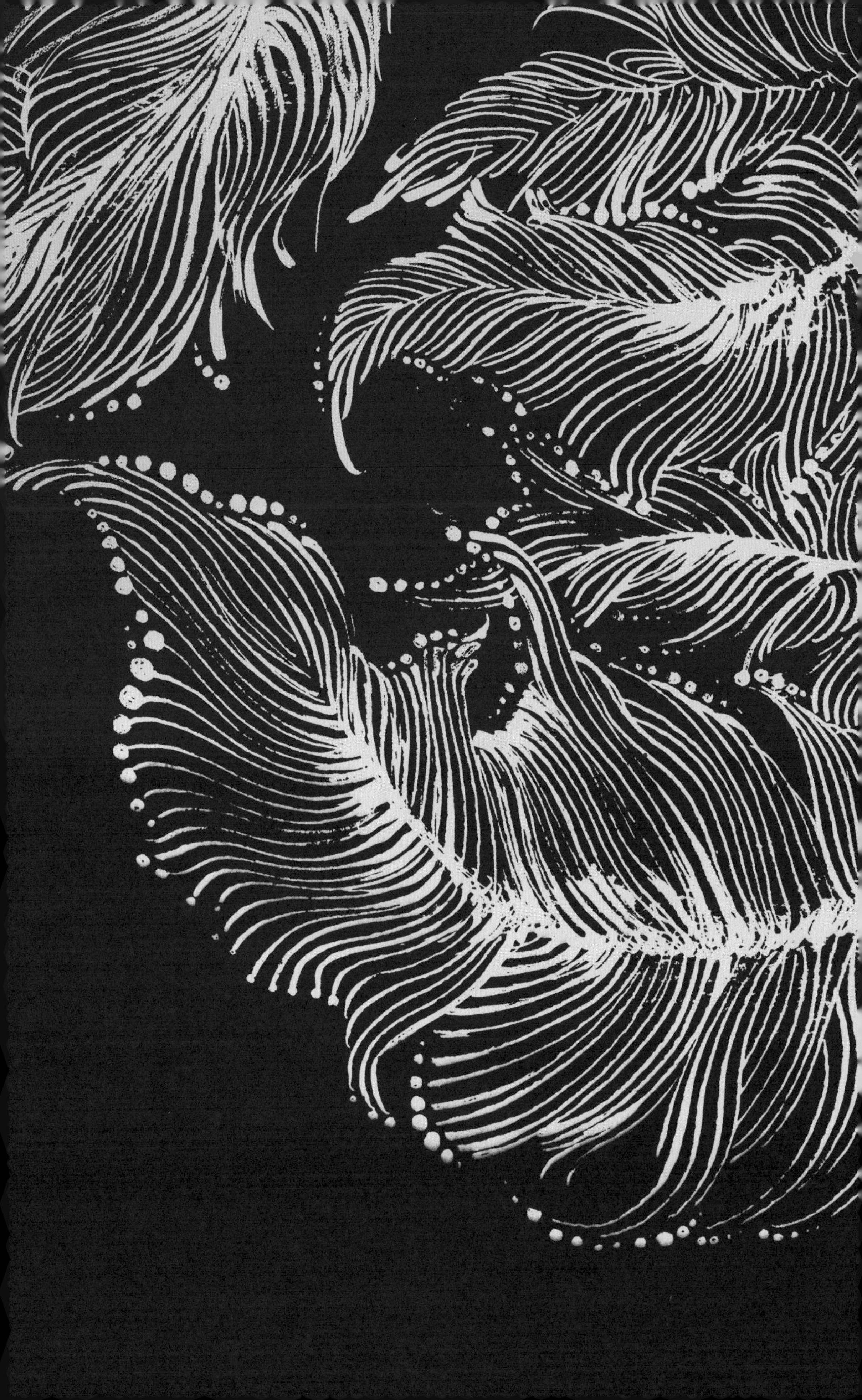

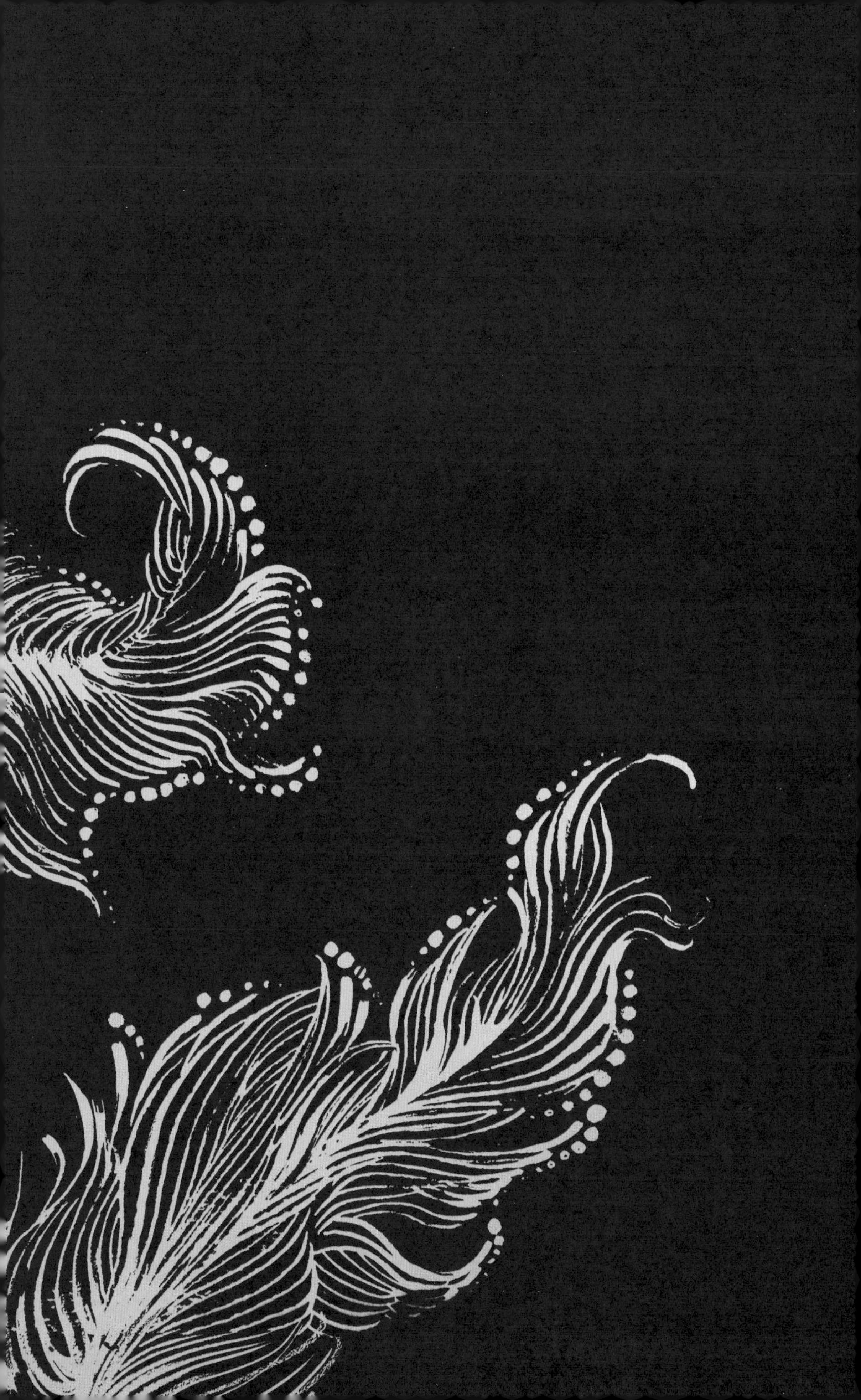

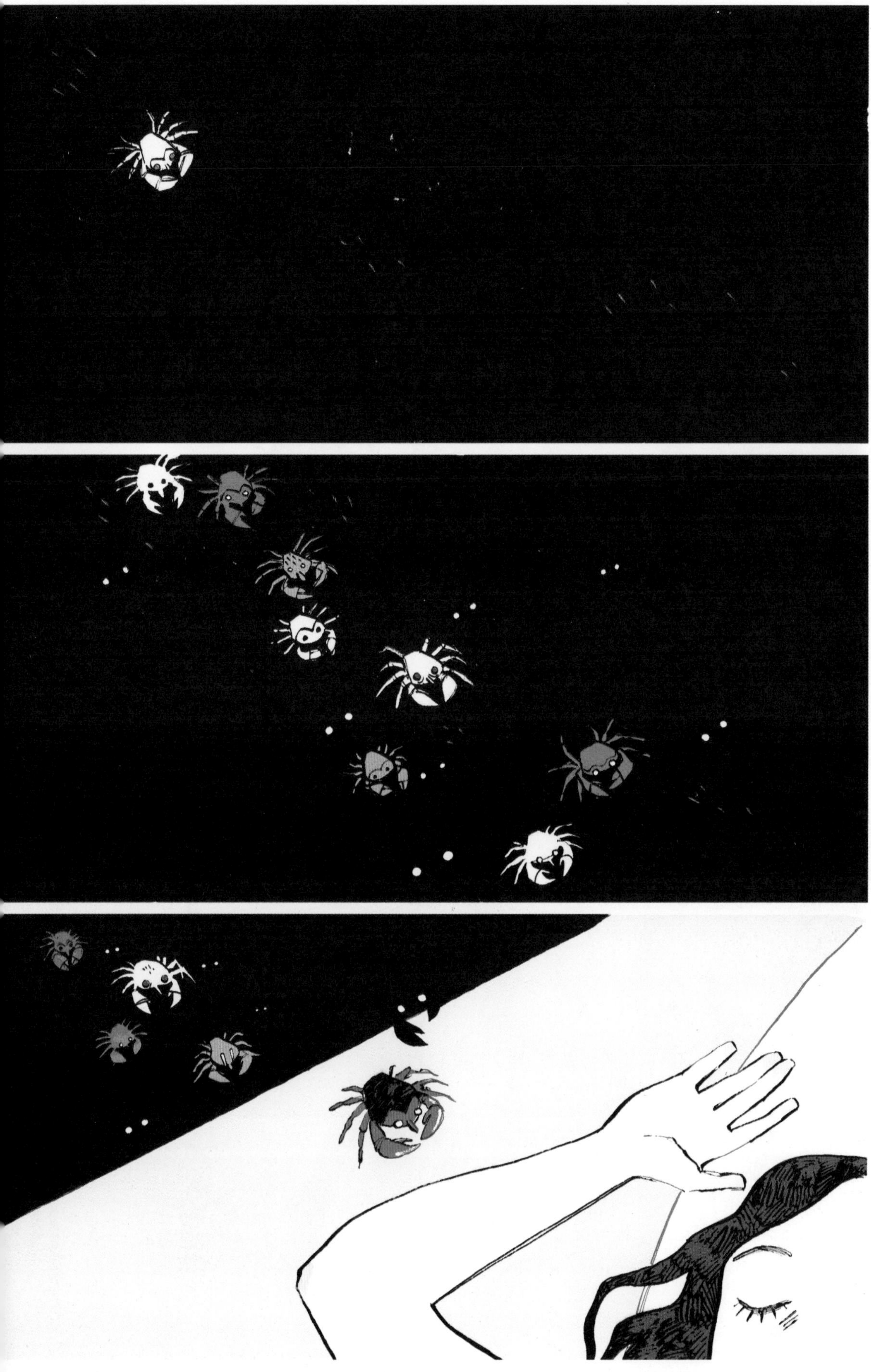

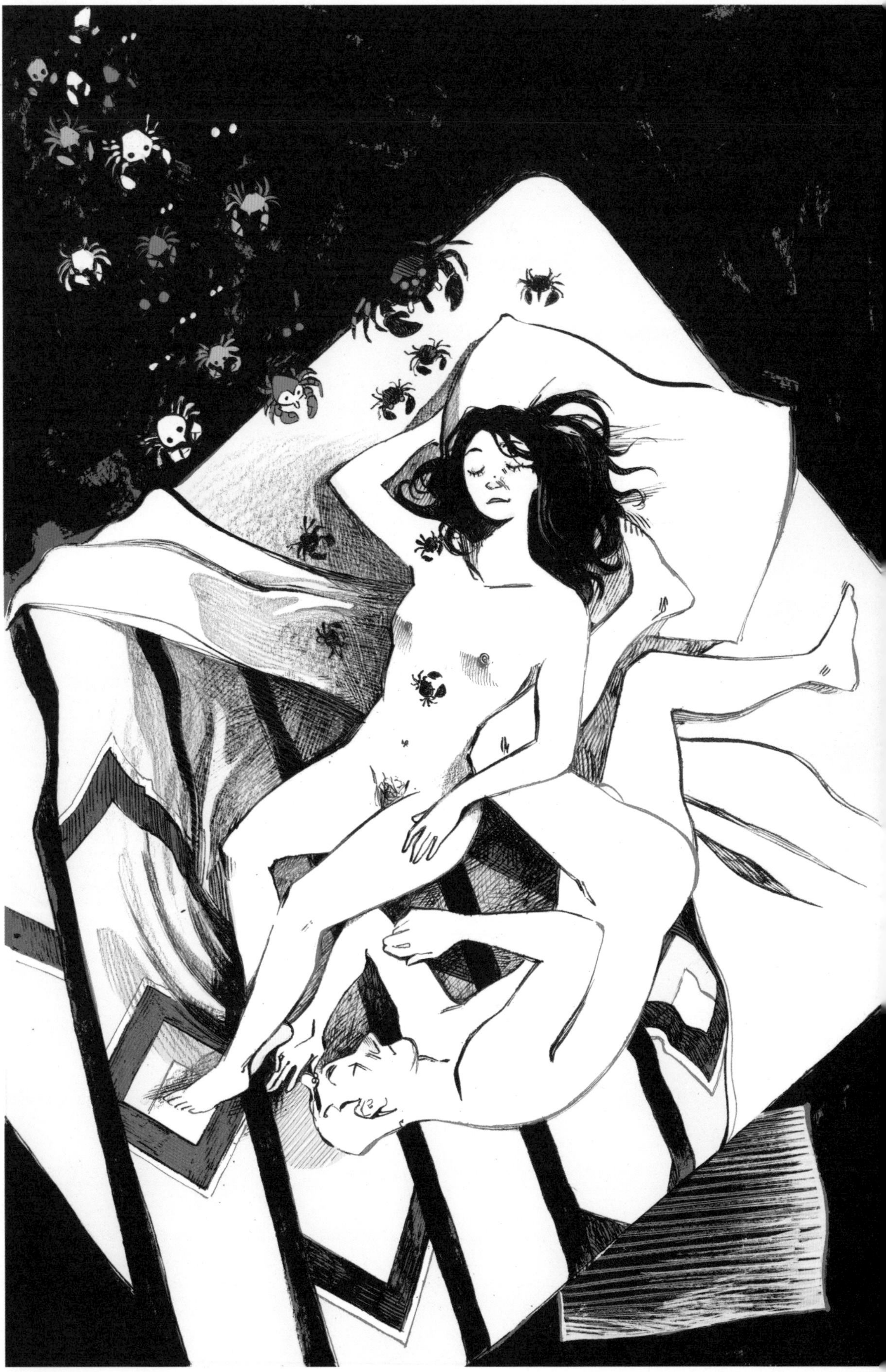

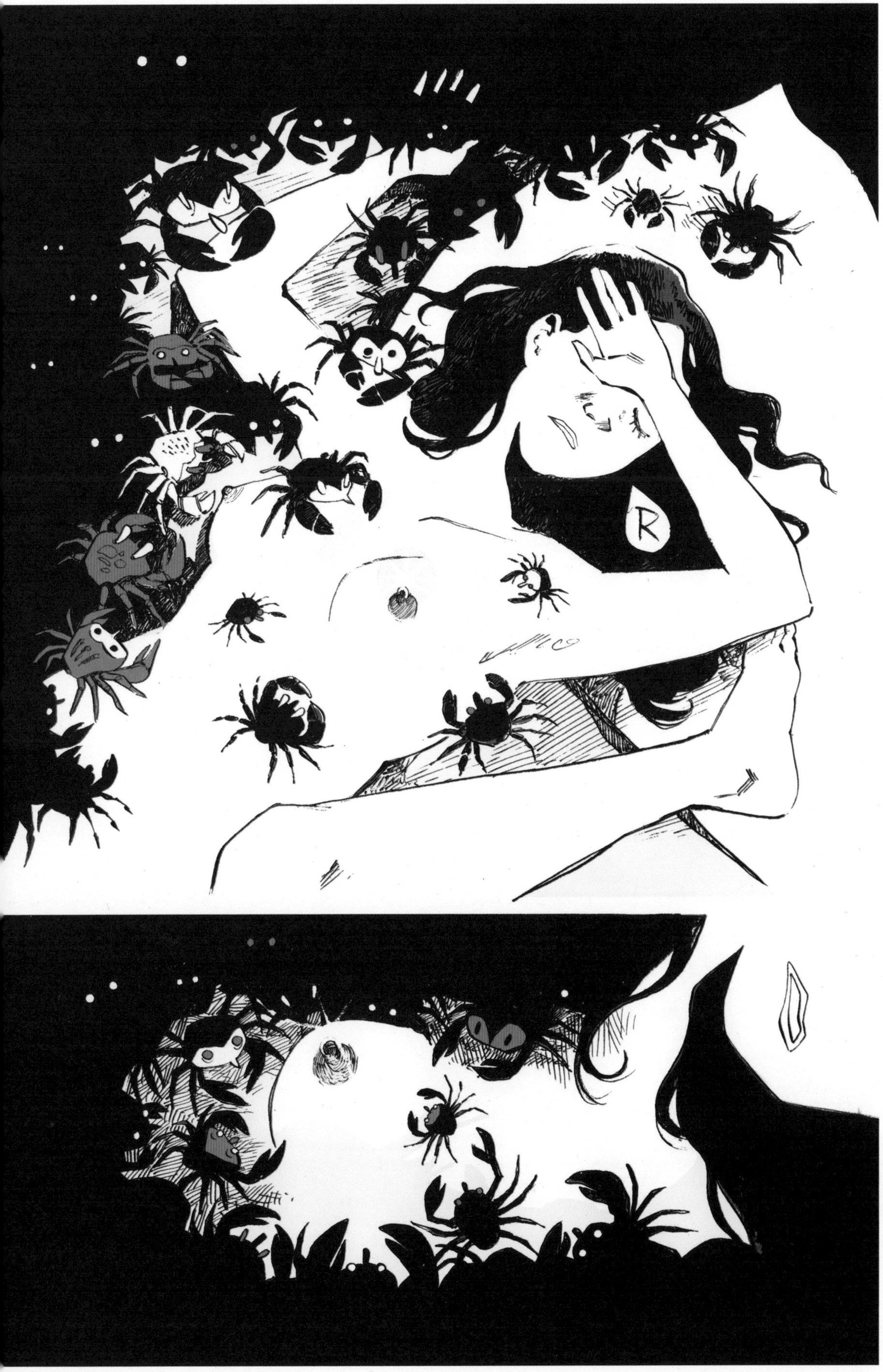
R

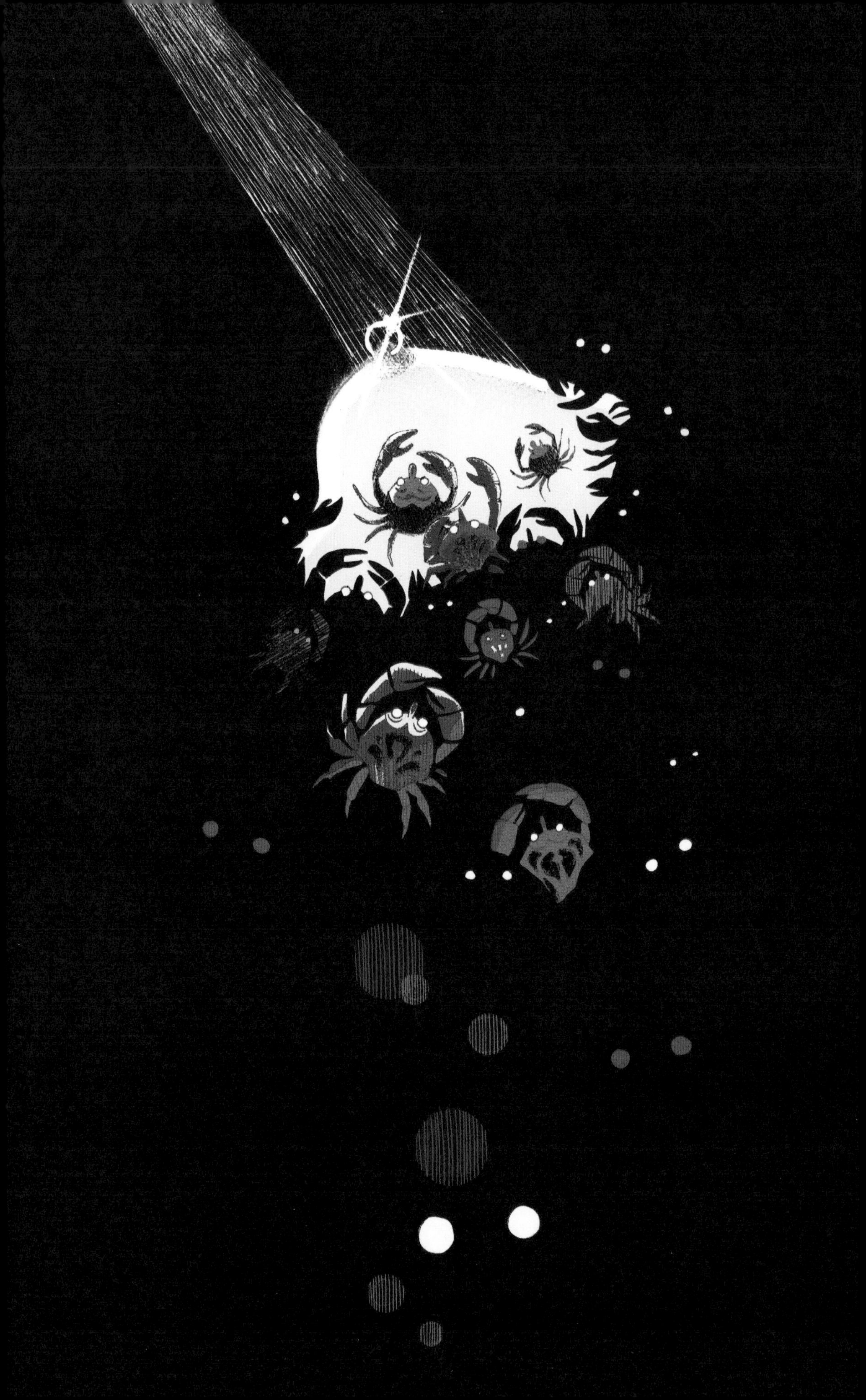

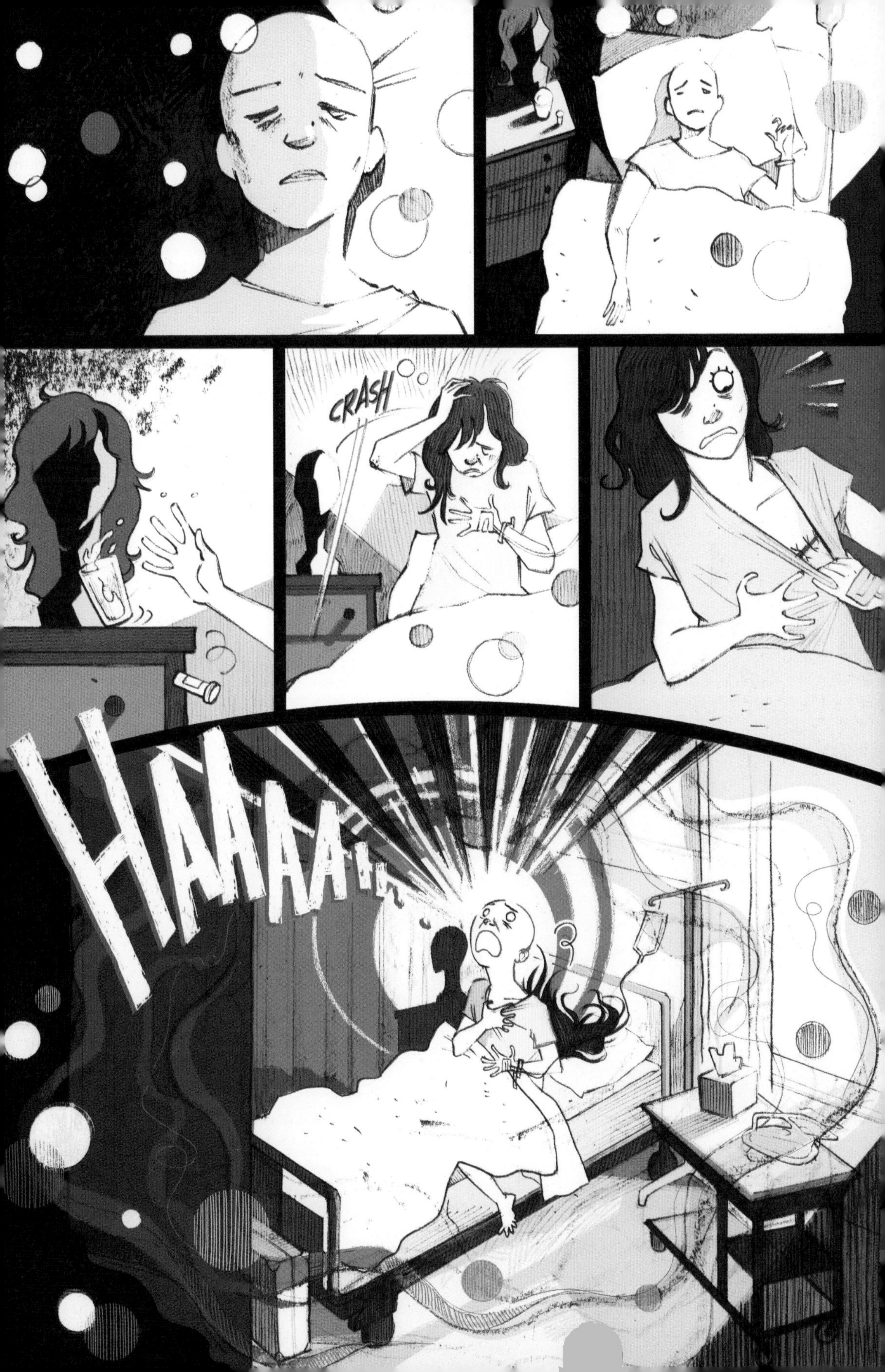
CRASH
HAAAA

-Give it to me!
-Madam, you've lost your mind!

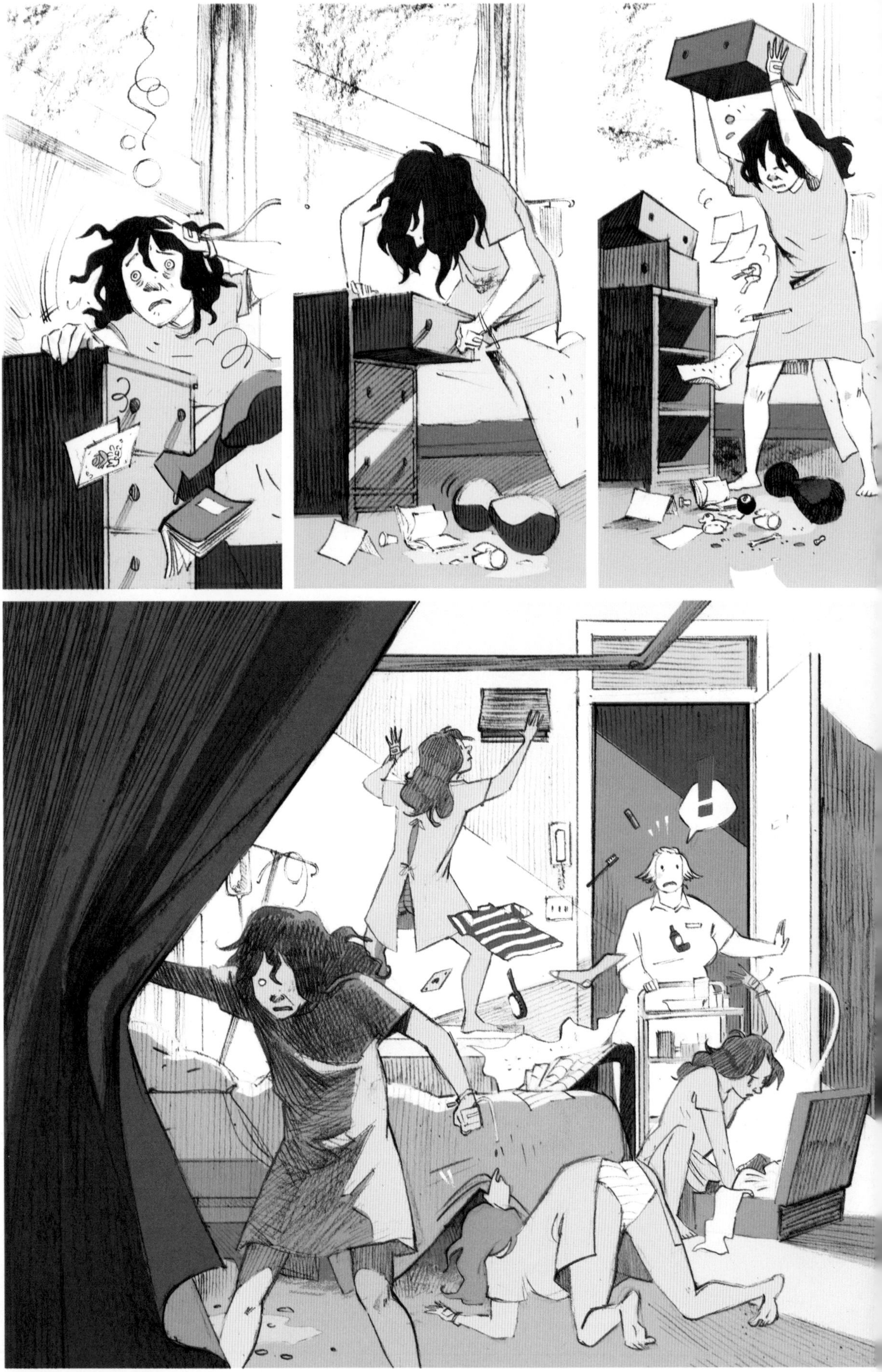

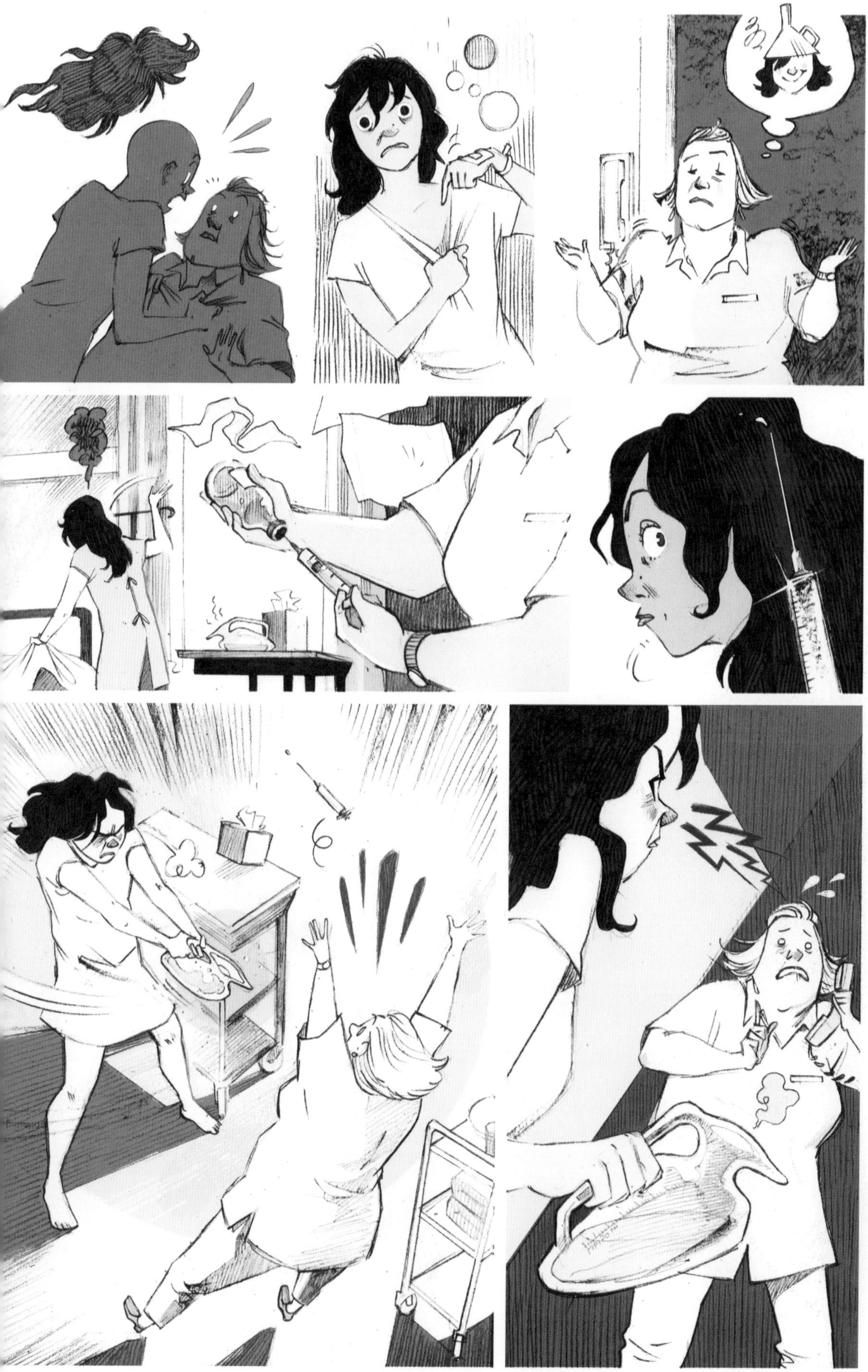

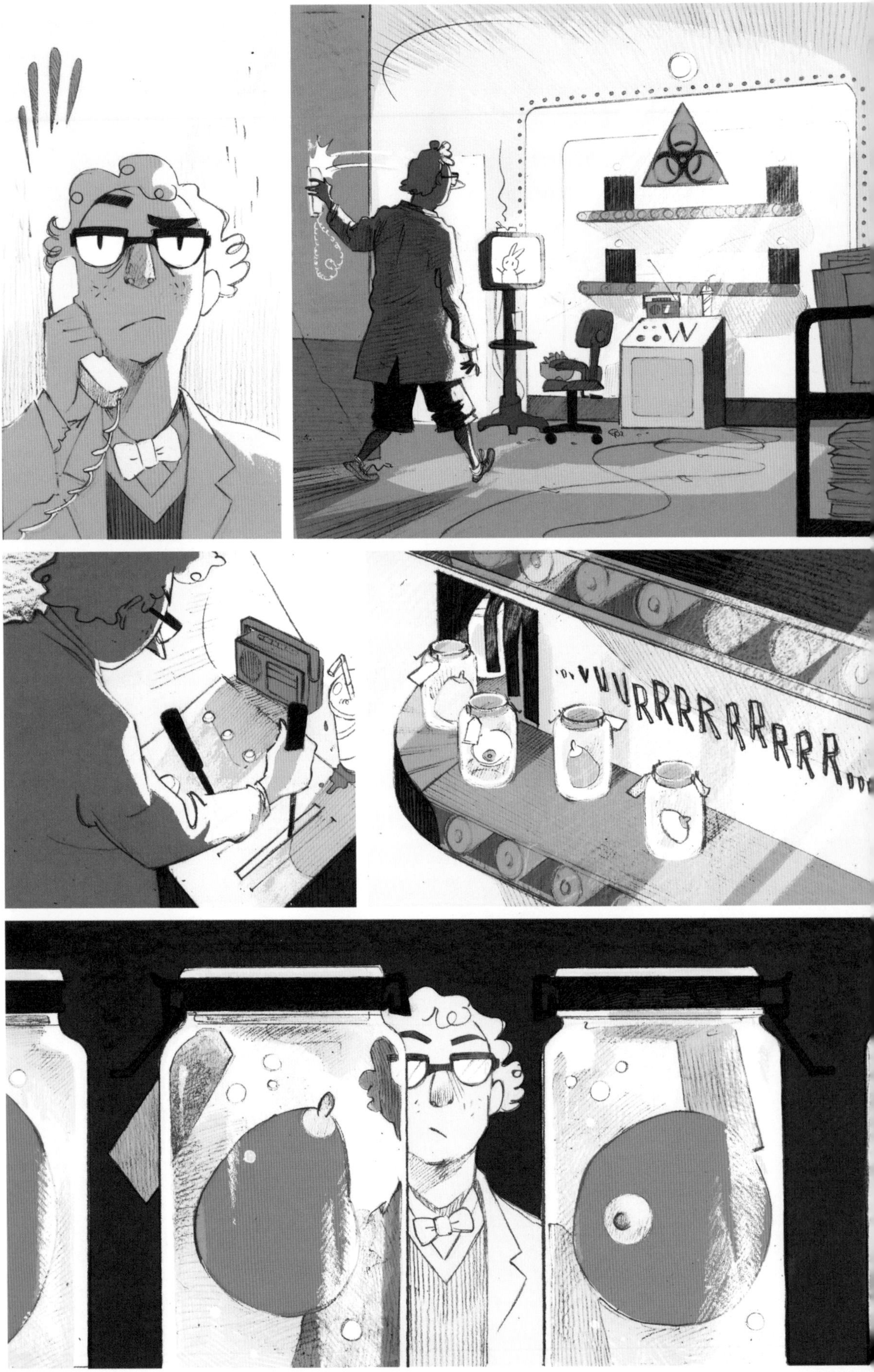
...VVUURRRRRRRRRR...

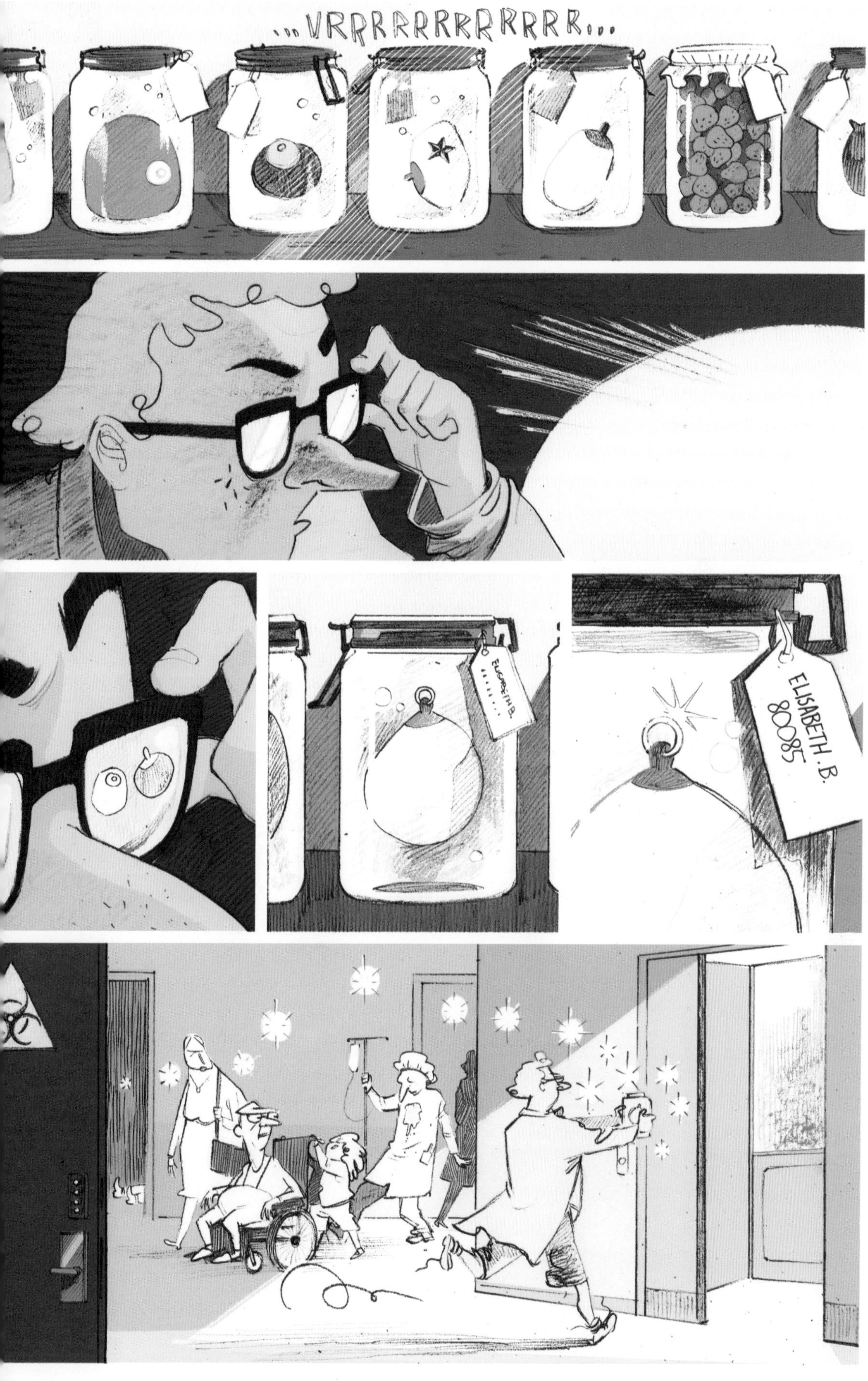
...VRRRRRRRRRRRR...
ELISABETH. B.
80085

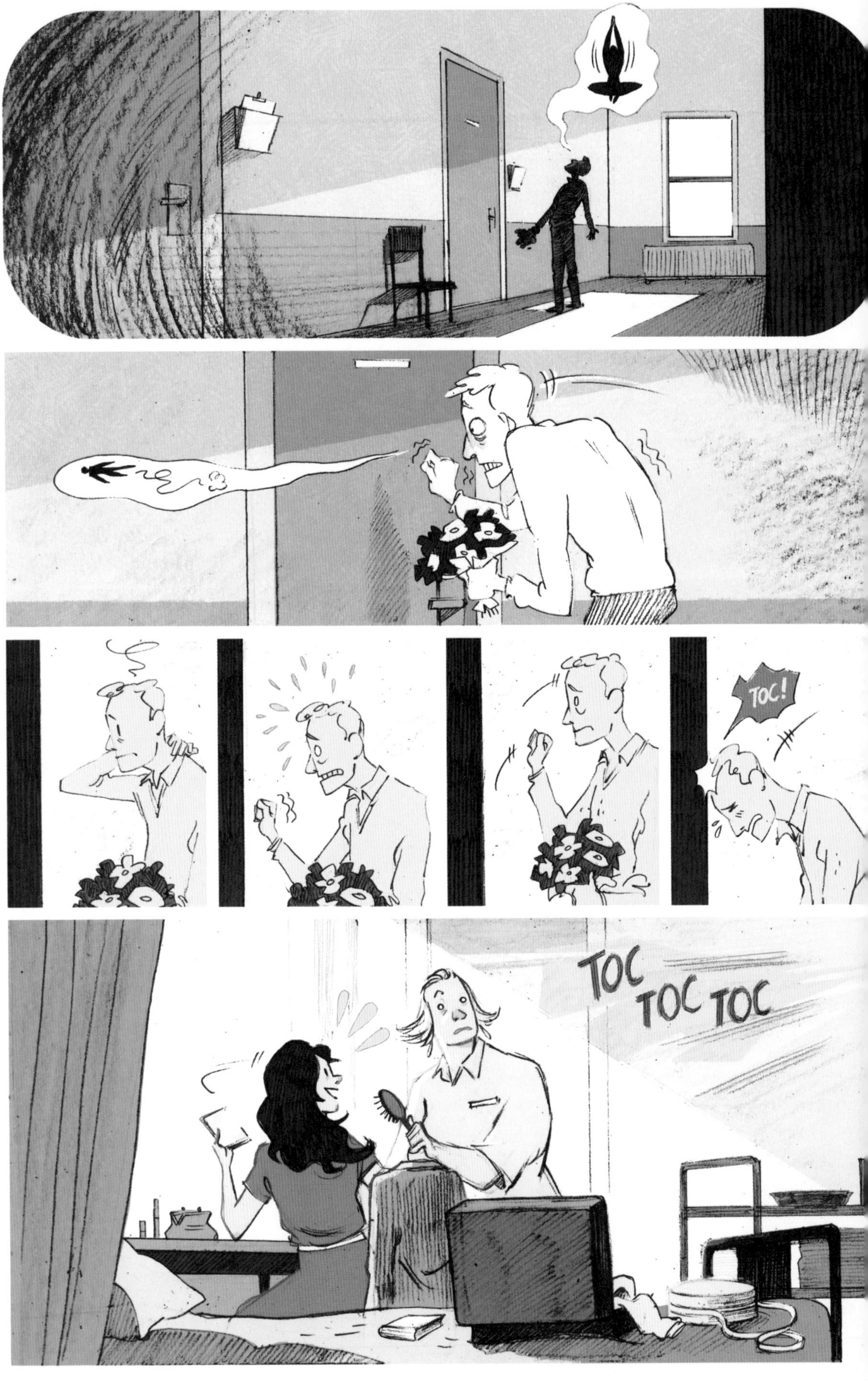
TOC!
TOC
TOC TOC

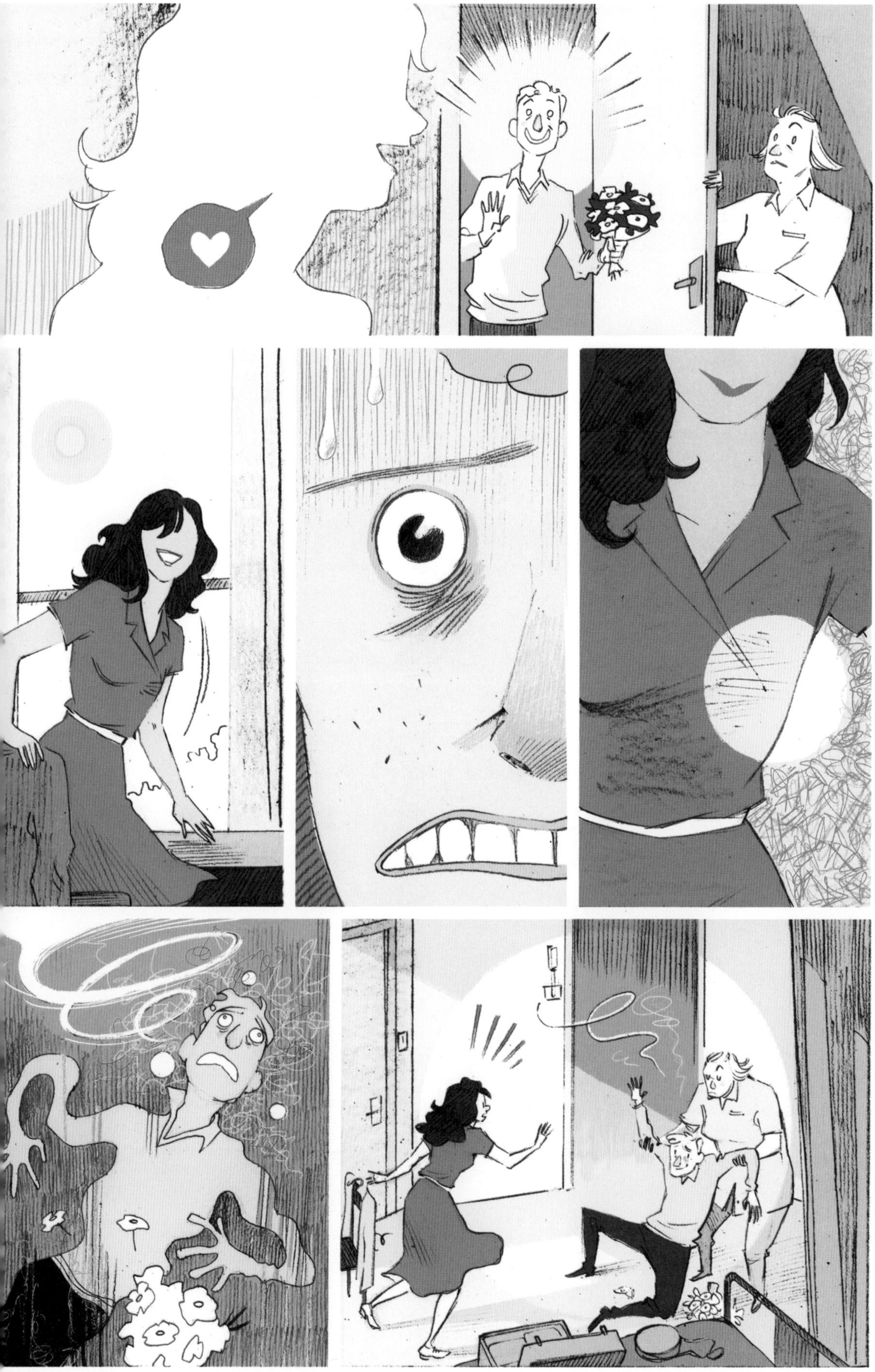

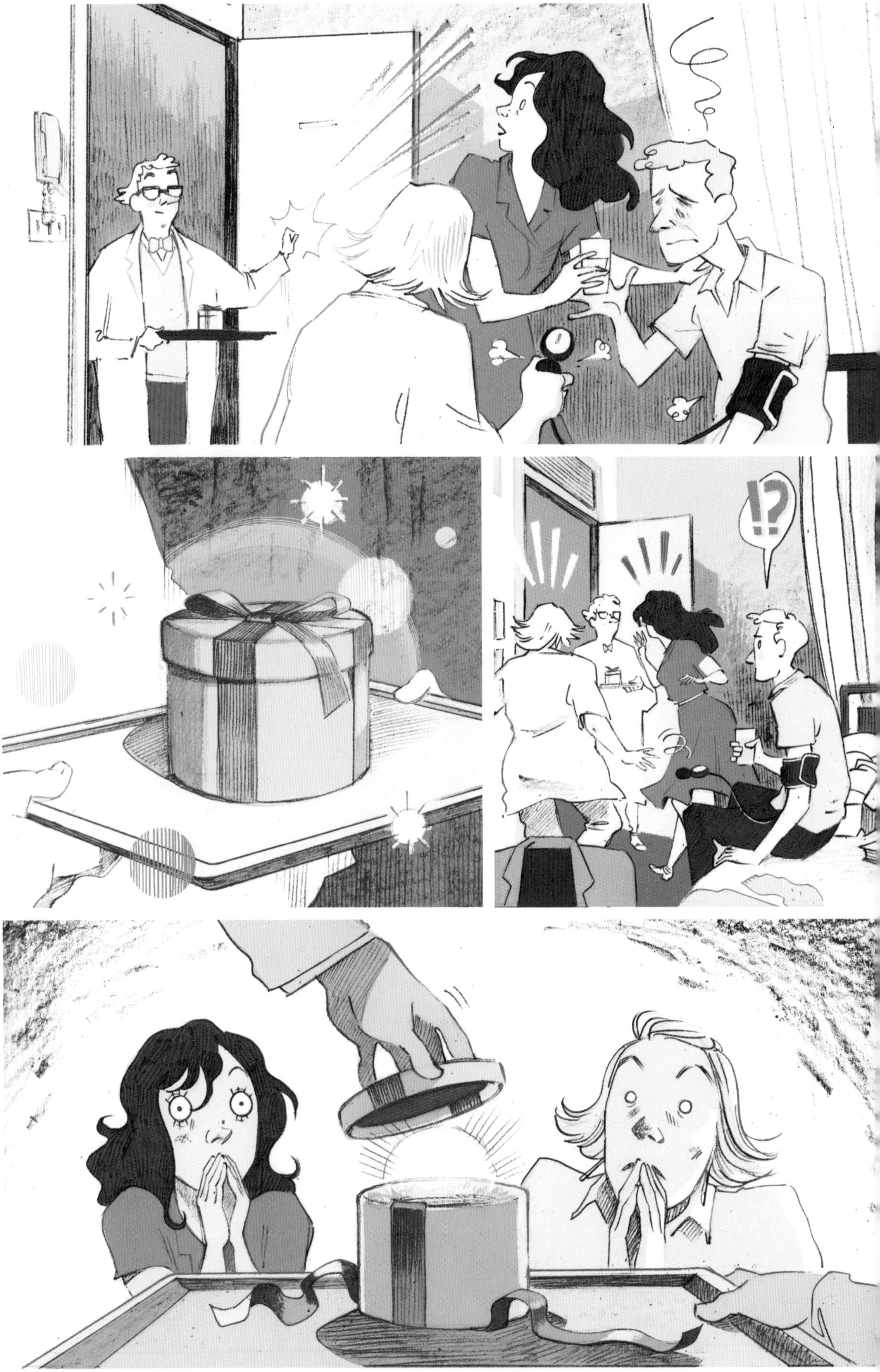
!?

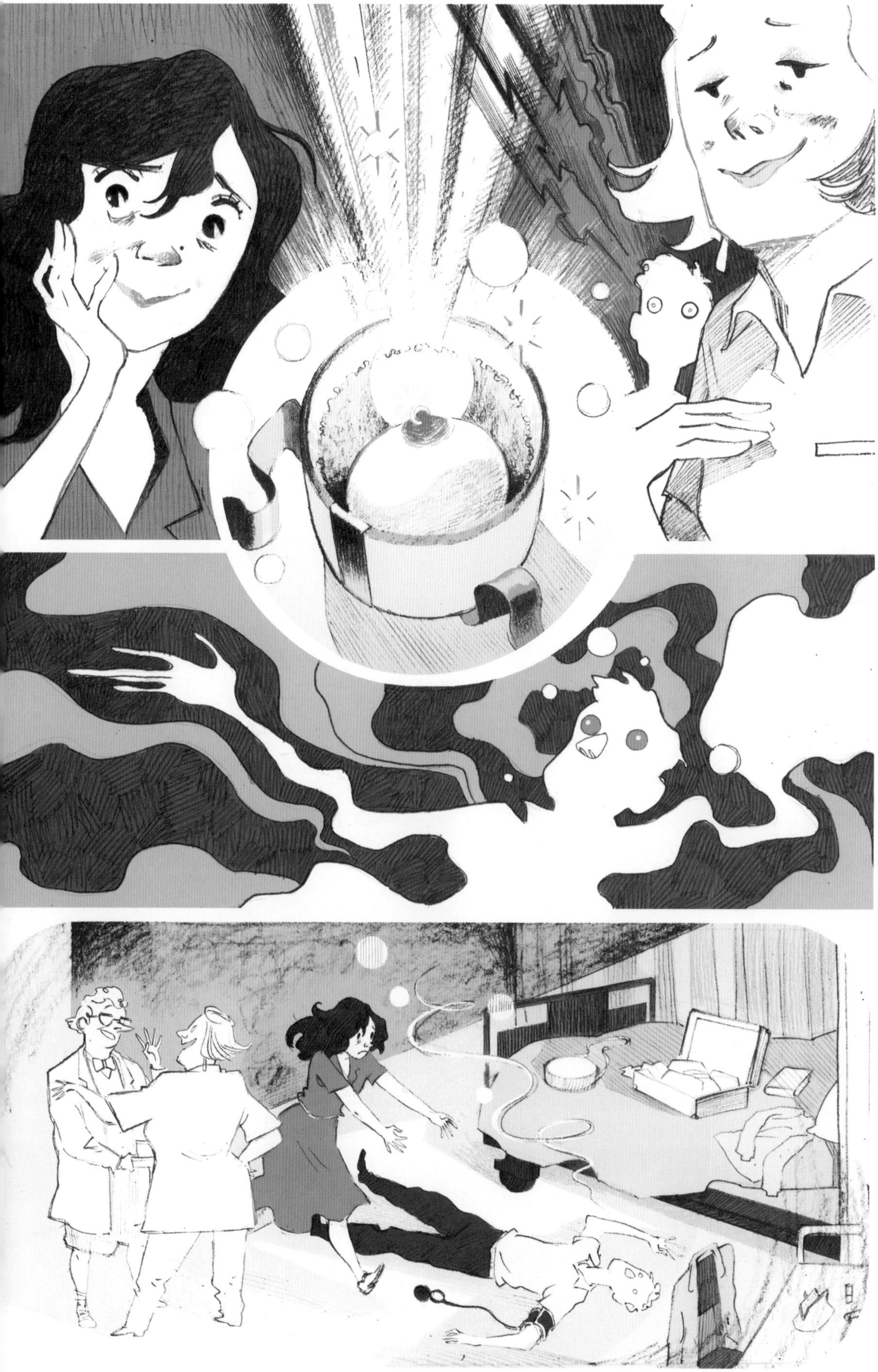

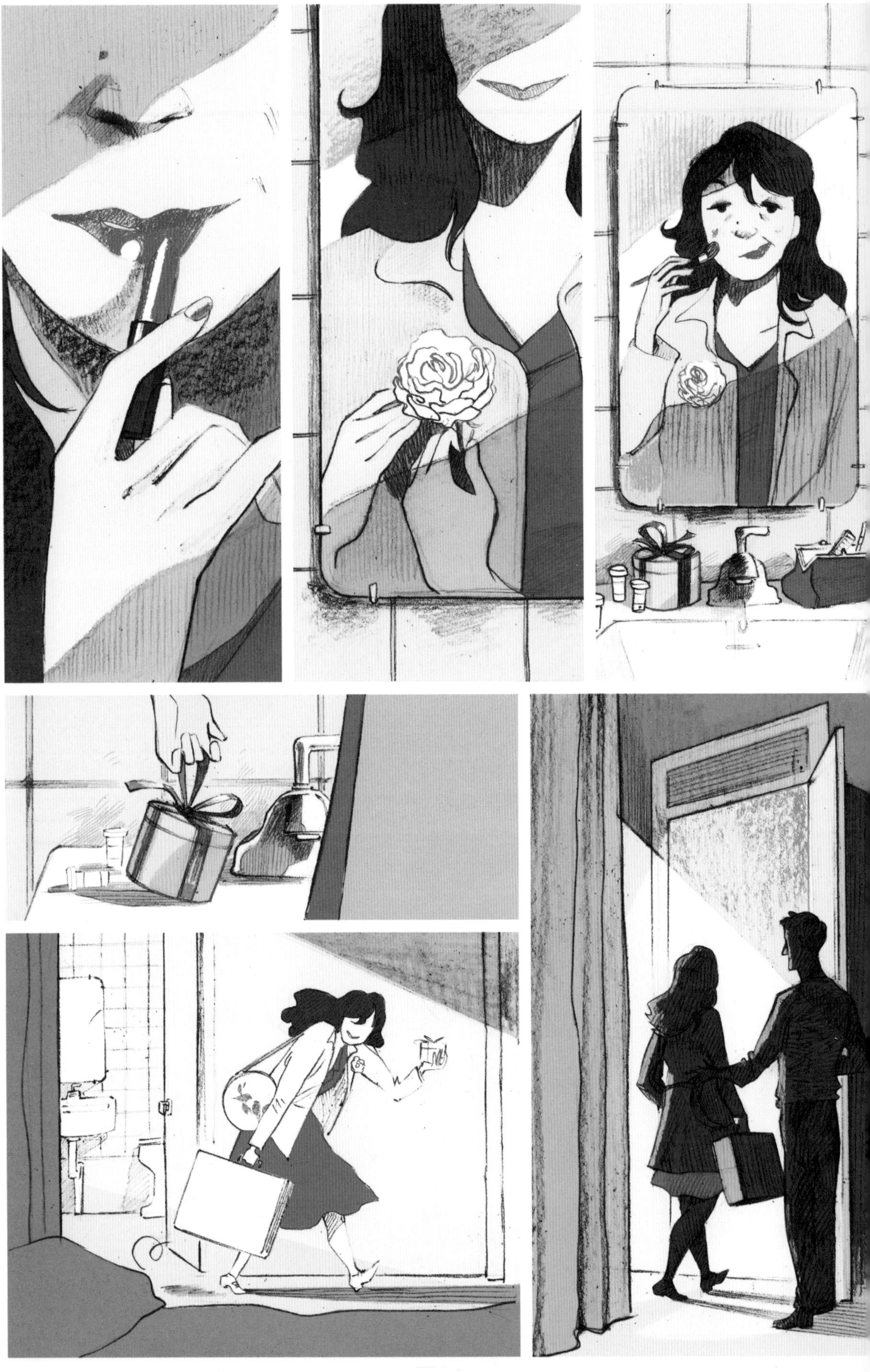

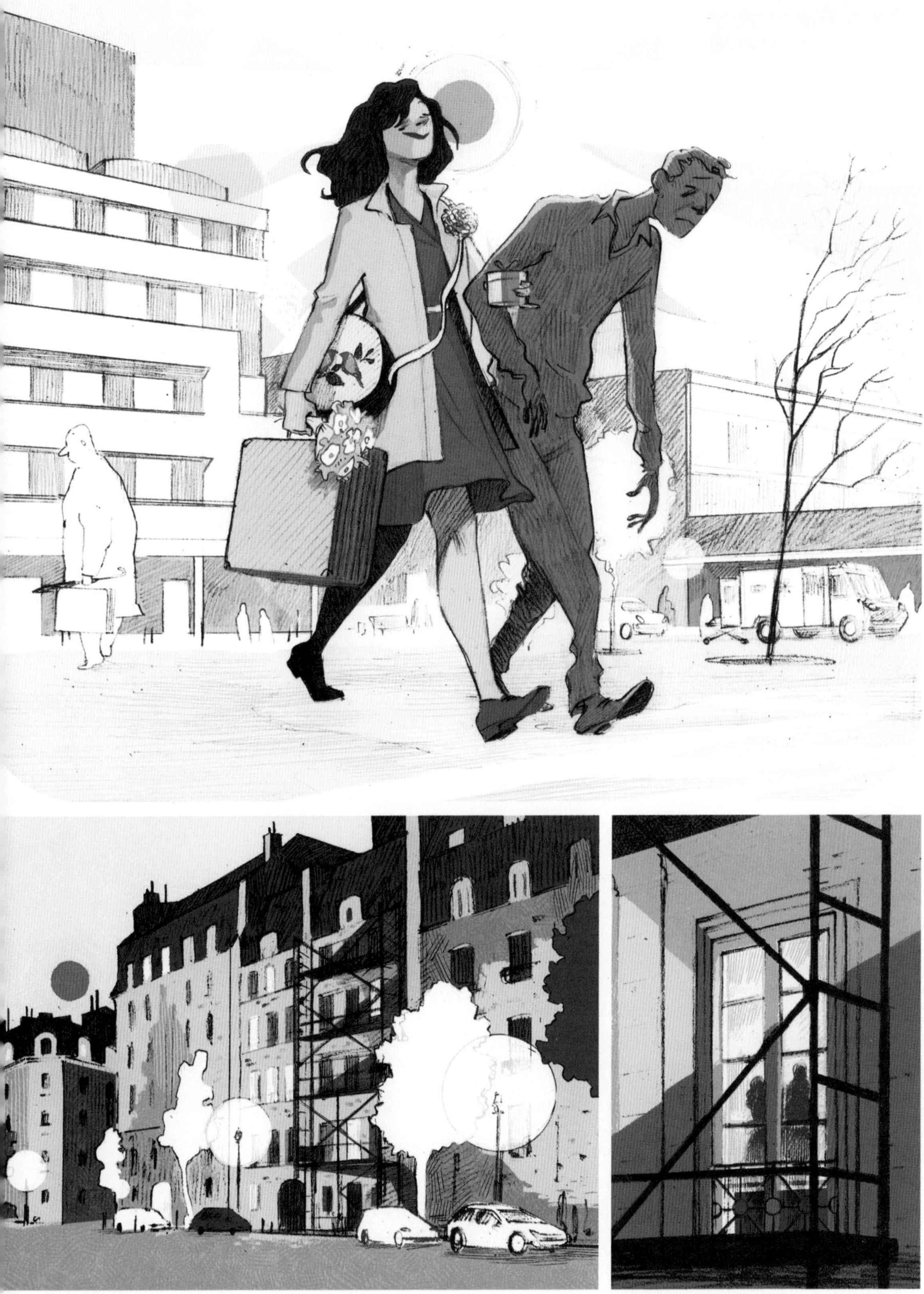

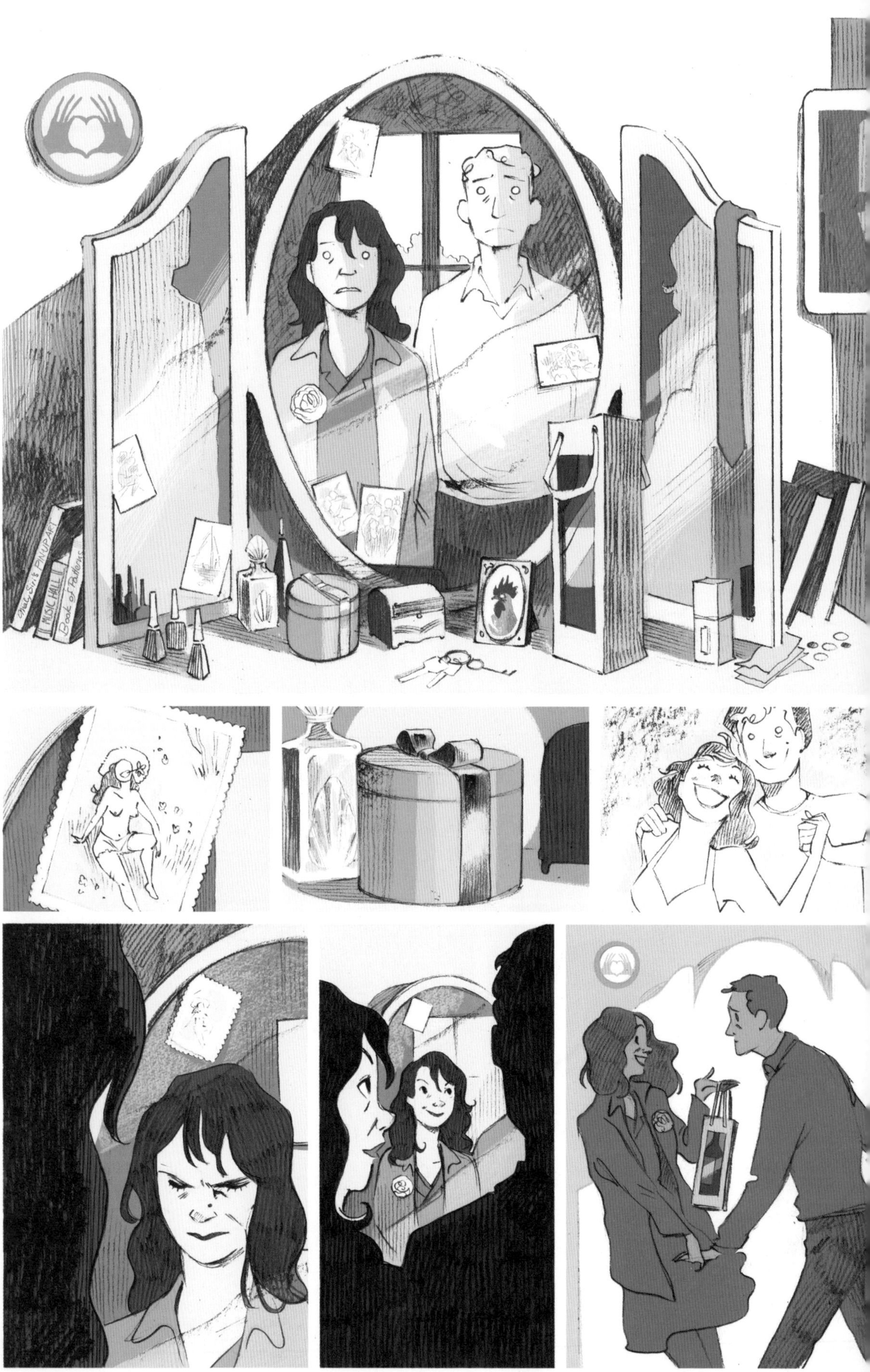
PINUP ART
MUSIC HALL
Book of Patterns

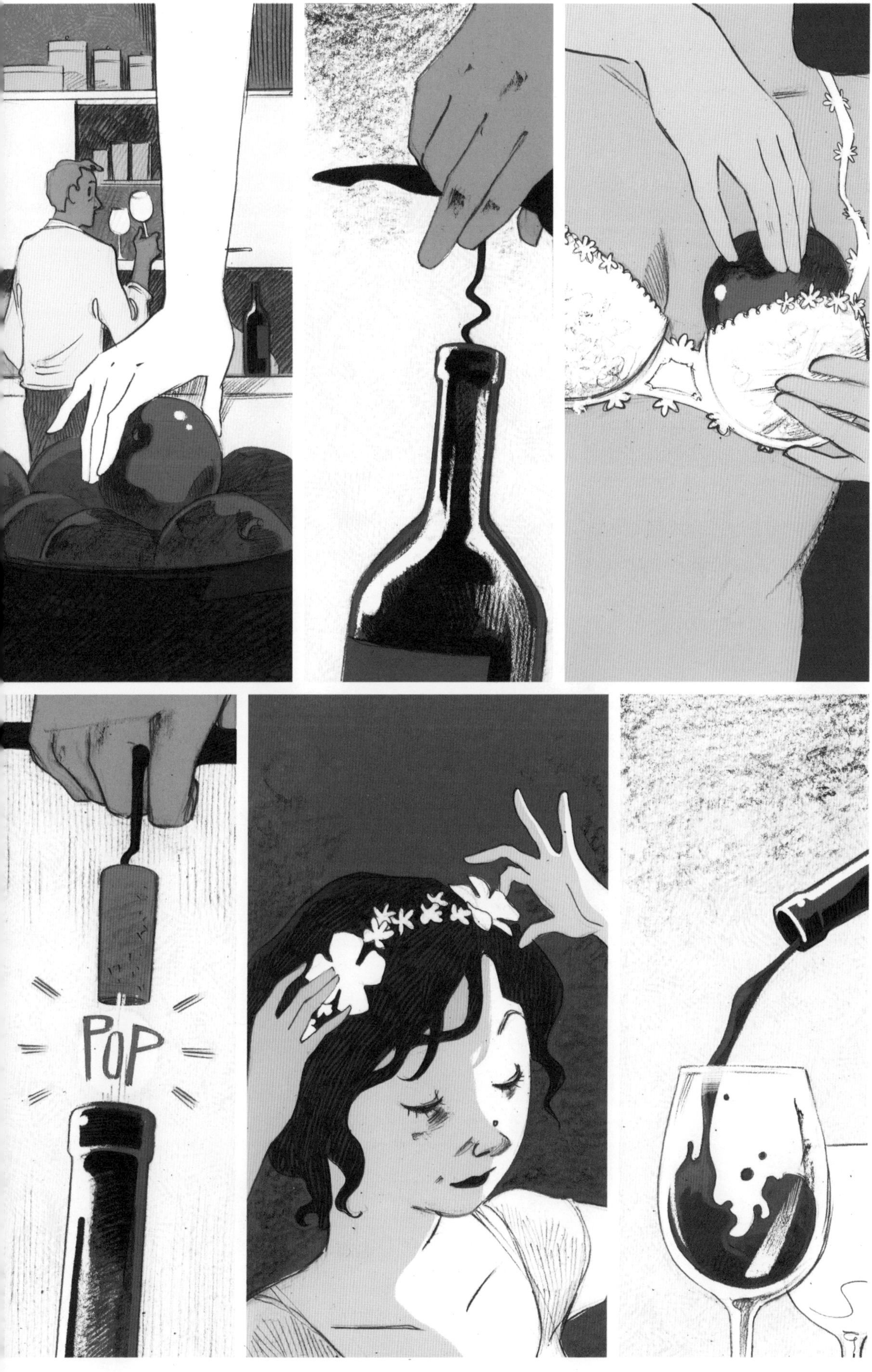
POP

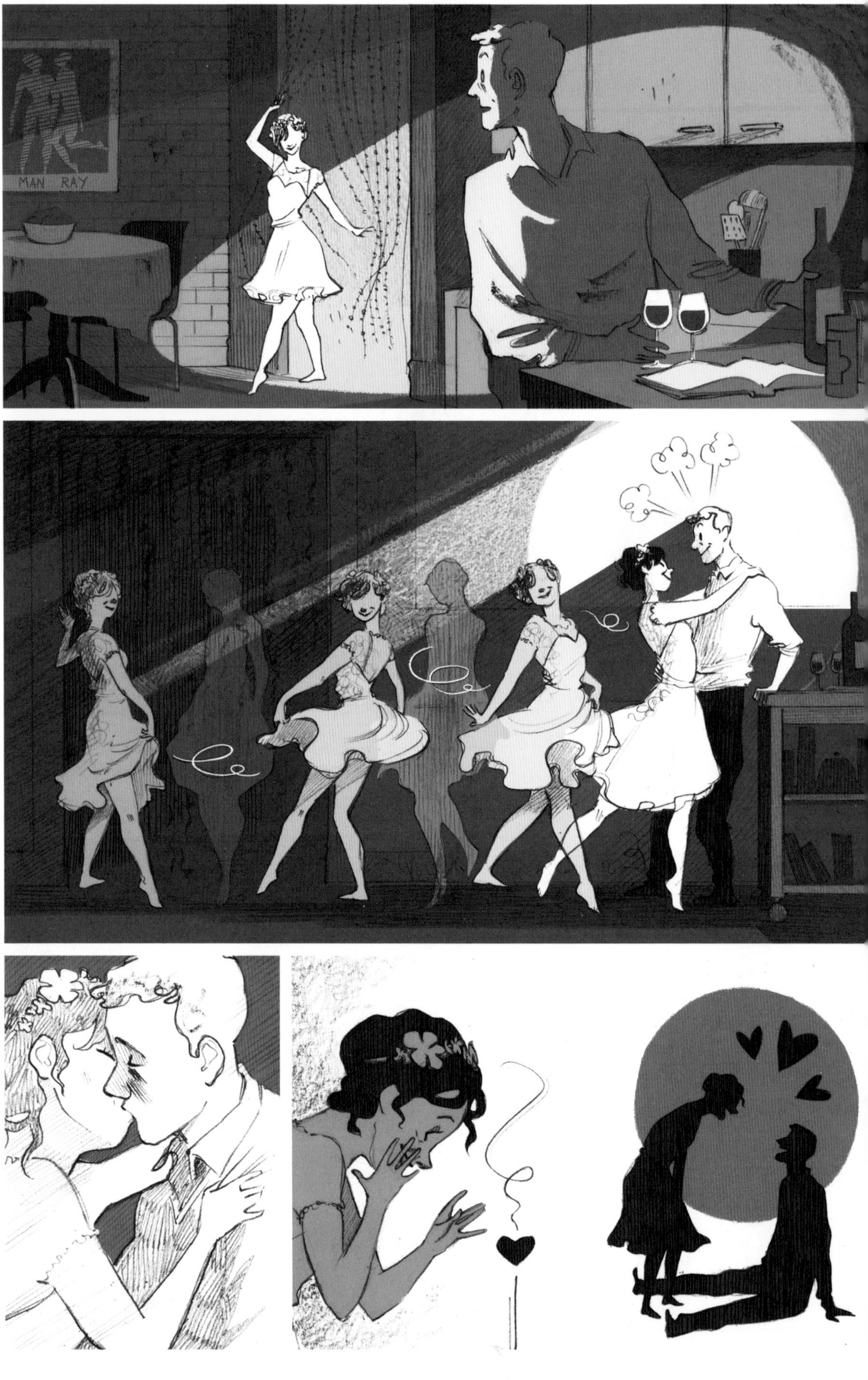
MAN RAY

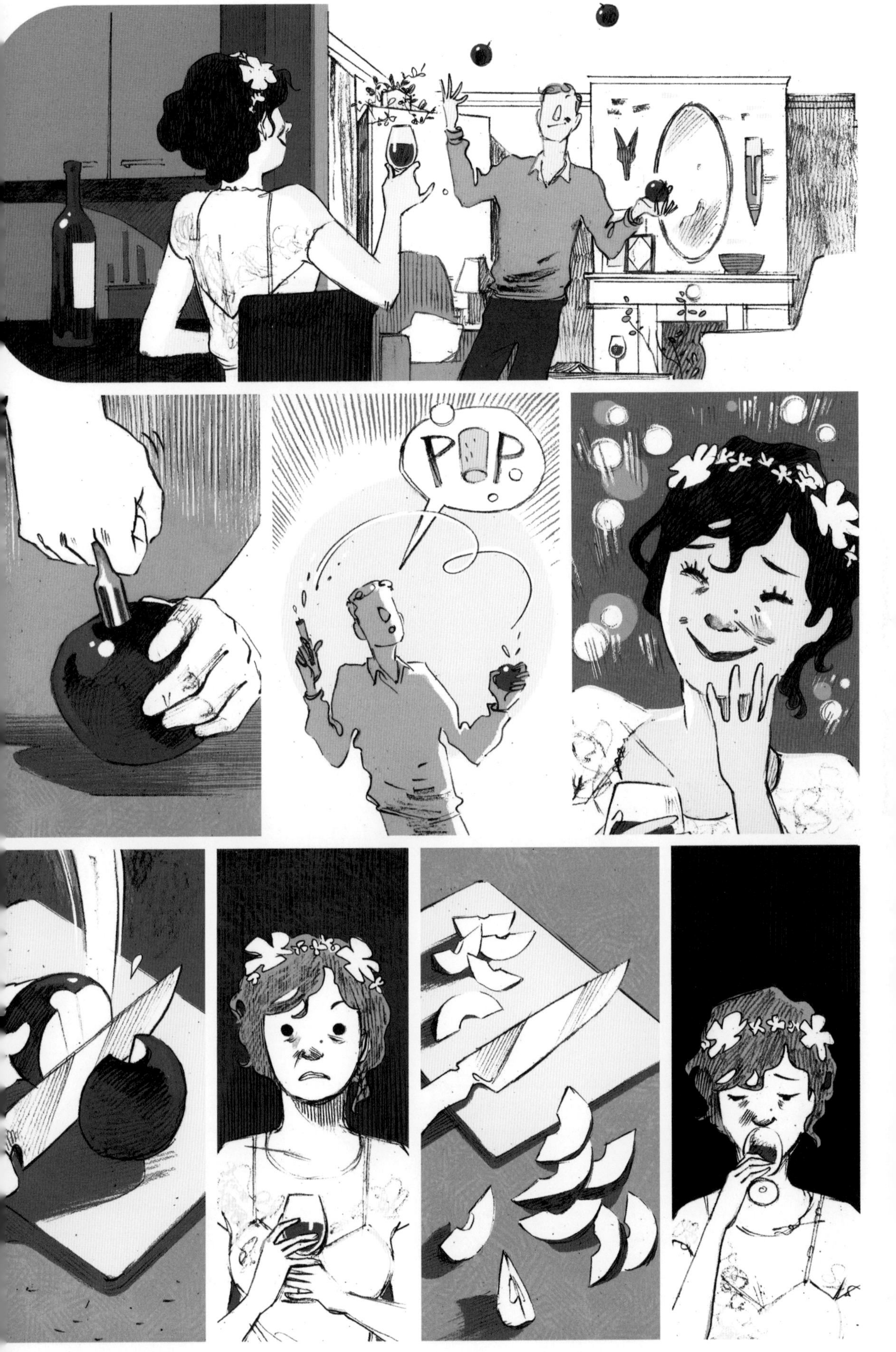
POP.

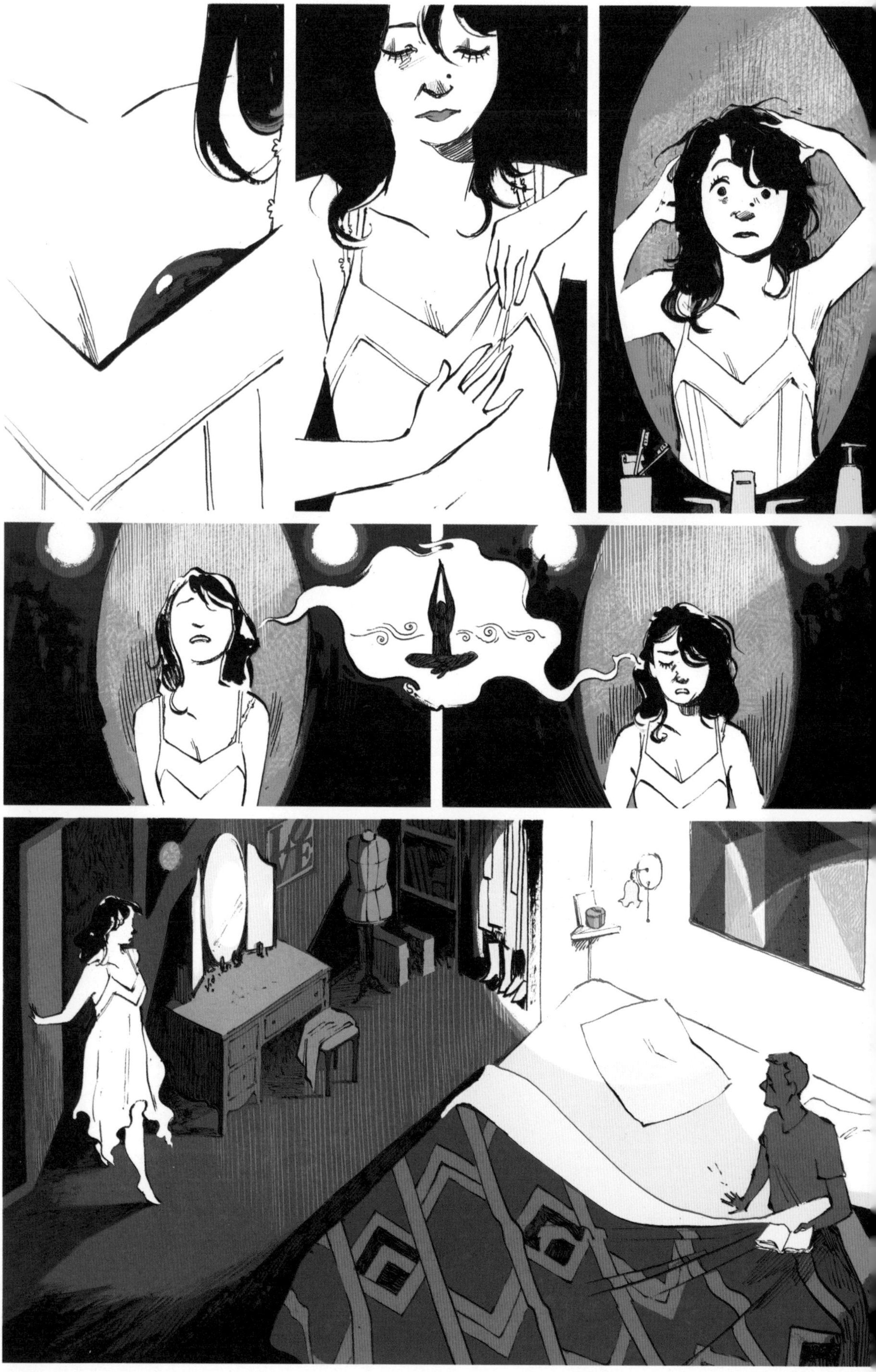
LOVE

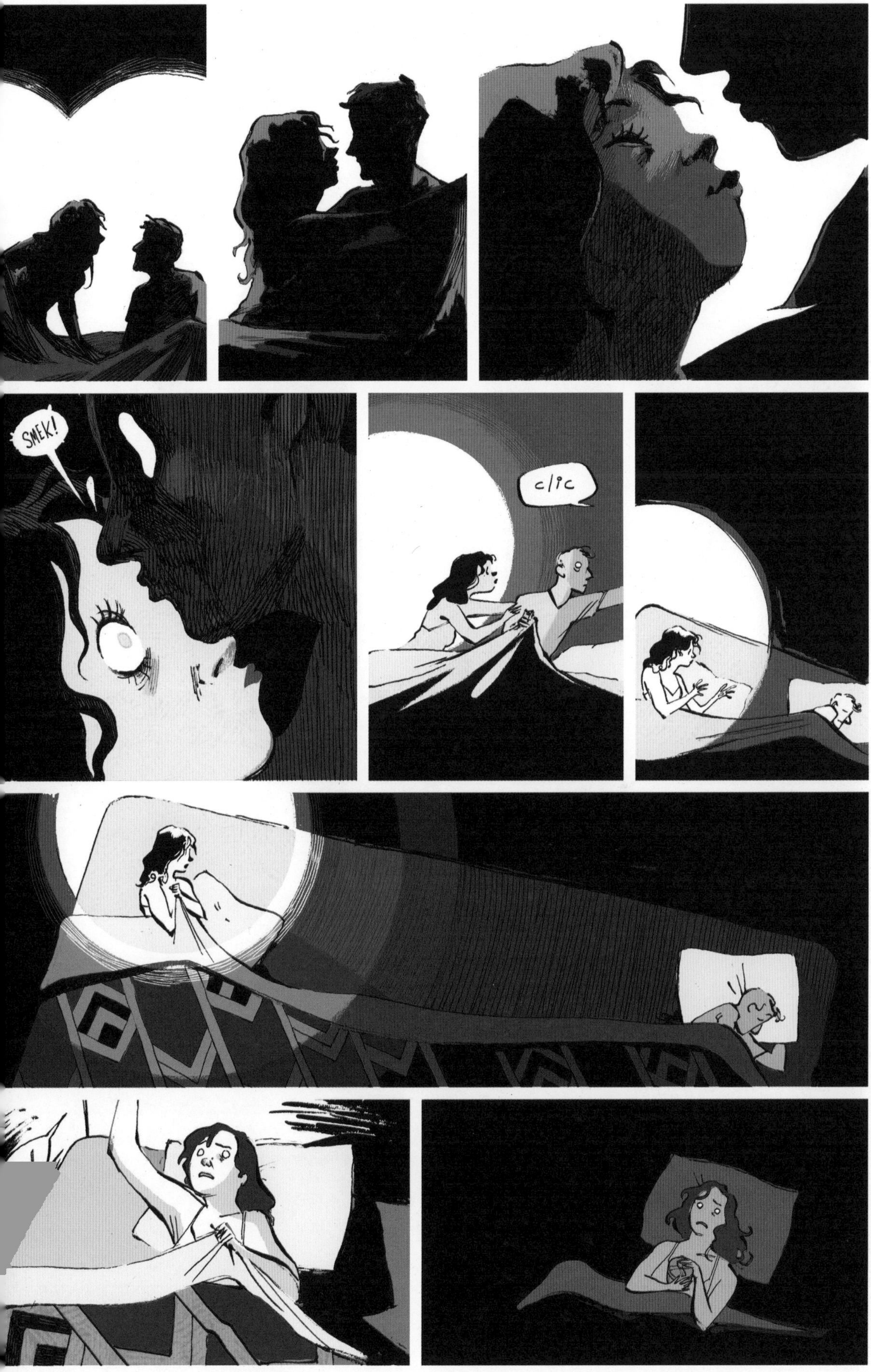
SMEK!
clic

-Big Sister is watching us.
-Be careful! She wants them in a row, two by two.

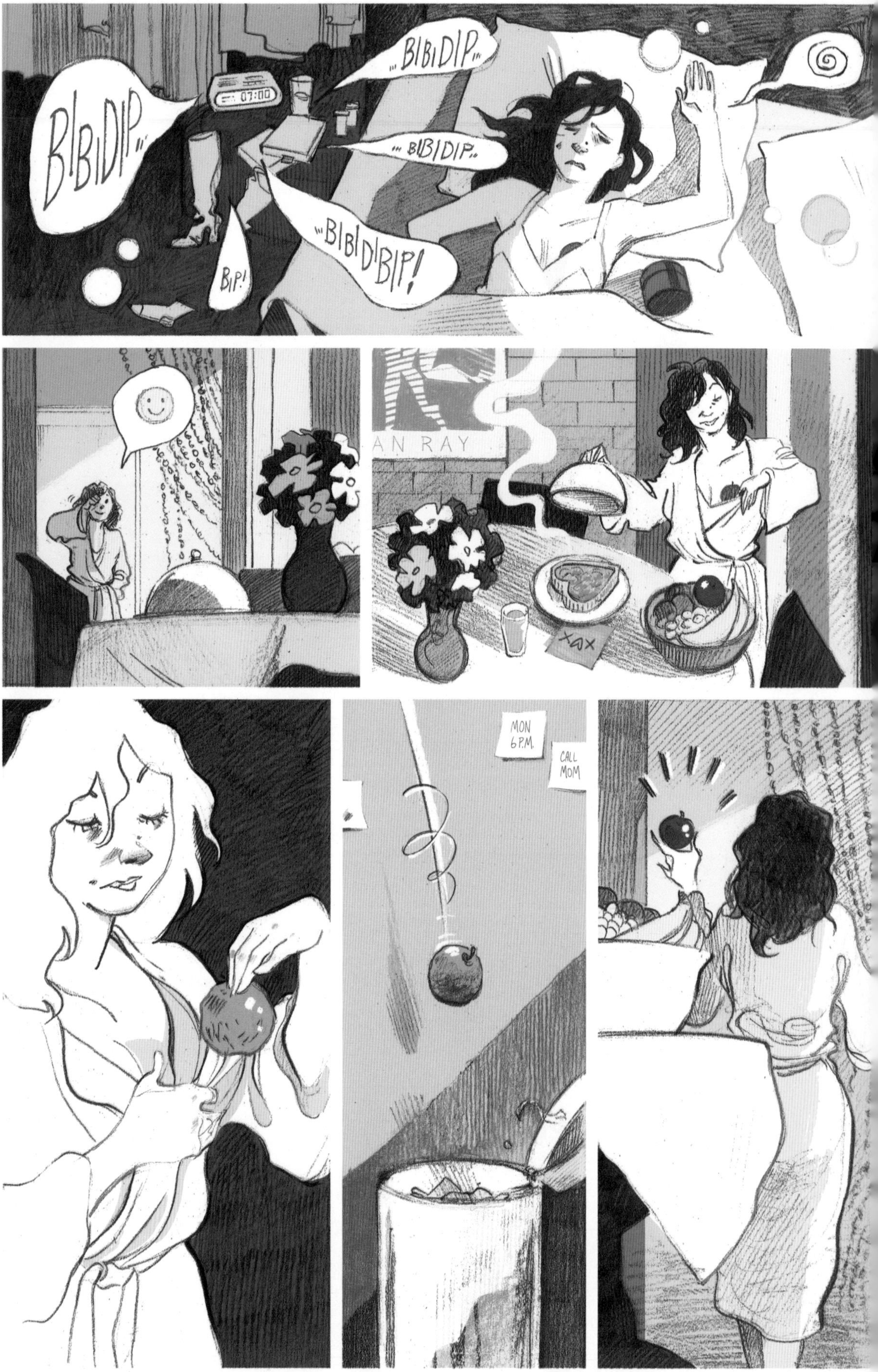
BIBIDIP...
...BIBIDIP...
...BIBIDIP...
...BIBIDIBIP!
BIP!
AN RAY
XOX
MON
6 P.M.
CALL
MOM

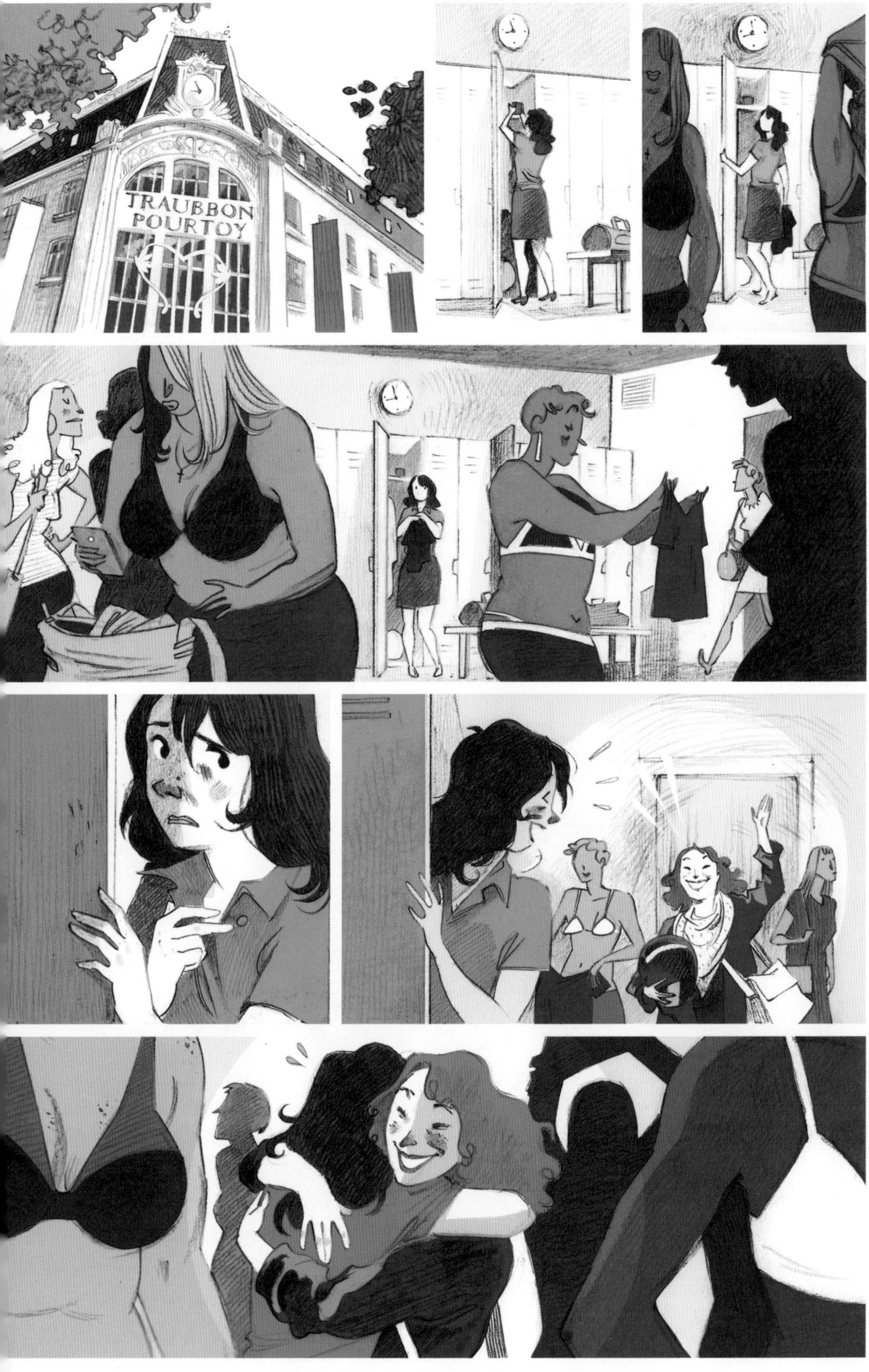
TRAUBBON
POURTOY

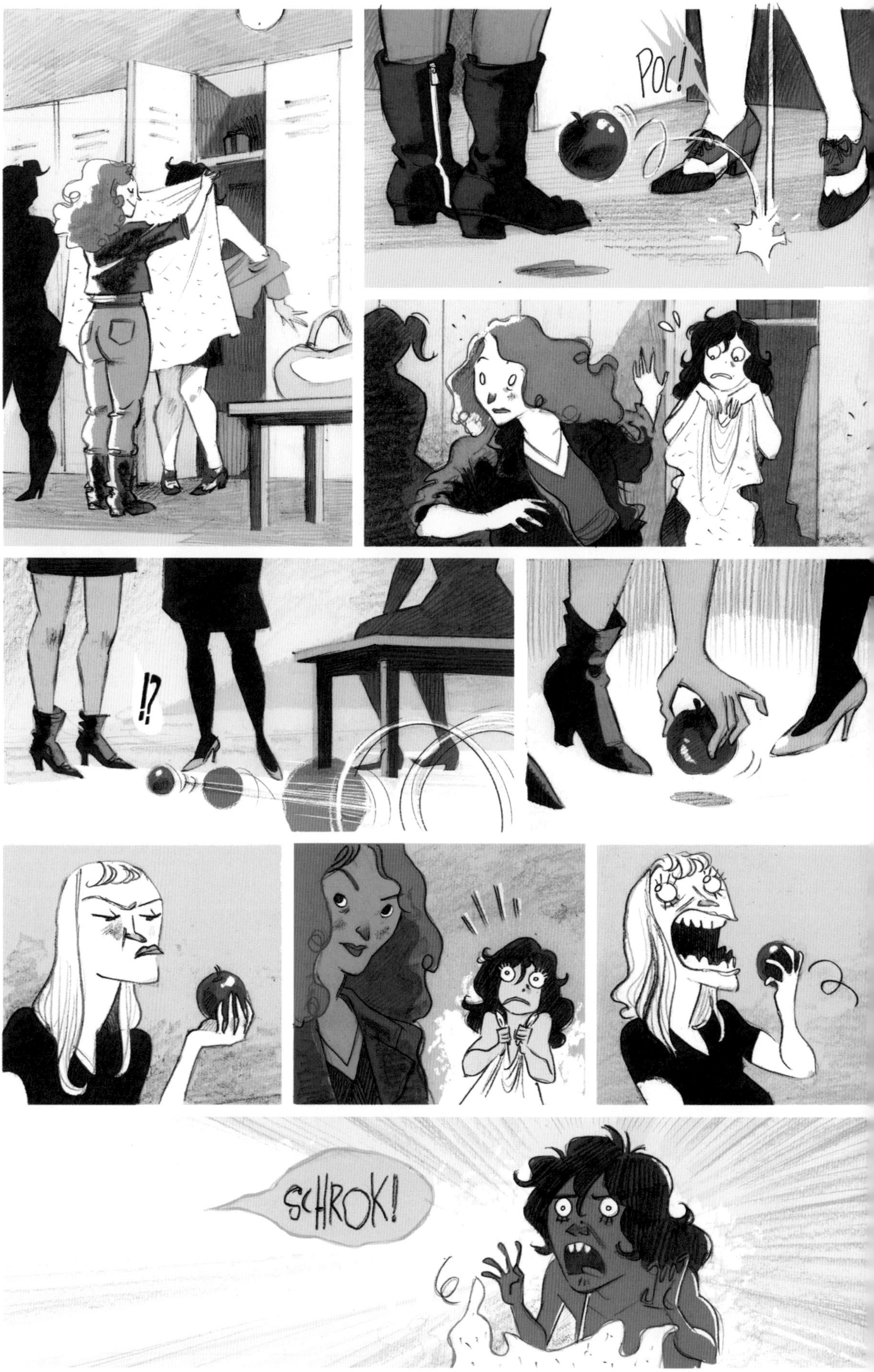
POC!
!?
SCHROK!

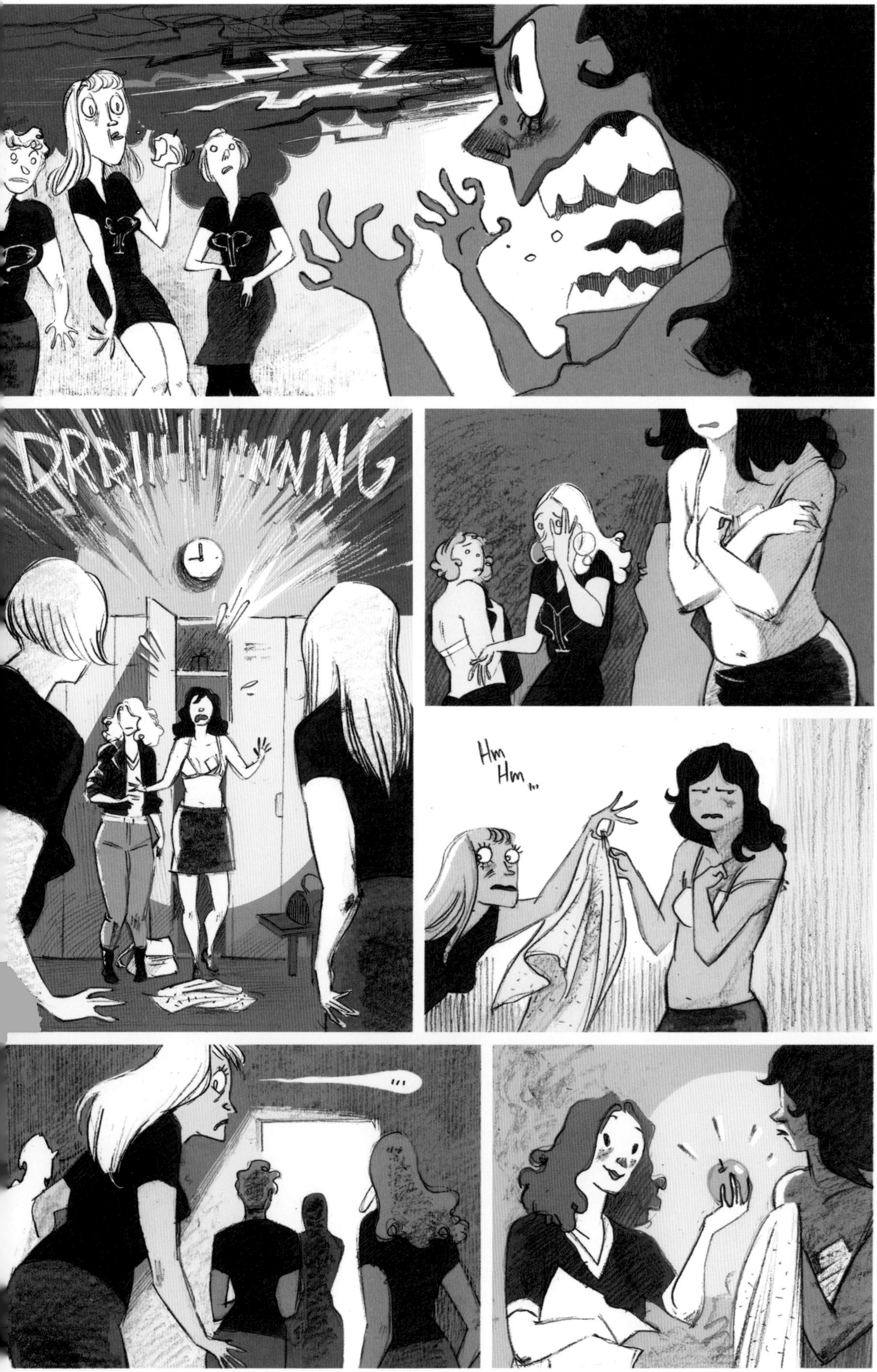
DRRIIIIIINNNG
Hm
Hm...

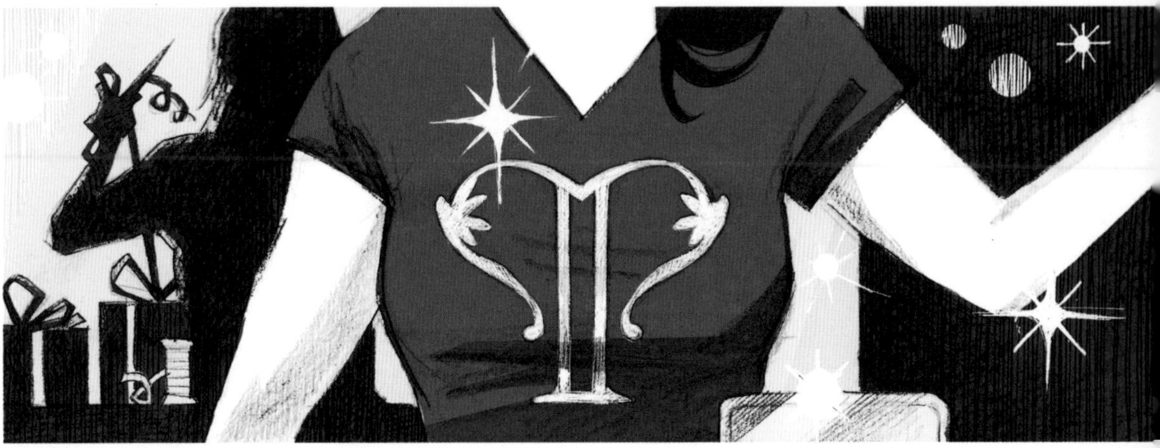

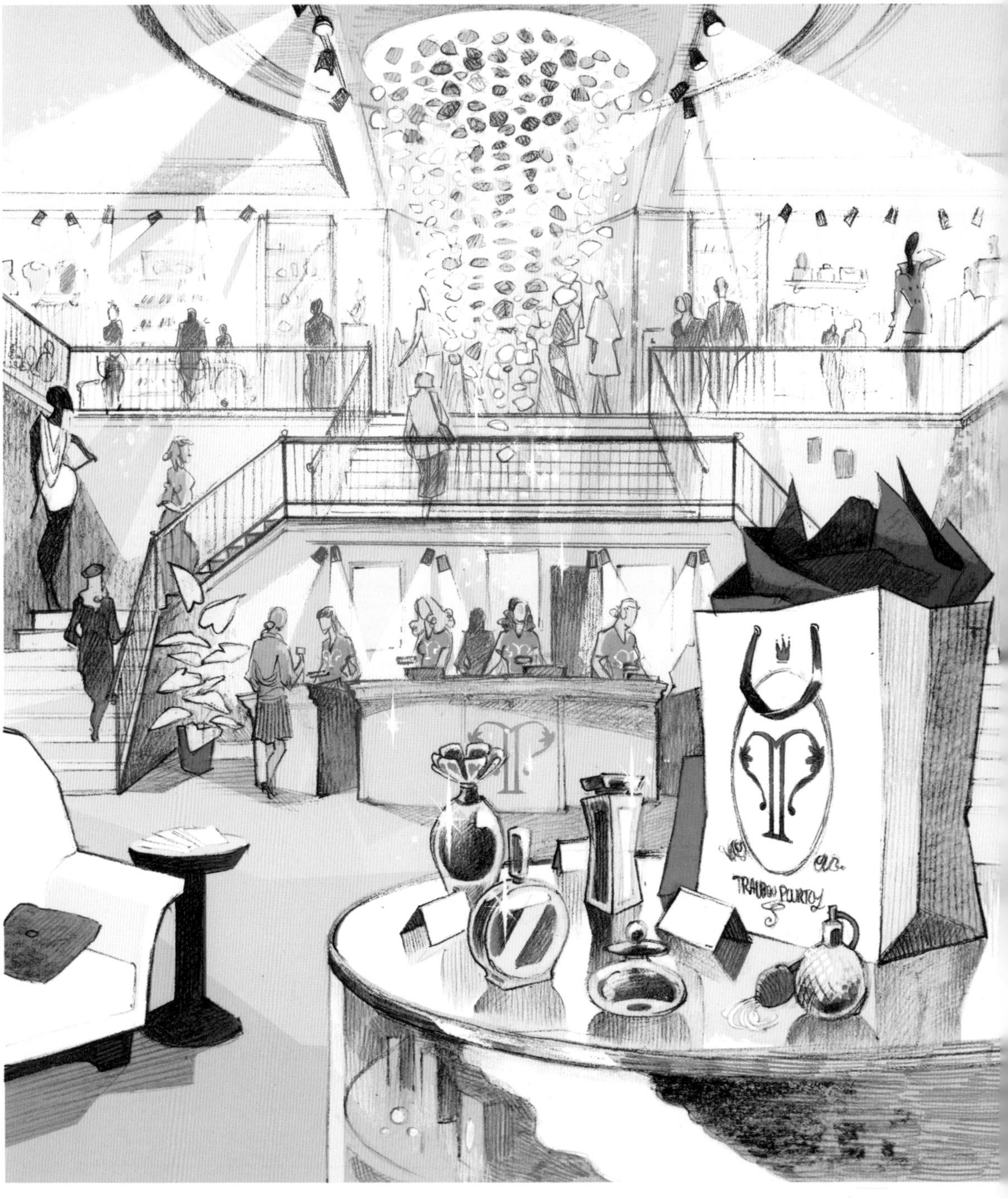

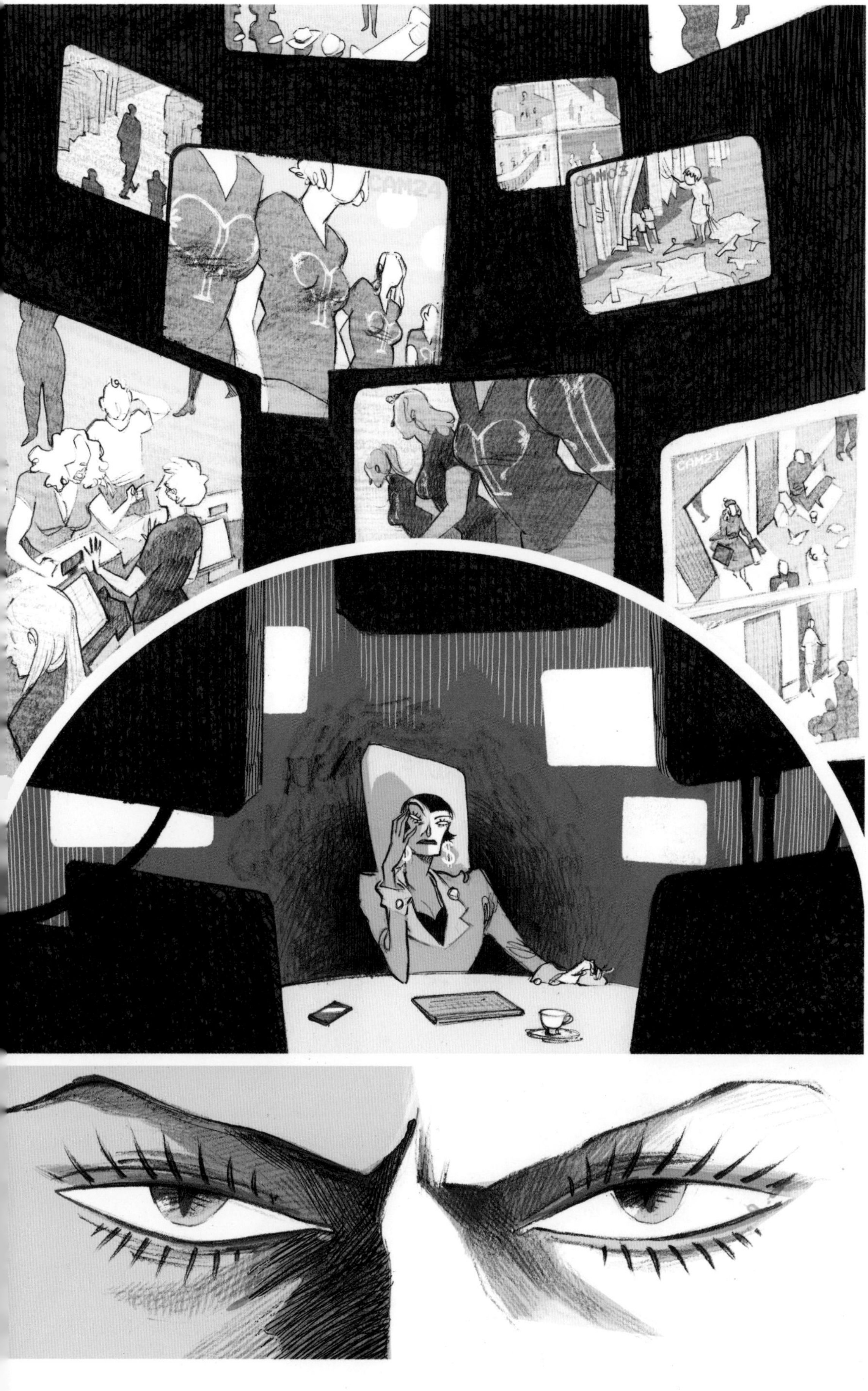
CAM24
CAM03
CAM21

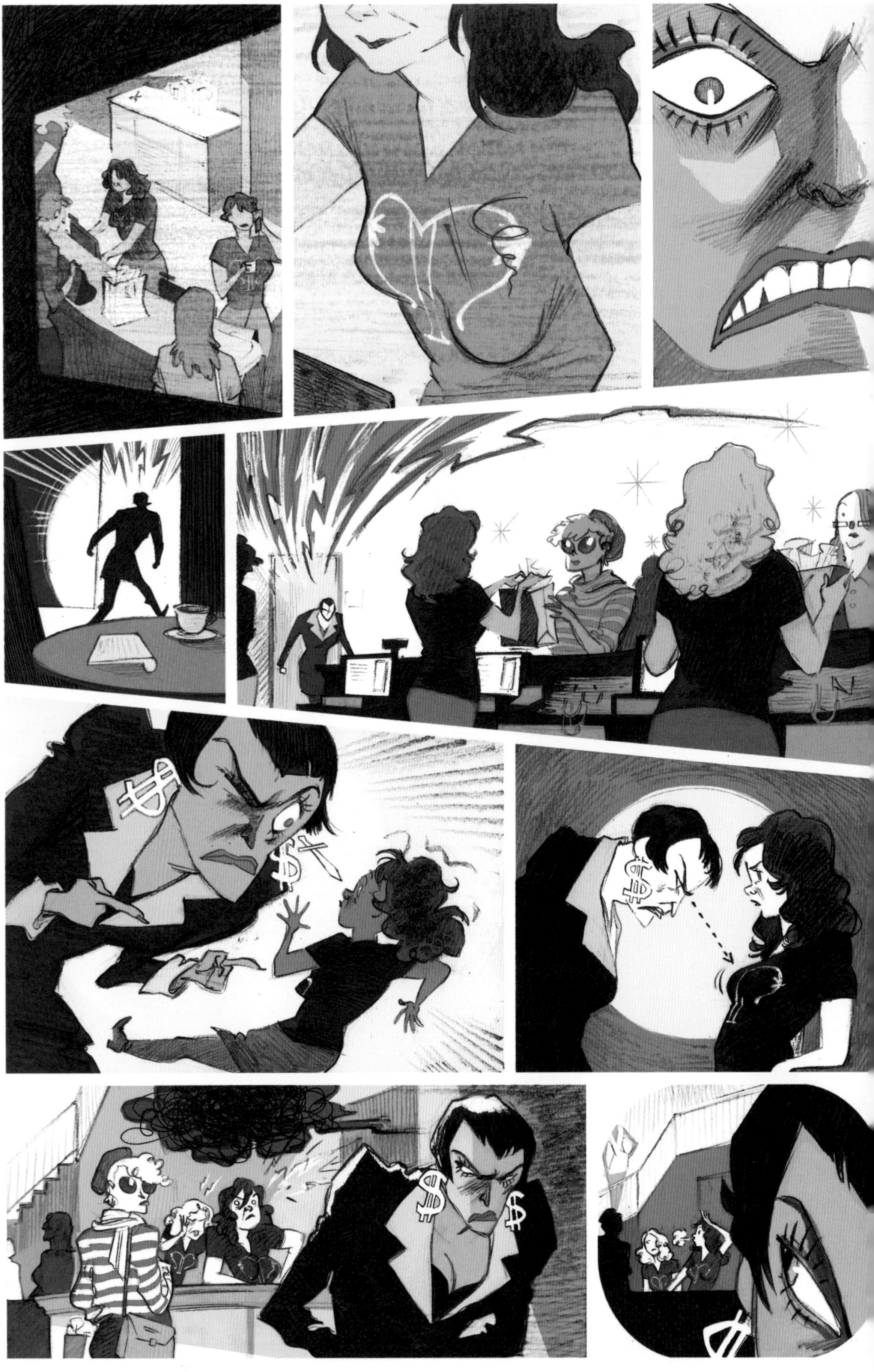

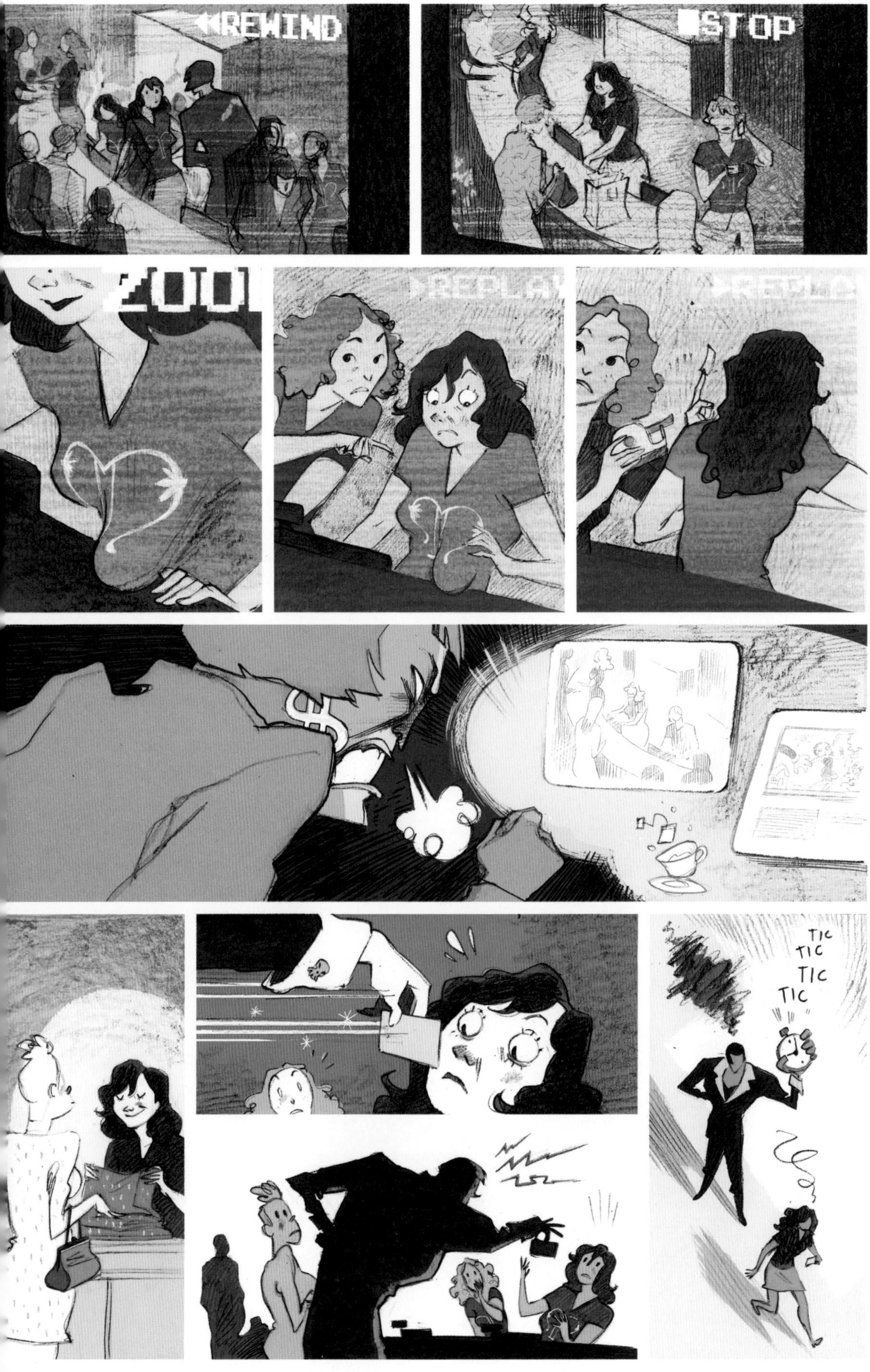
◄◄REWIND
■STOP
ZOOM
►REPLAY
►REPLAY
TIC
TIC
TIC
TIC

-State-of-the-art technology with retractable nipple.
With this breast, my beauty, you will be the envy of all.

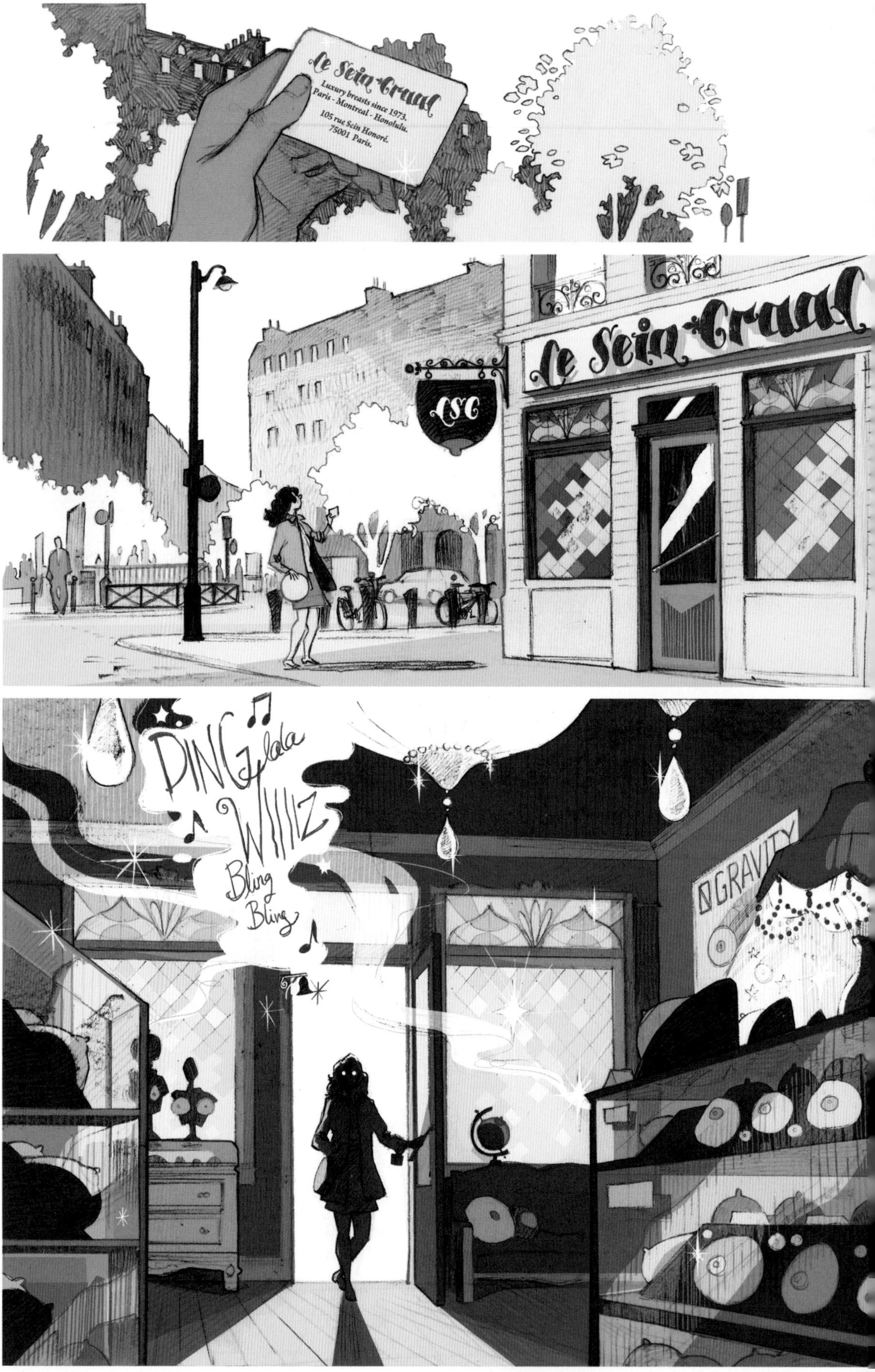
Le Sein Graal
Luxury breasts since 1973.
Paris - Montreal - Honolulu.
105 rue Sein Honoré.
75001 Paris.
Le Sein Graal
CSC
DING lala
WIIIZ
Bling Bling
0 GRAVITY

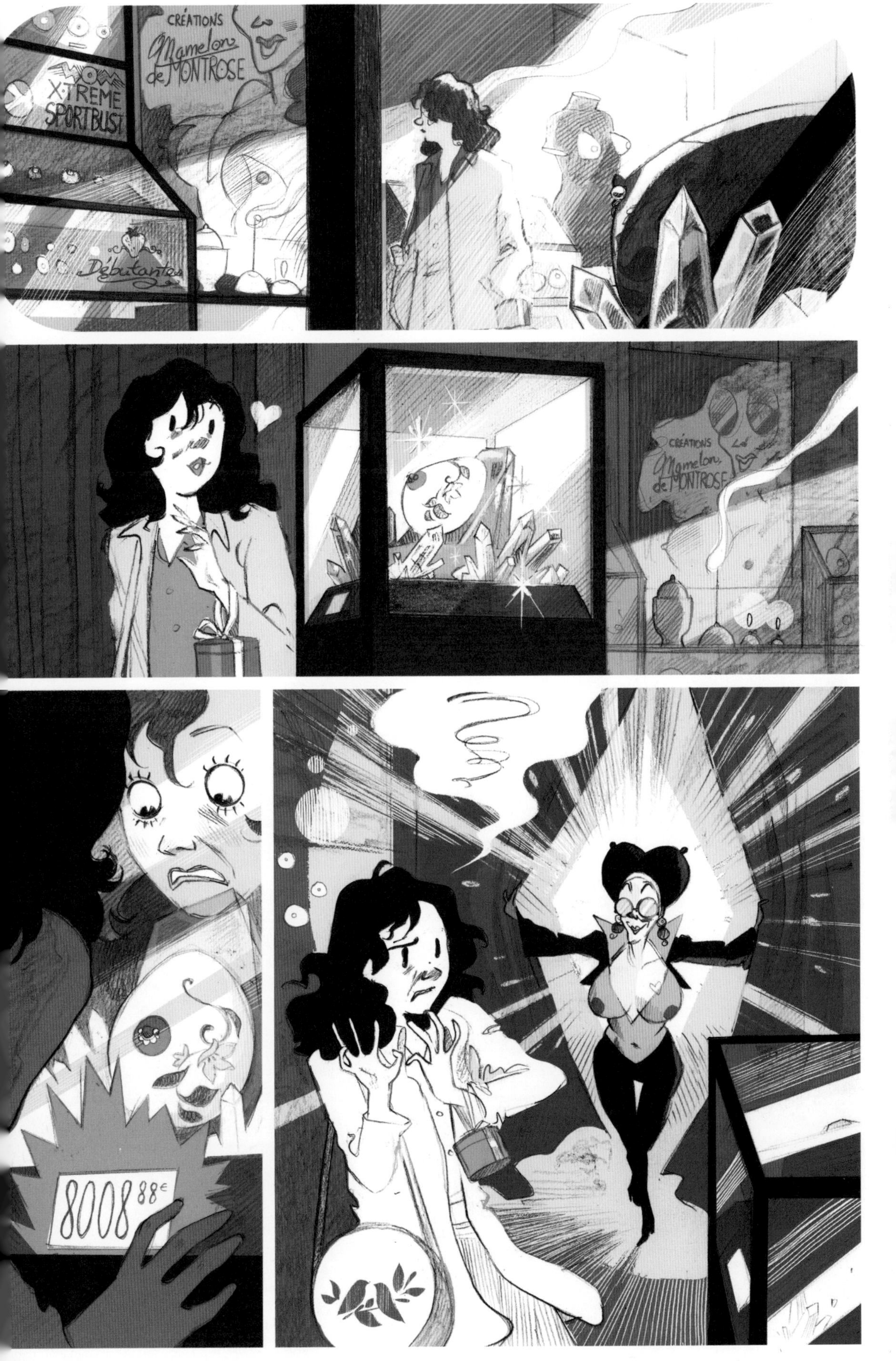

CRÉATIONS
Mamelon de MONTROSE
WOW X-TREME SPORTBUST
Débutantes
CRÉATIONS
Mamelon de MONTROSE
8008 88€

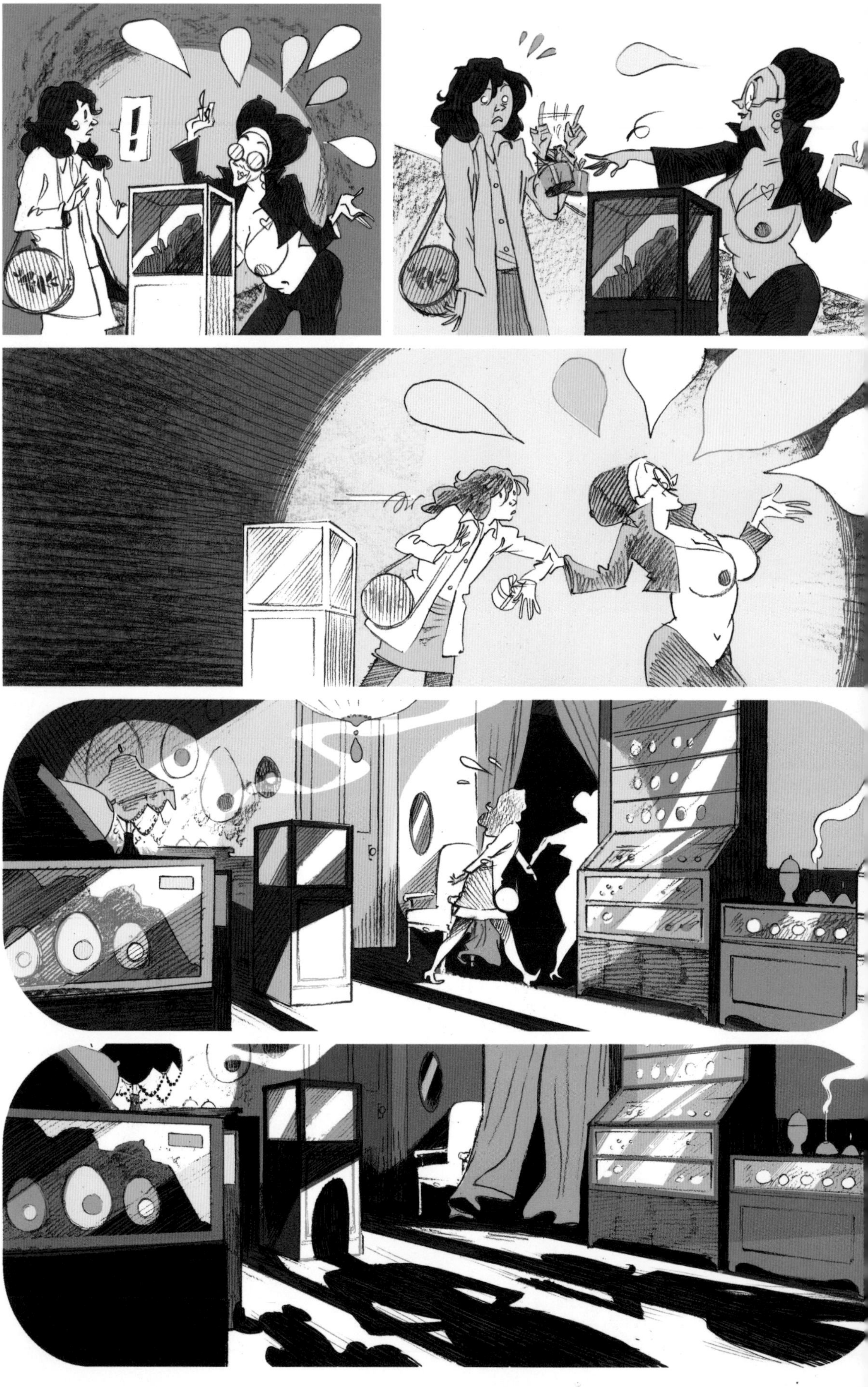
!

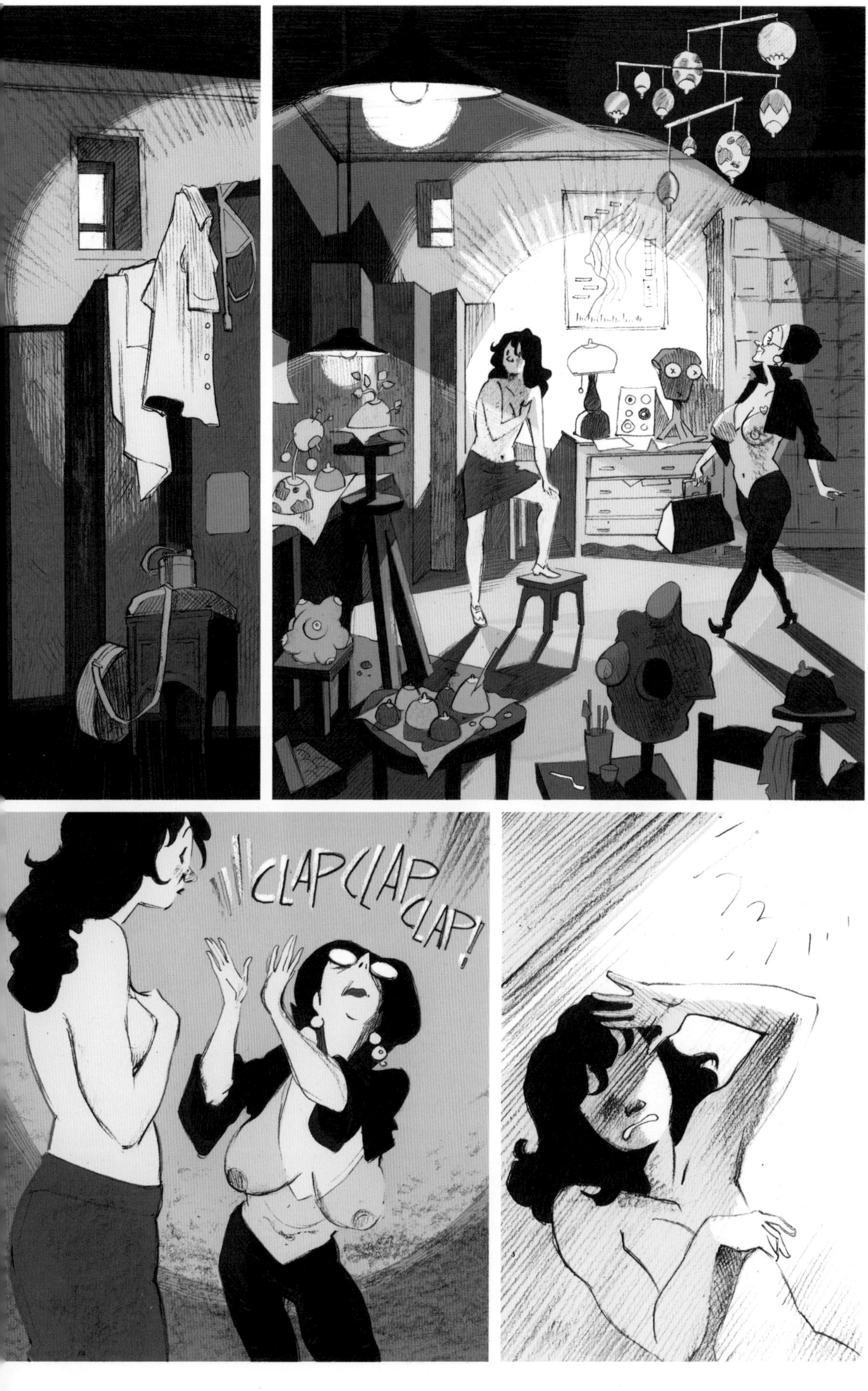
CLAP CLAP CLAP!

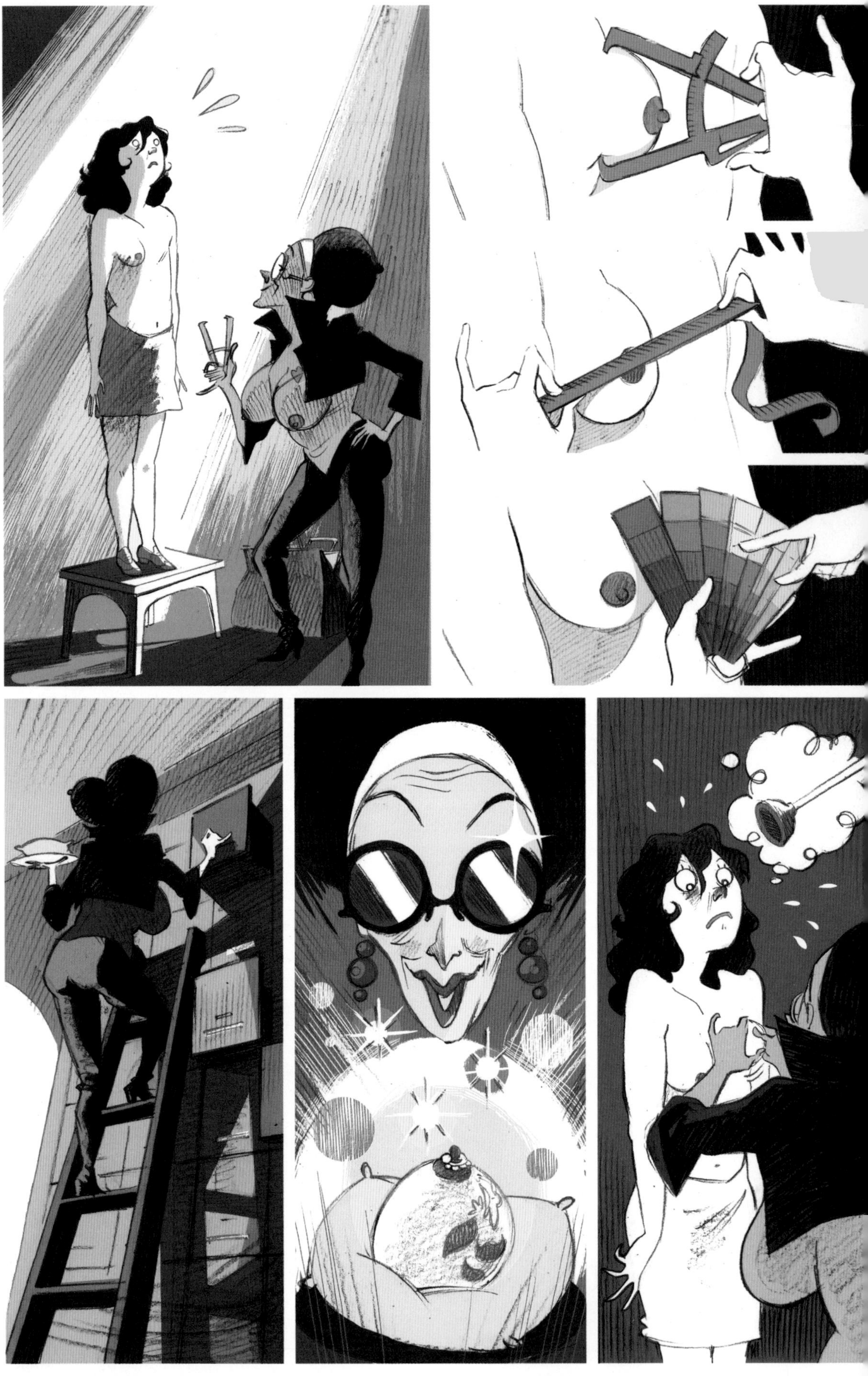

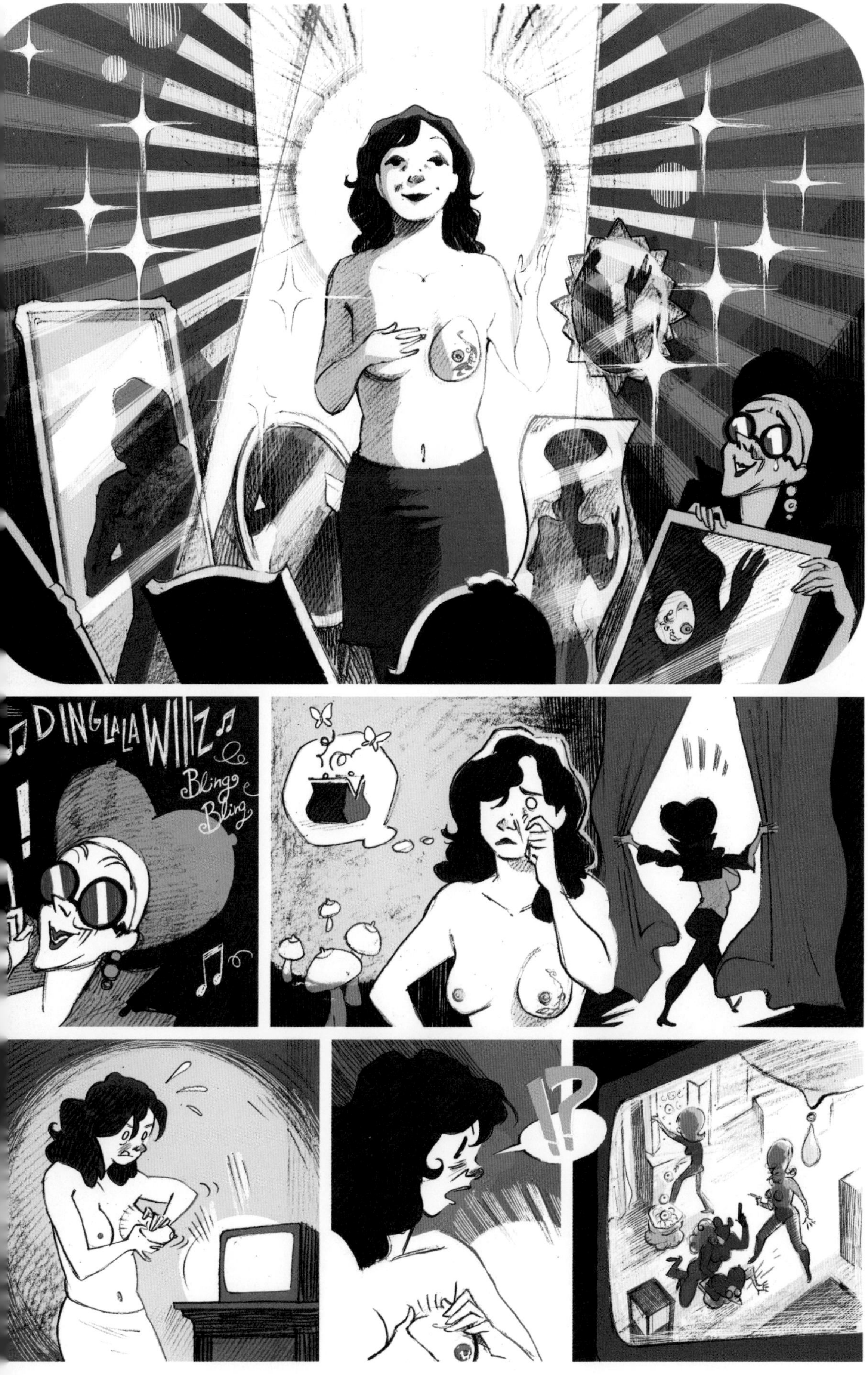
DING LALA WIIIZ
Bling Bling
!
!?

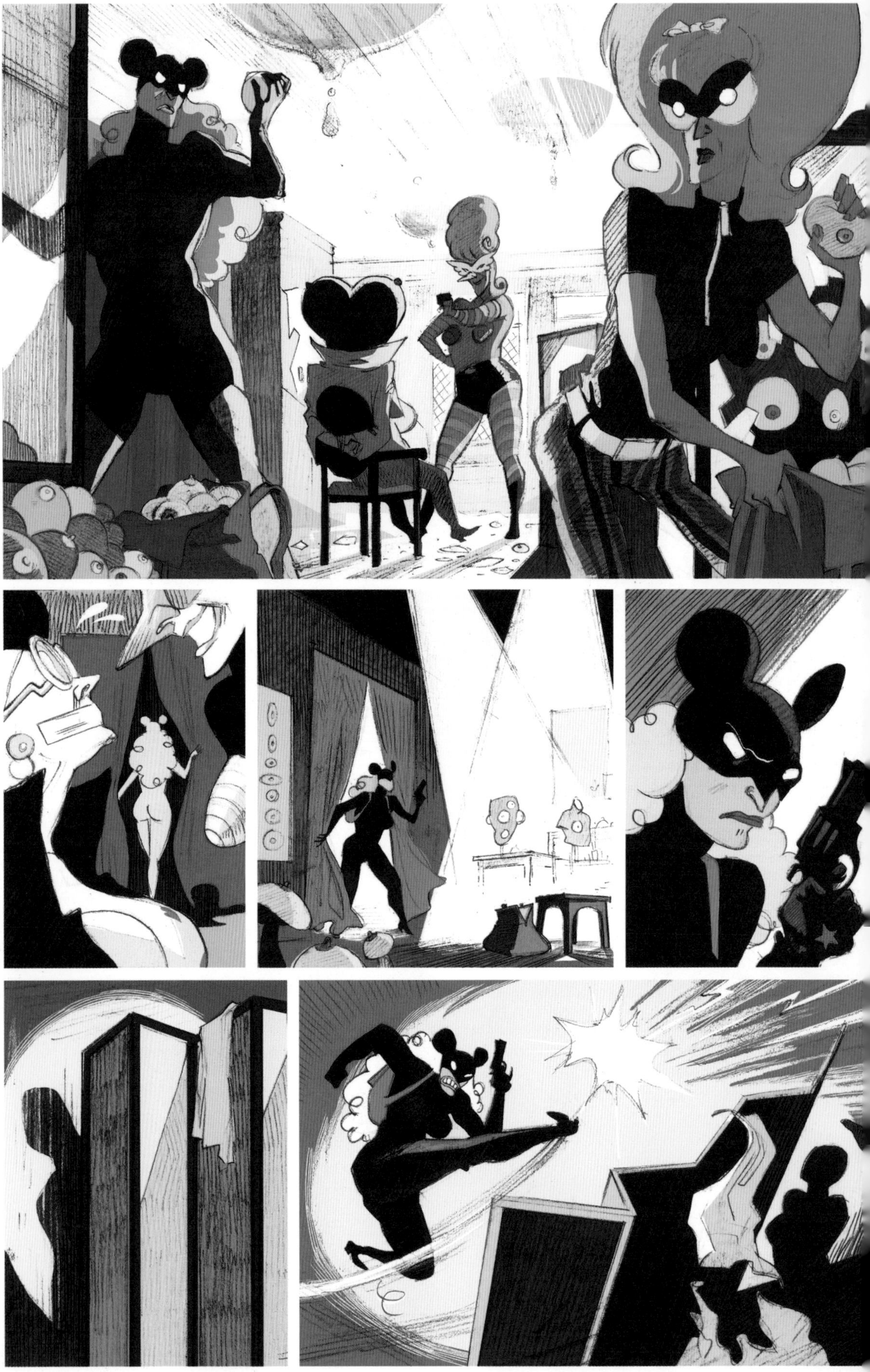

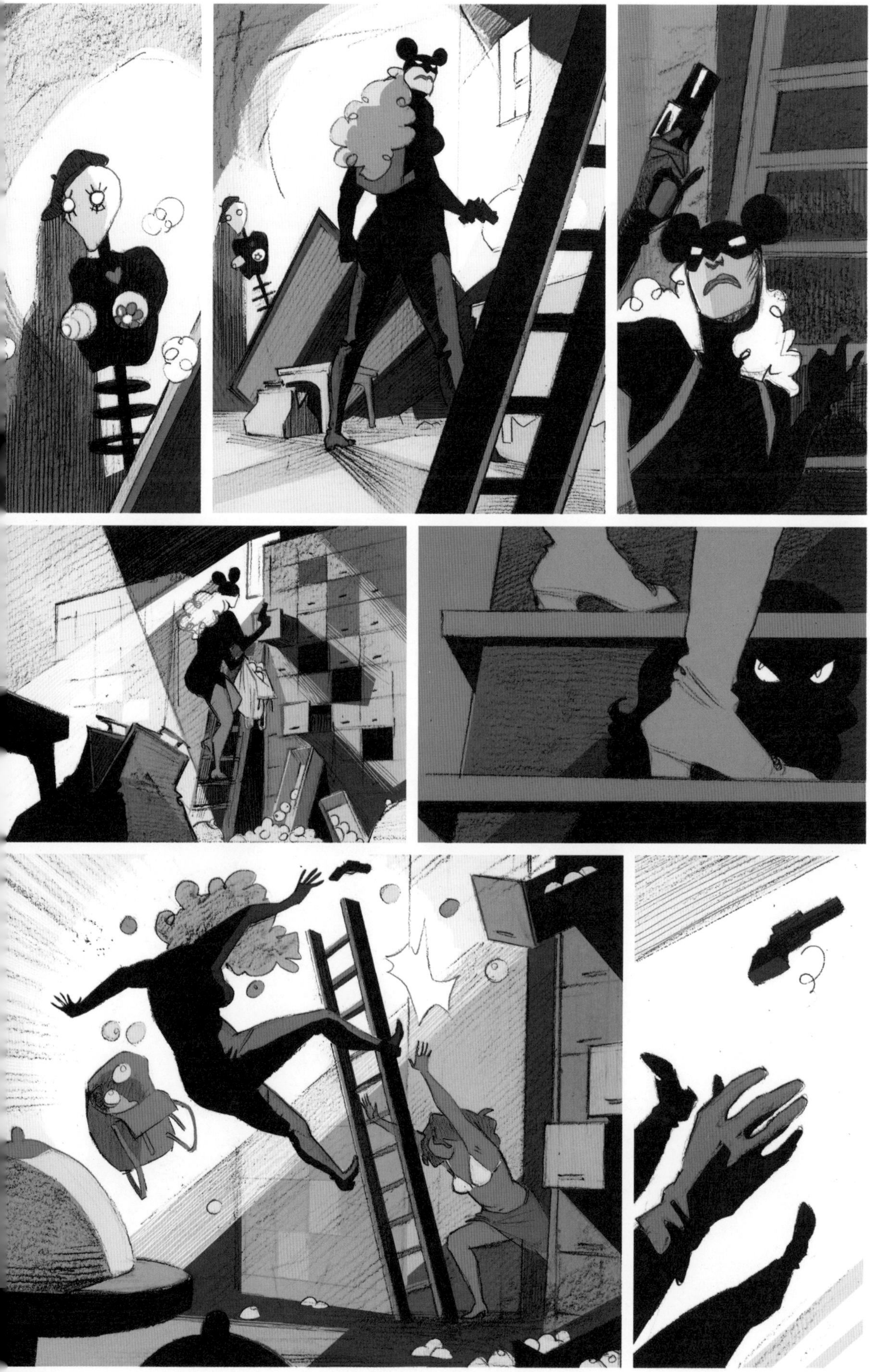

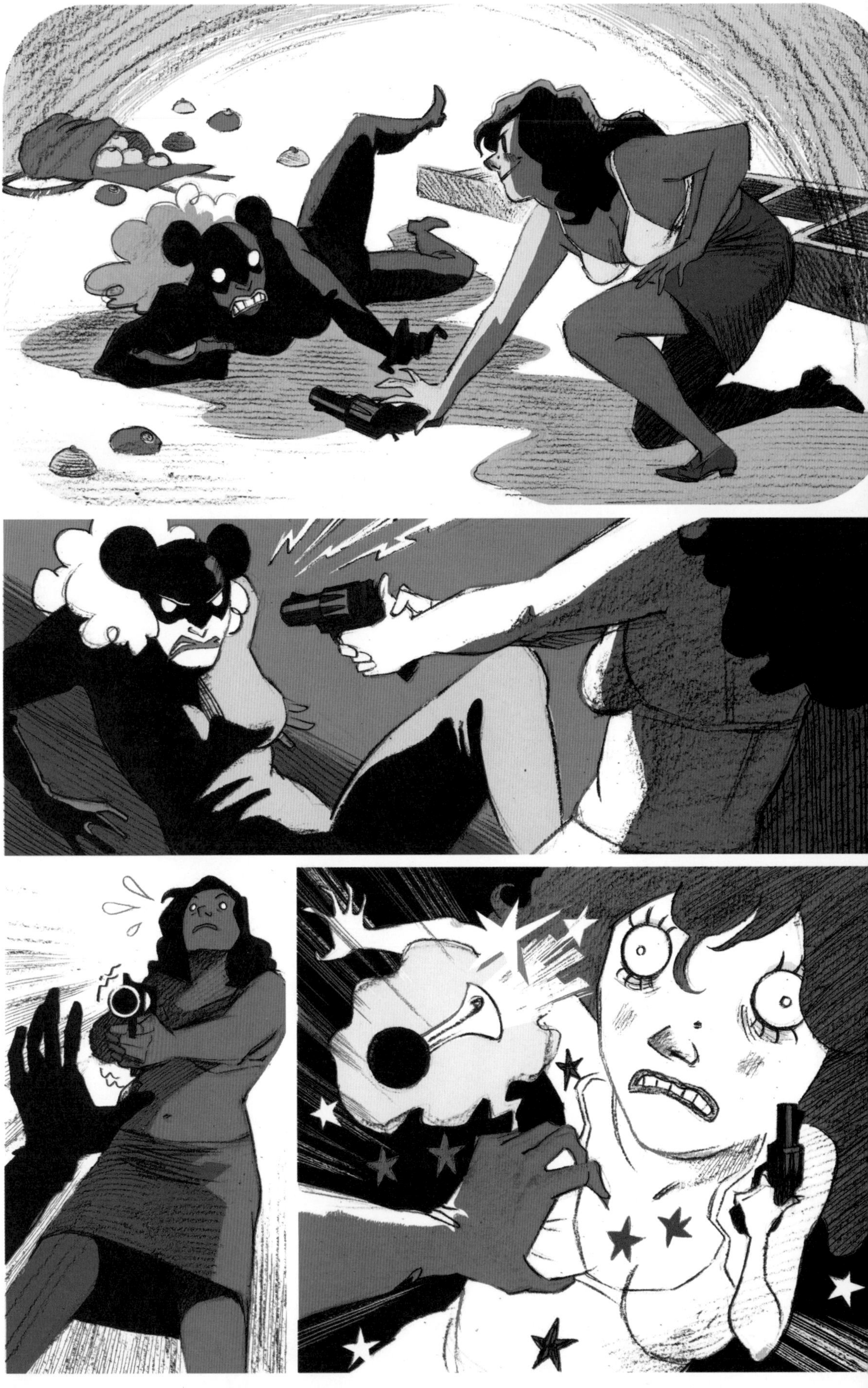

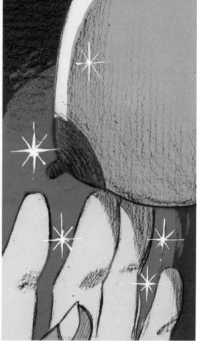

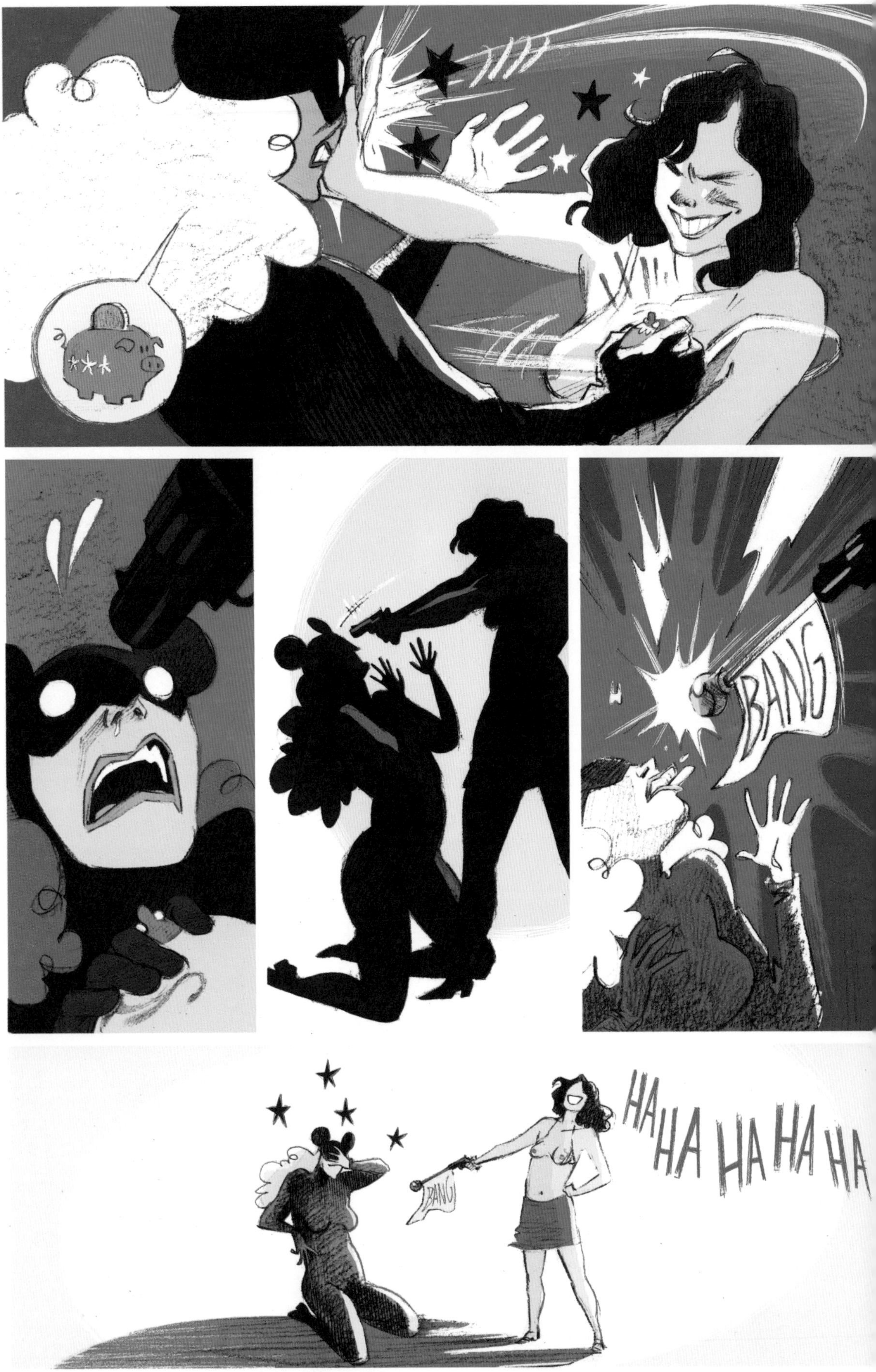
BANG
BANG
HA HA HA HA HA HA

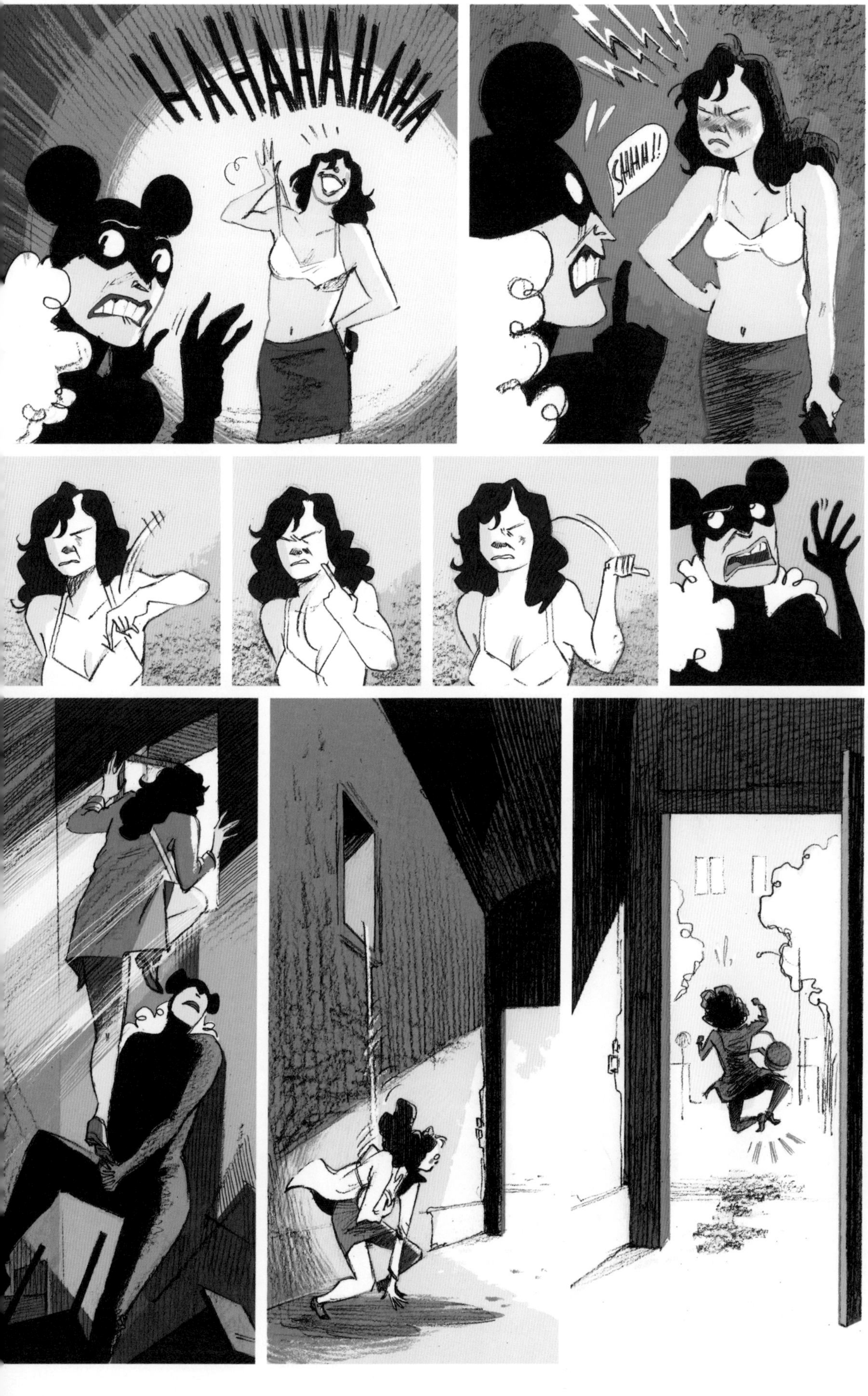
HAHAHAHAHAHA
SHHHH!!

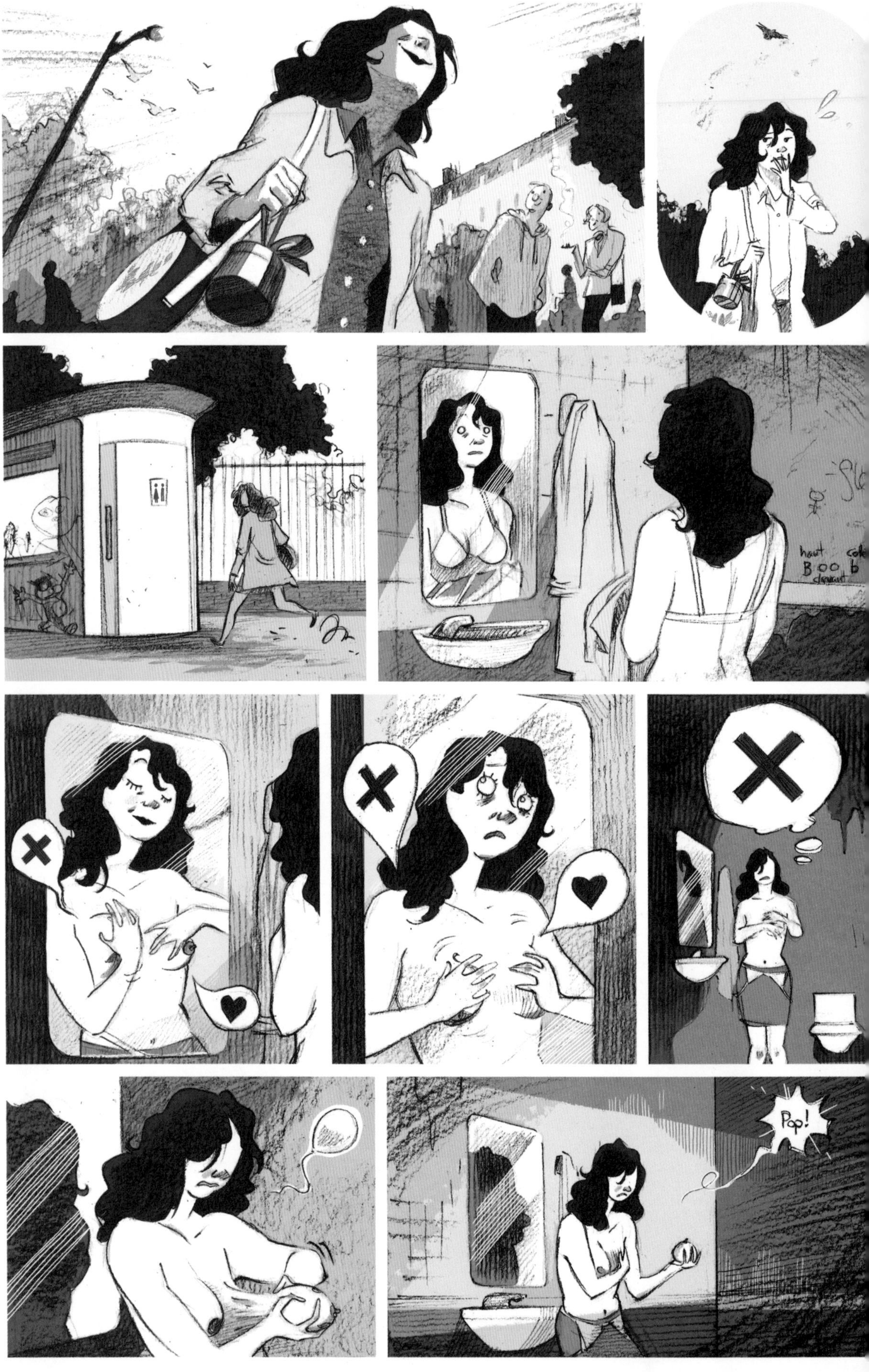
haut
Boob
devant
Pop!

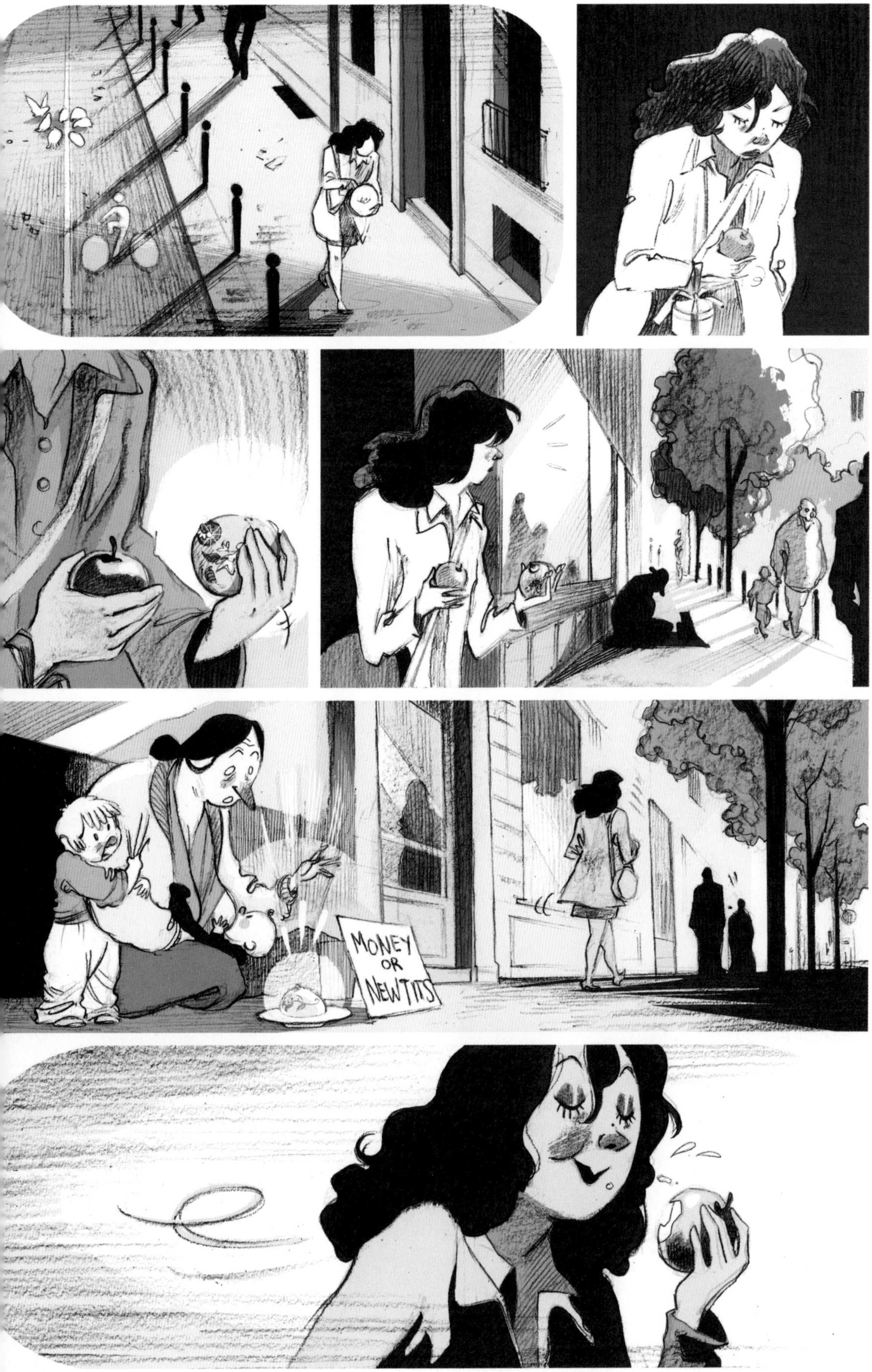
MONEY
OR
NEW TITS

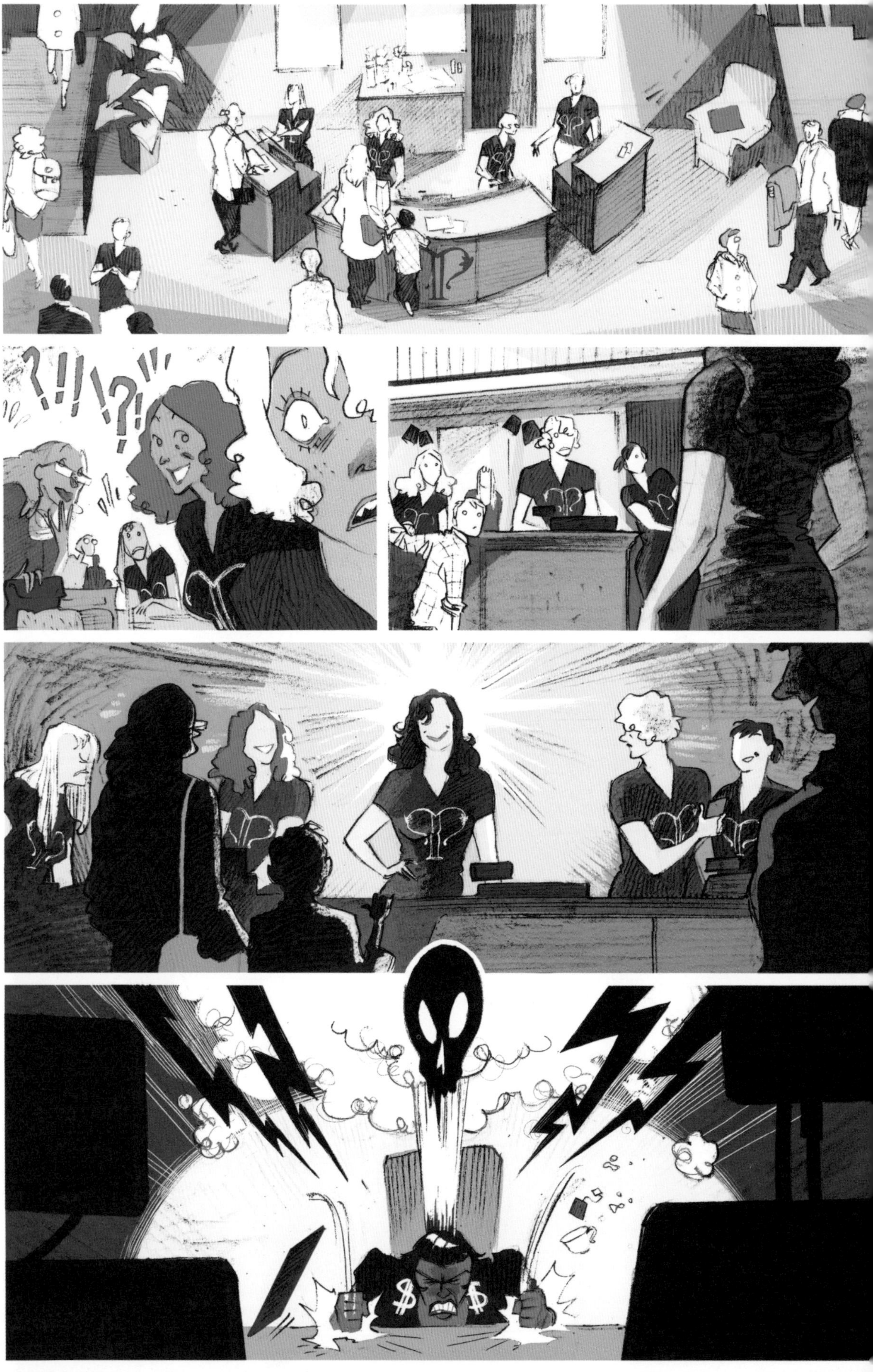
?!!!?!

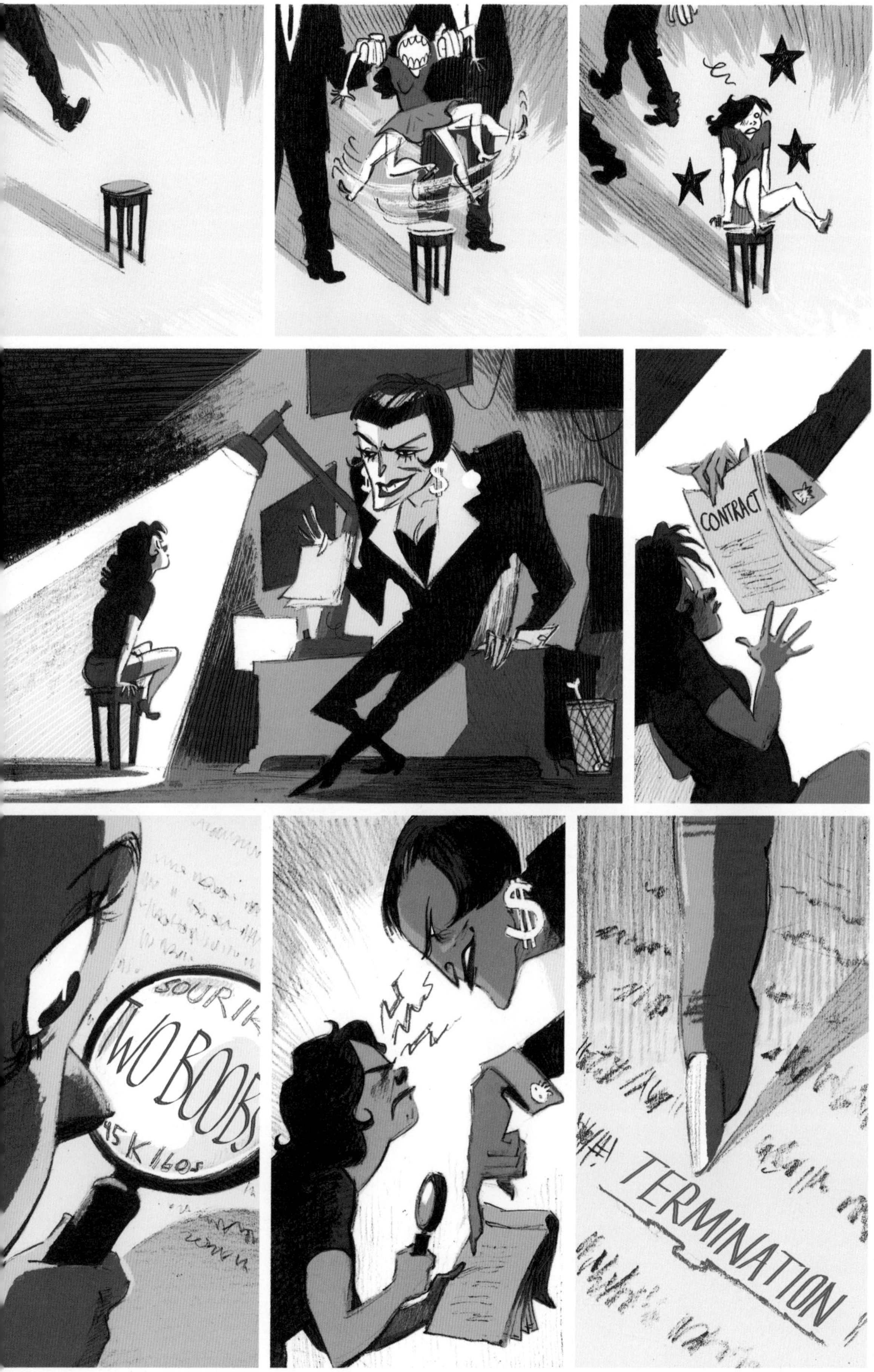
CONTRACT
SOURIK
TWO BOOKS
TERMINATION

-If you cannot look at me anymore,
I do not want to see you anymore!

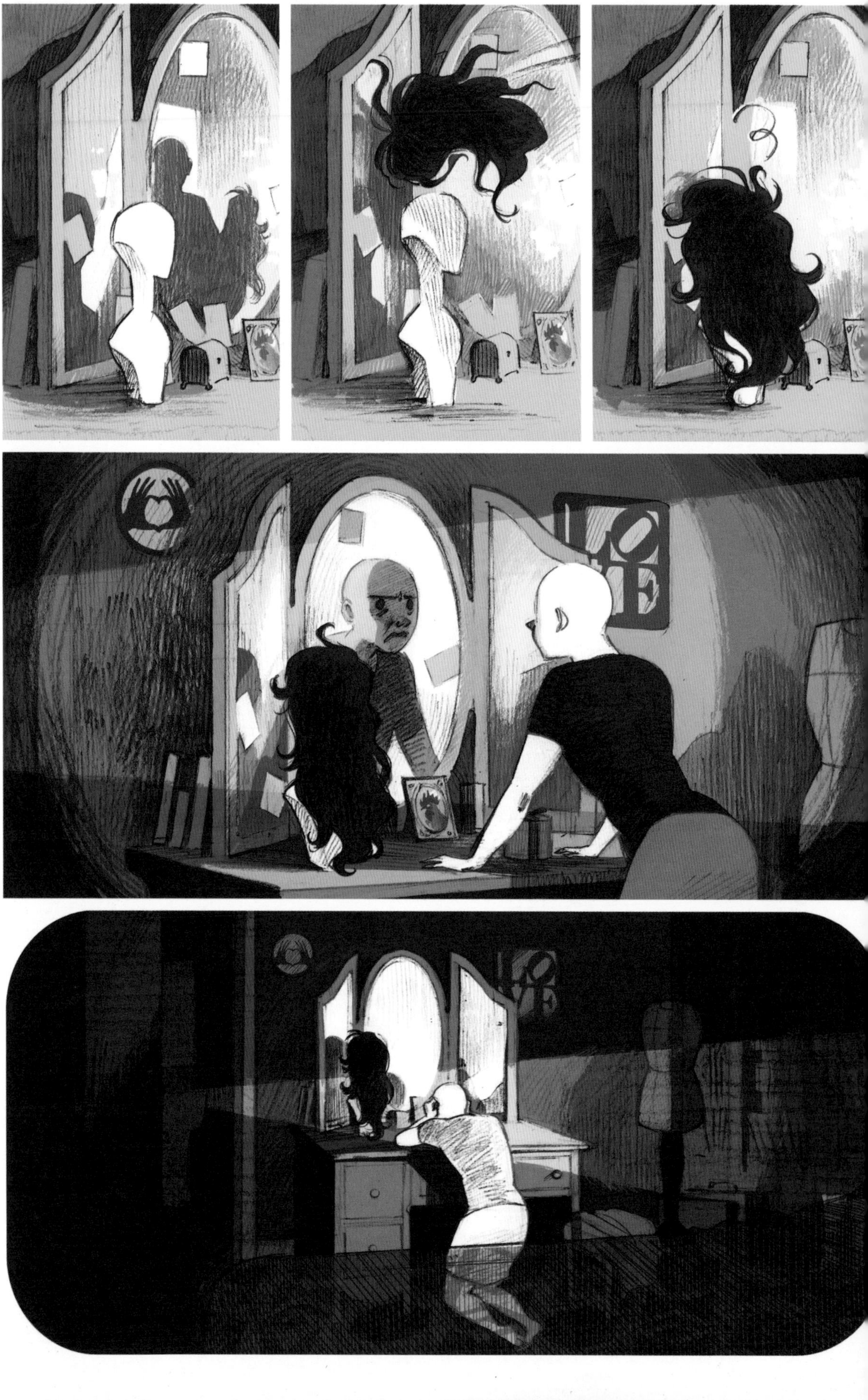

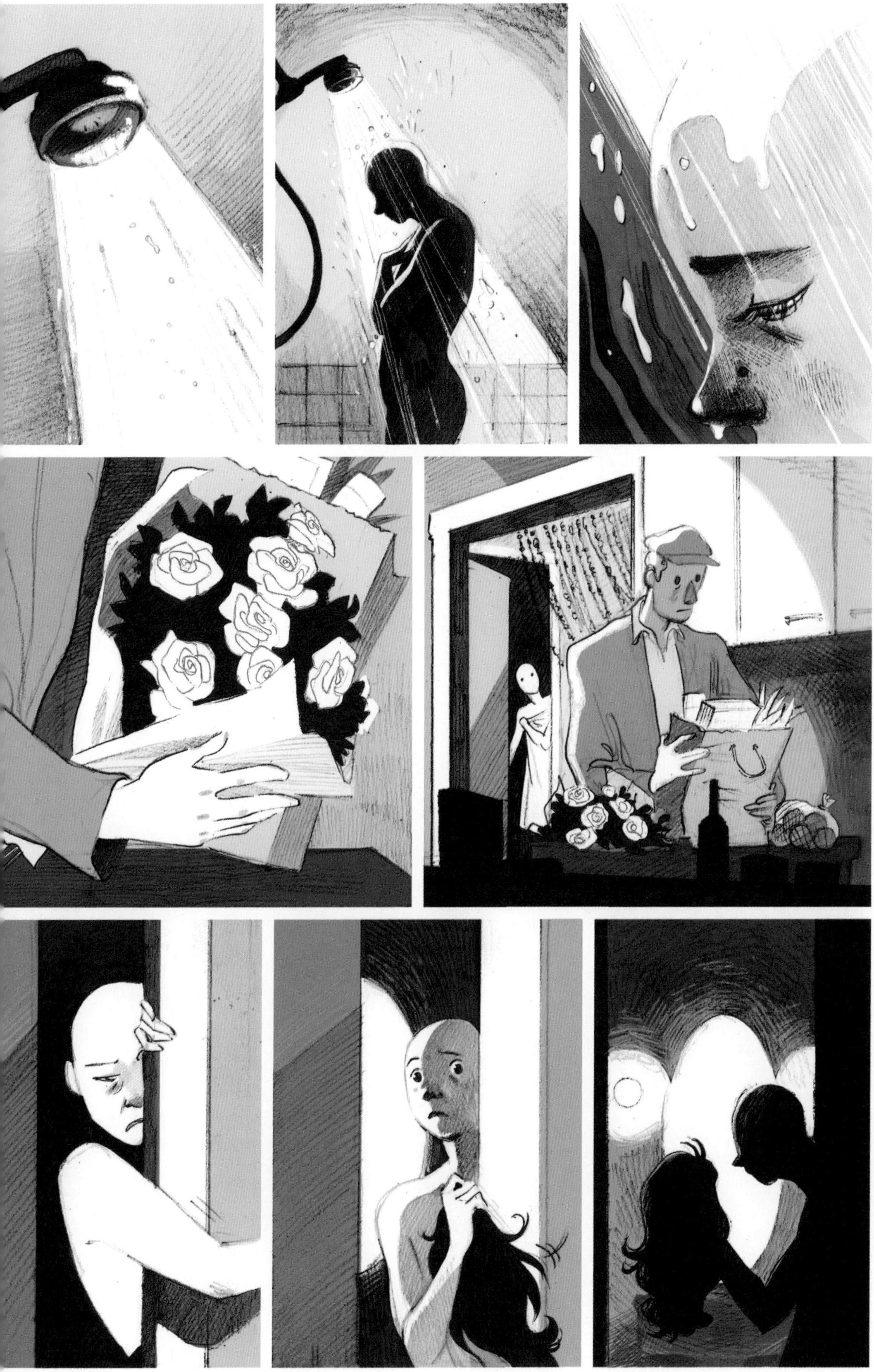

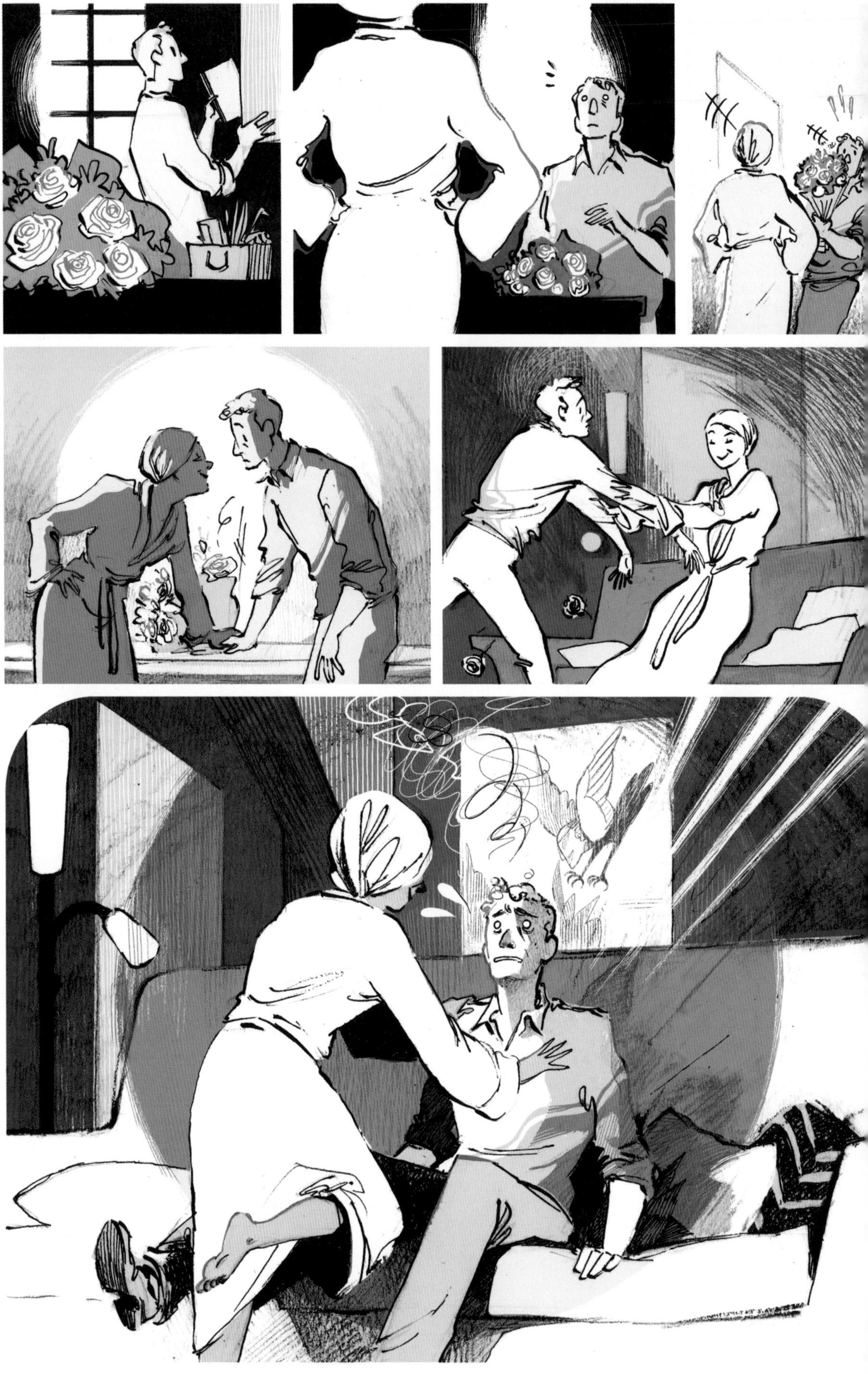

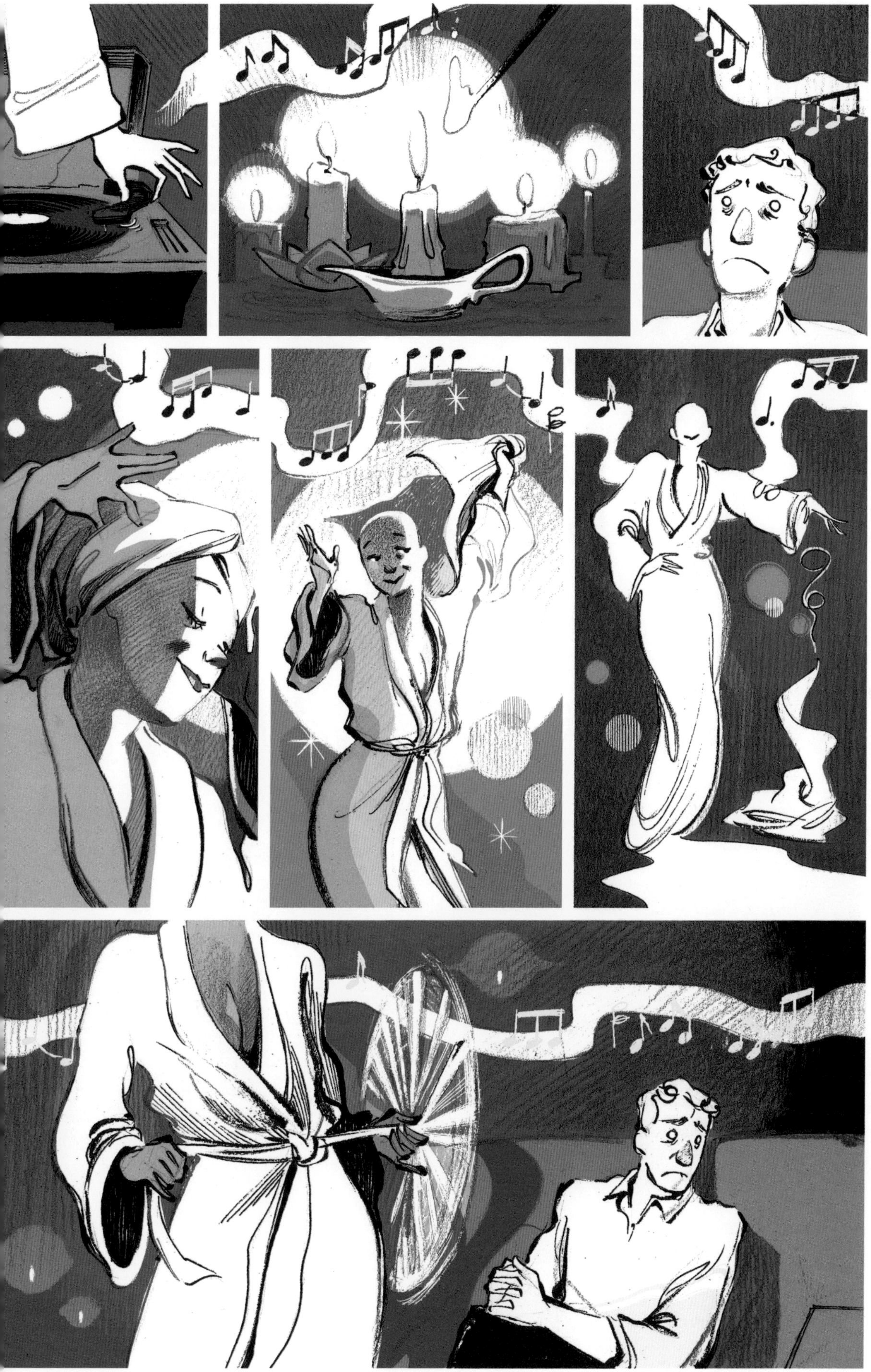

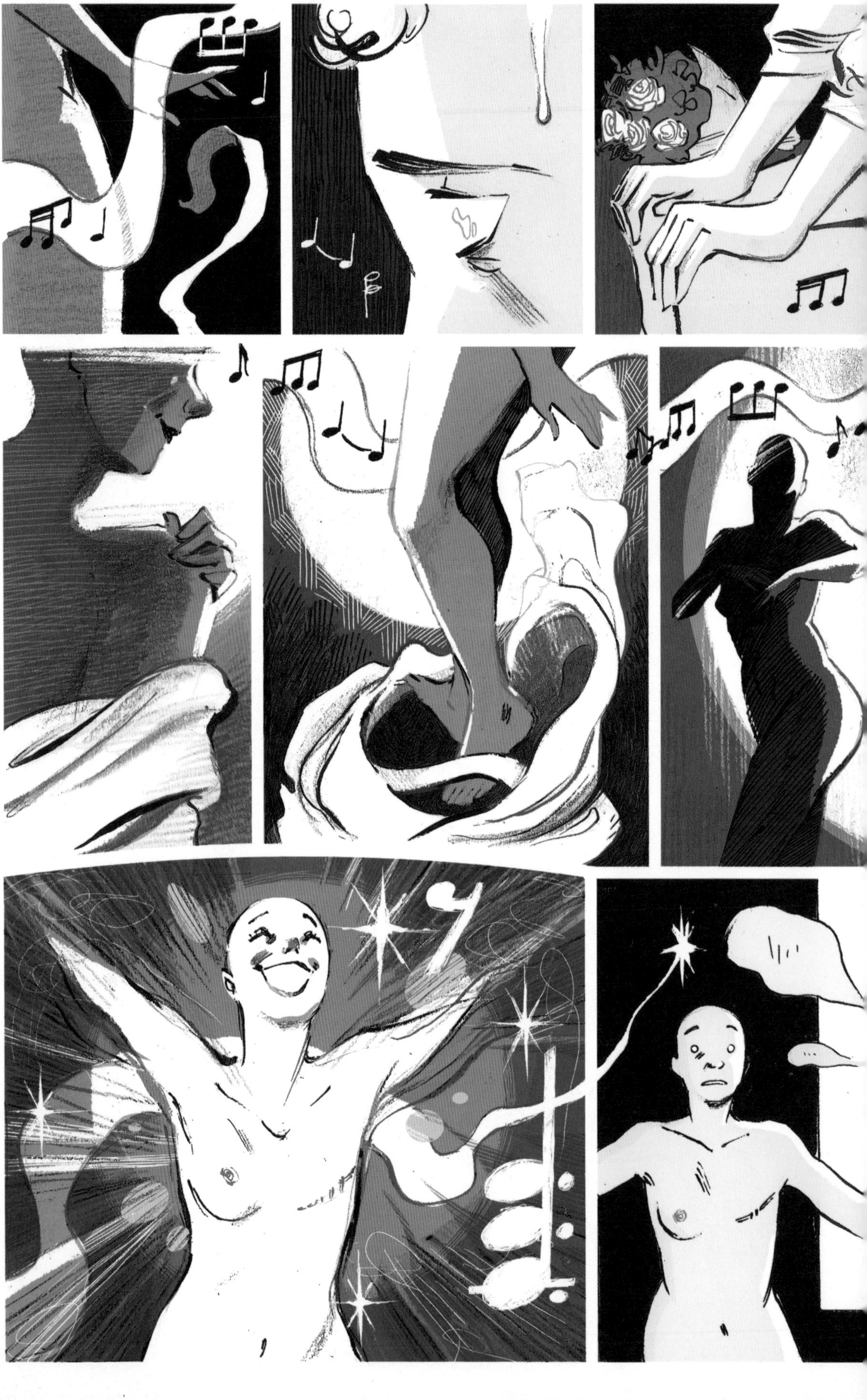

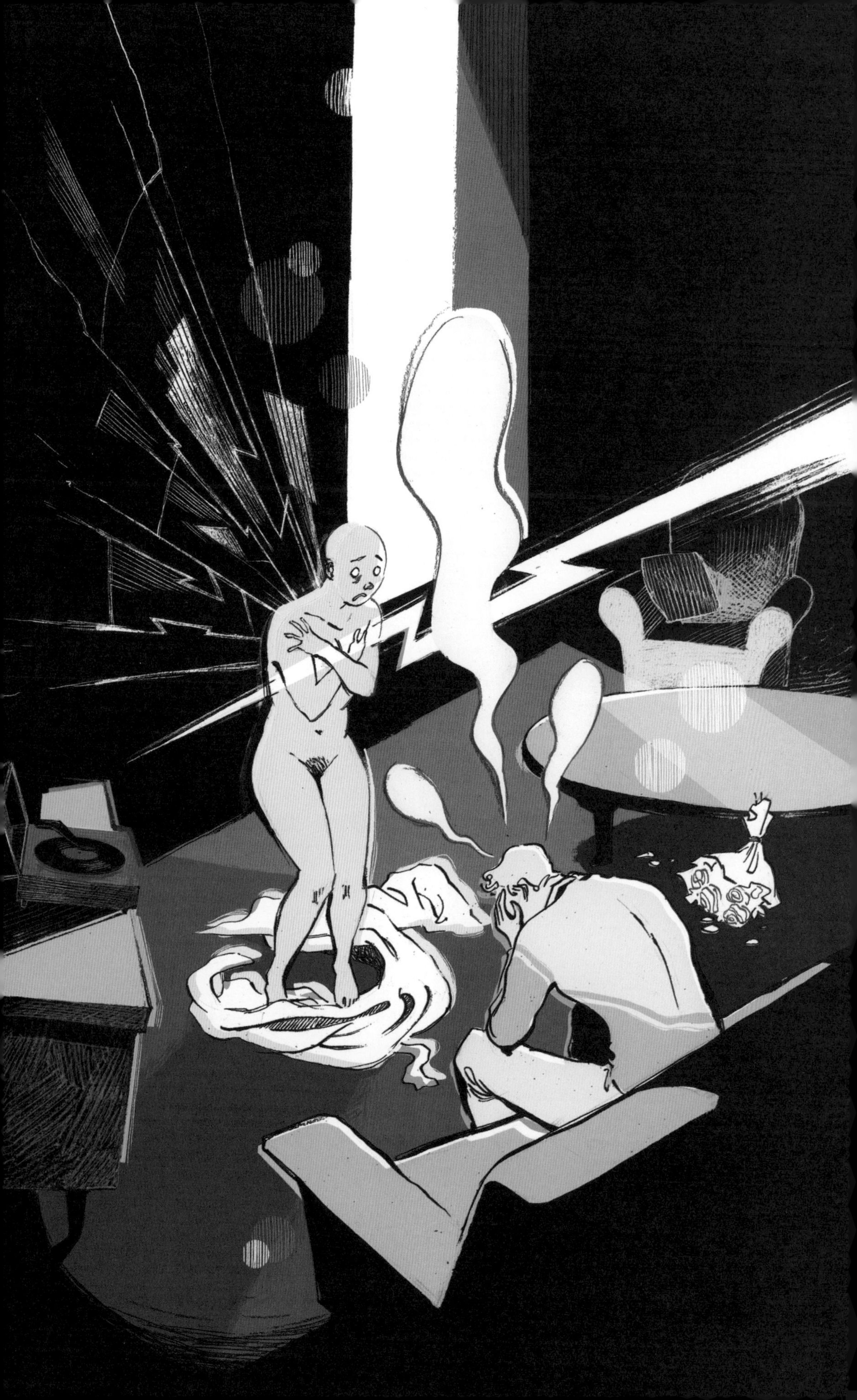

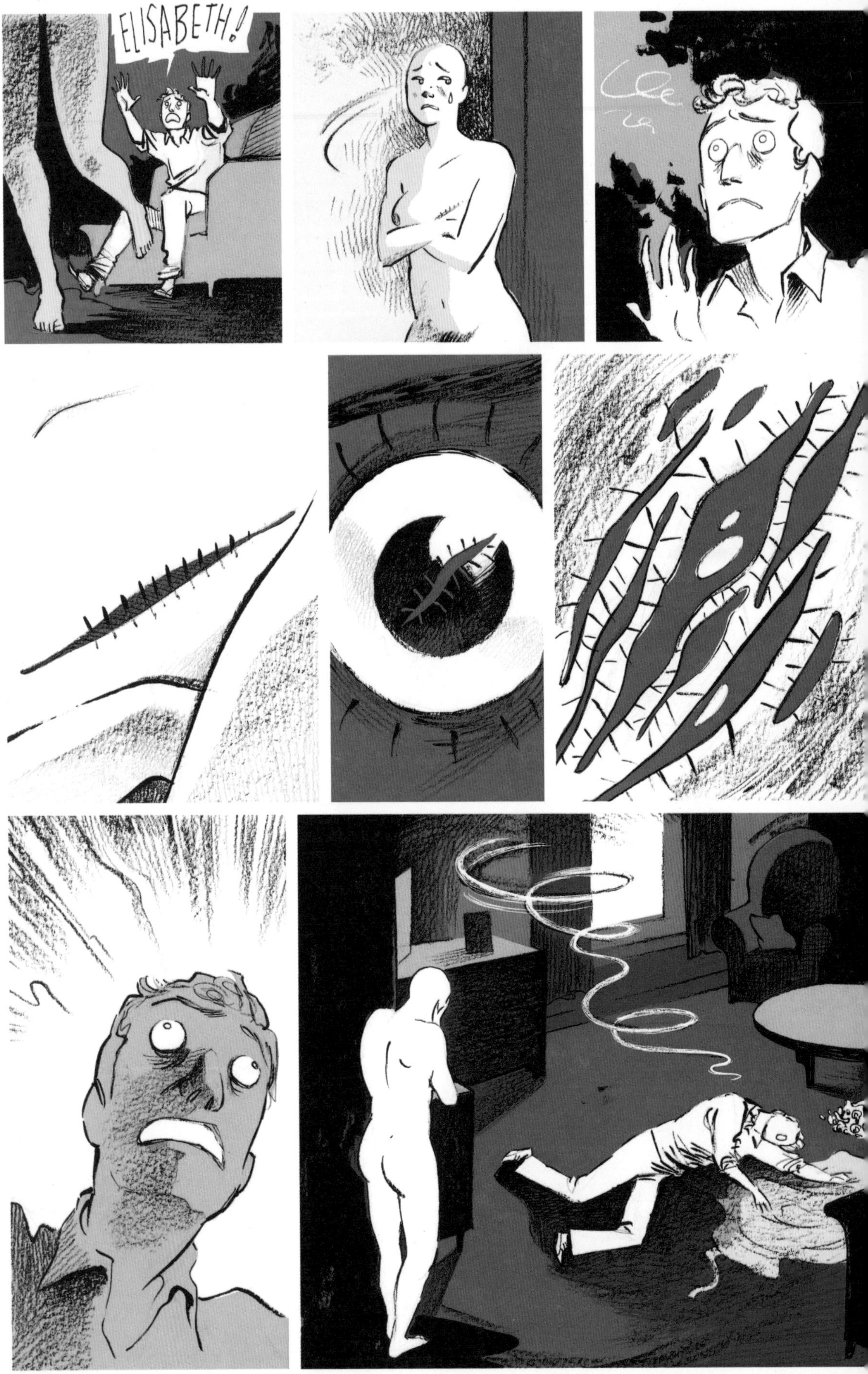
ELISABETH!

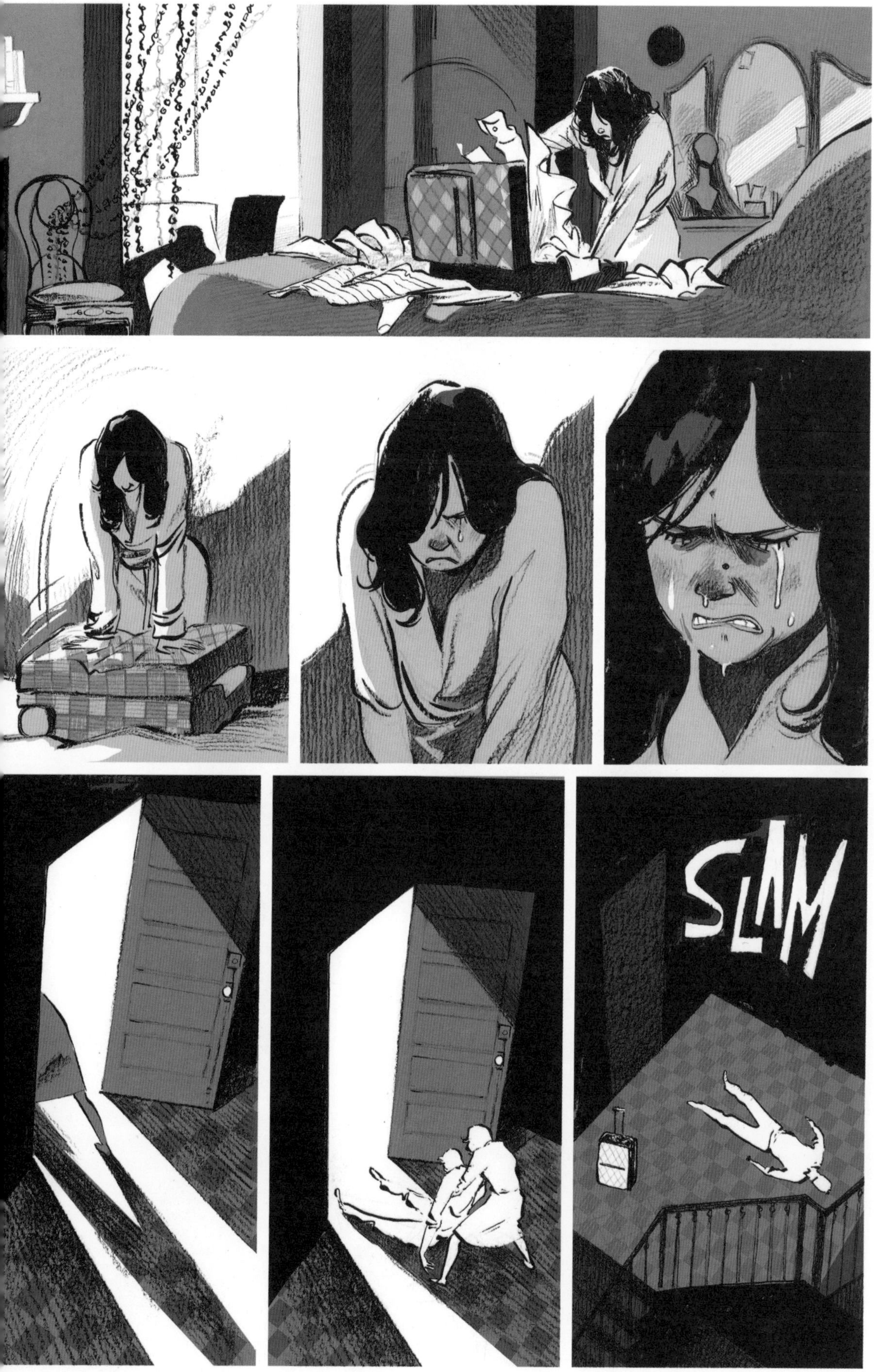
SLAM

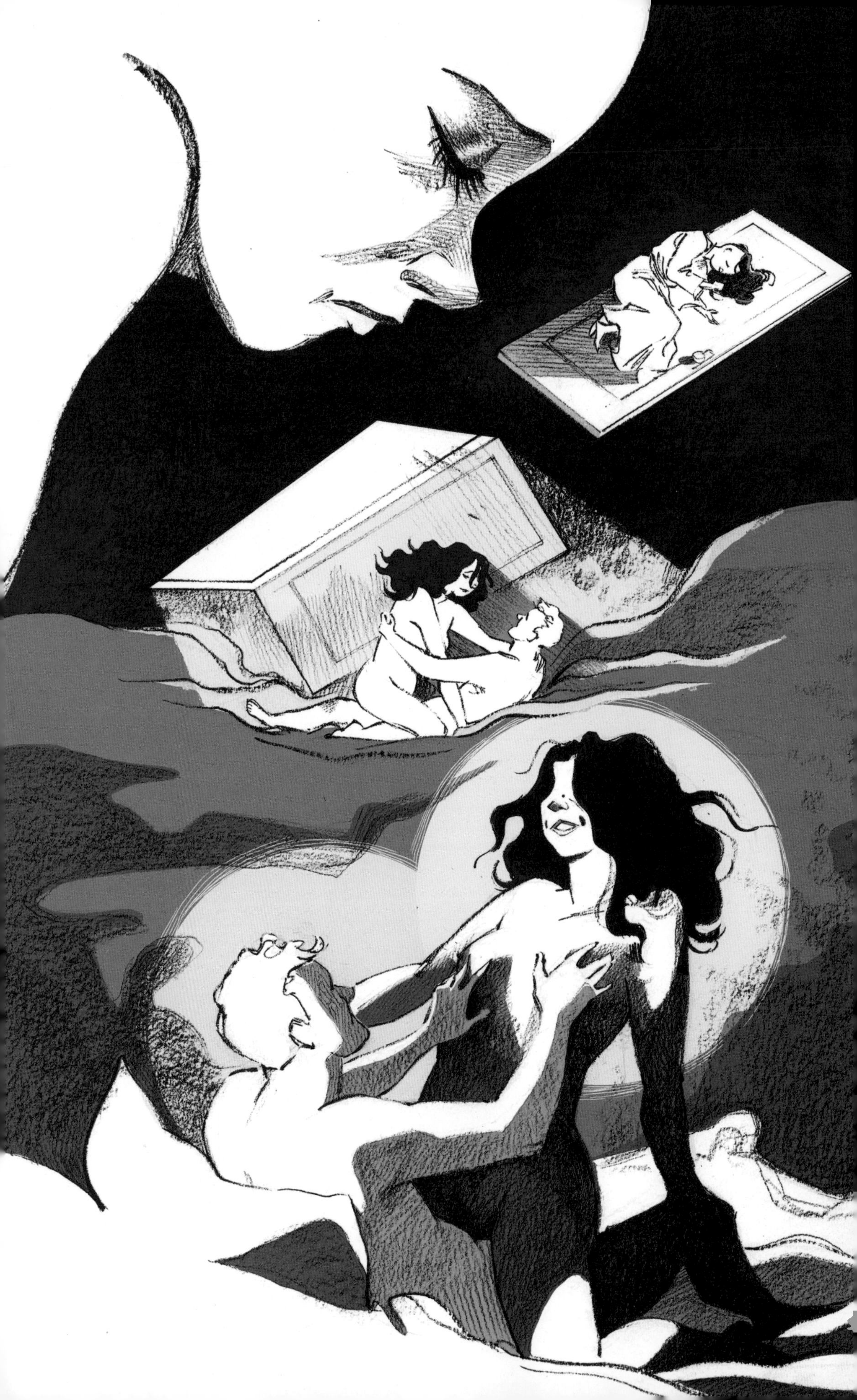

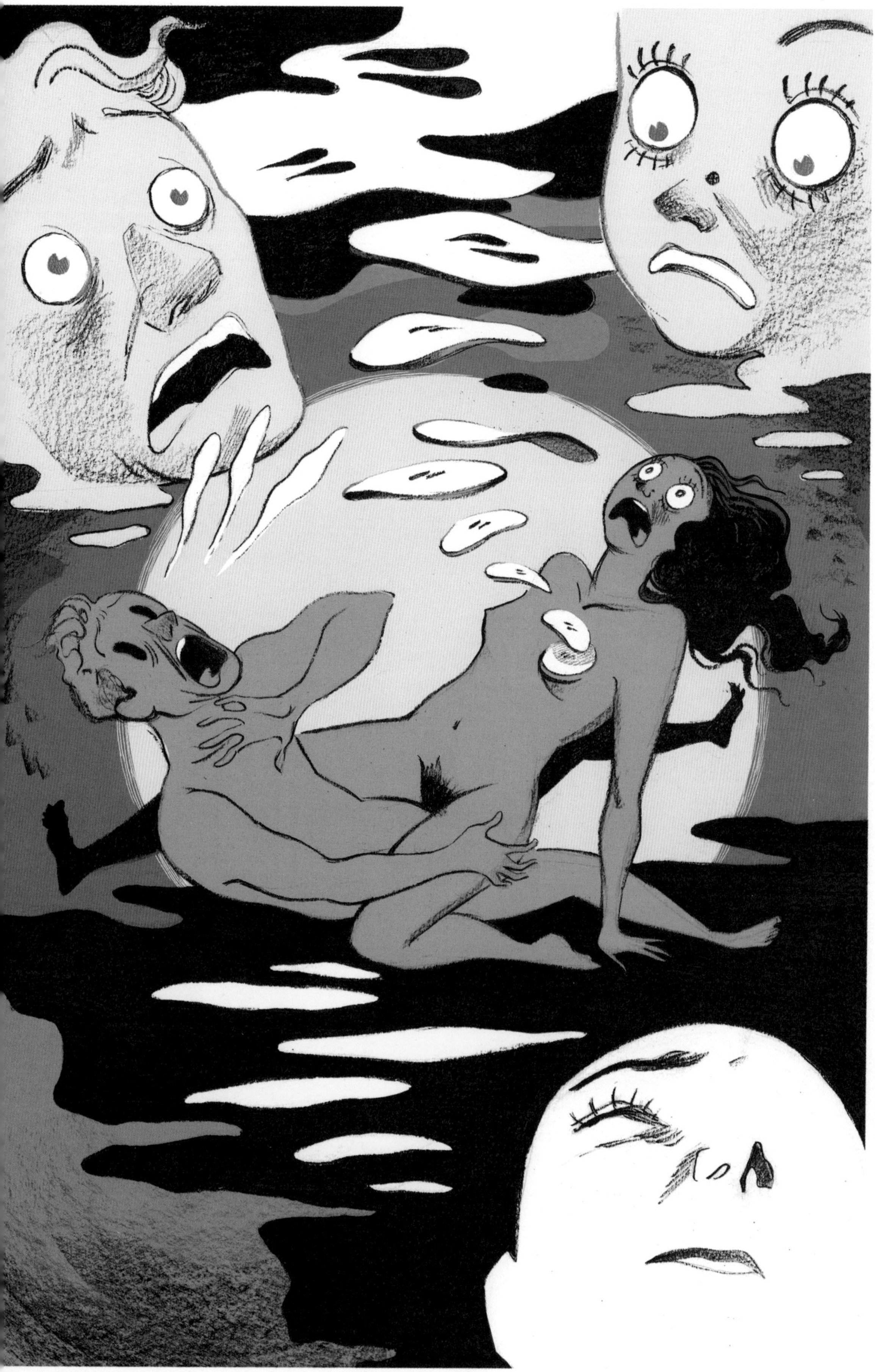

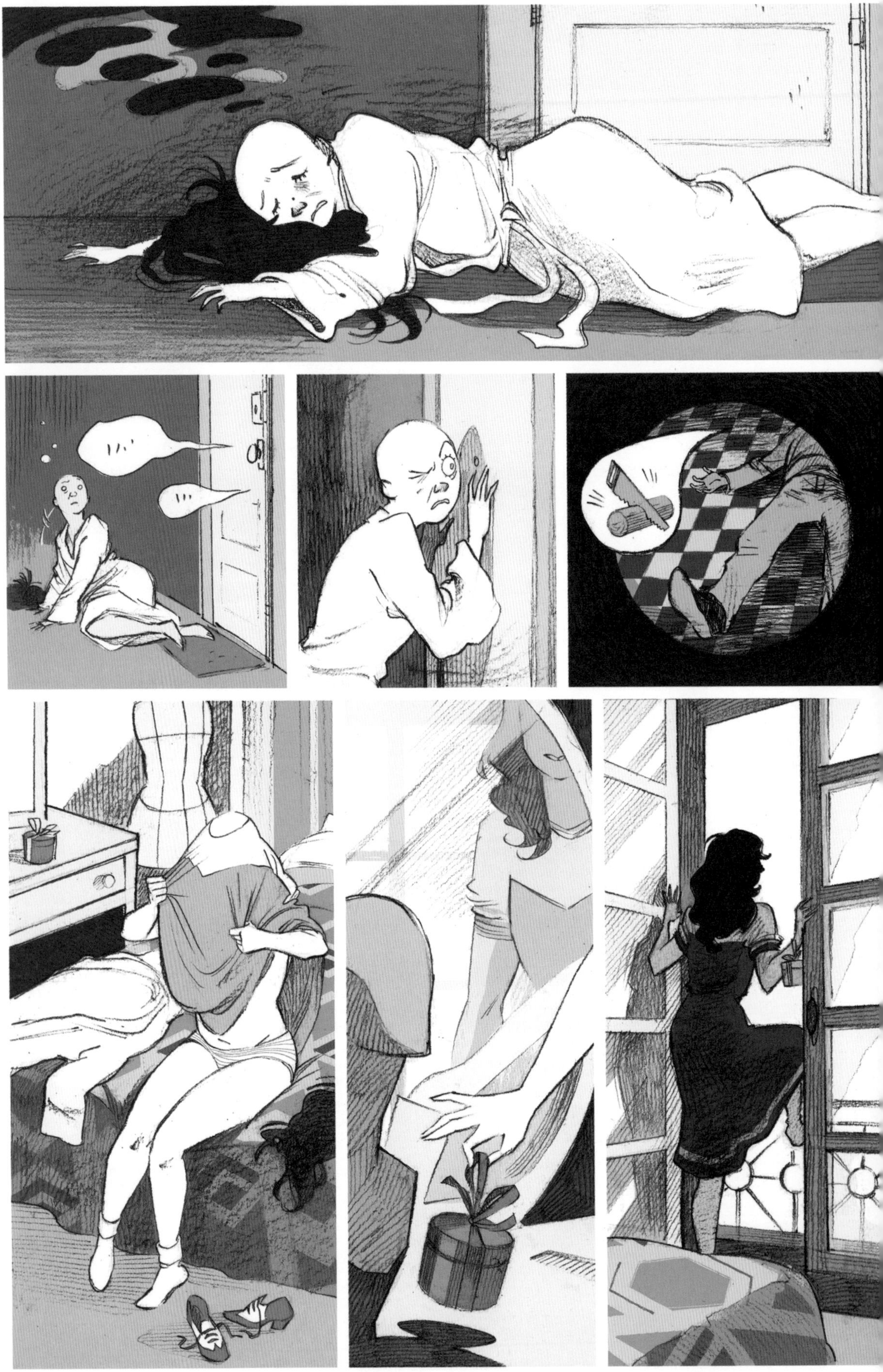

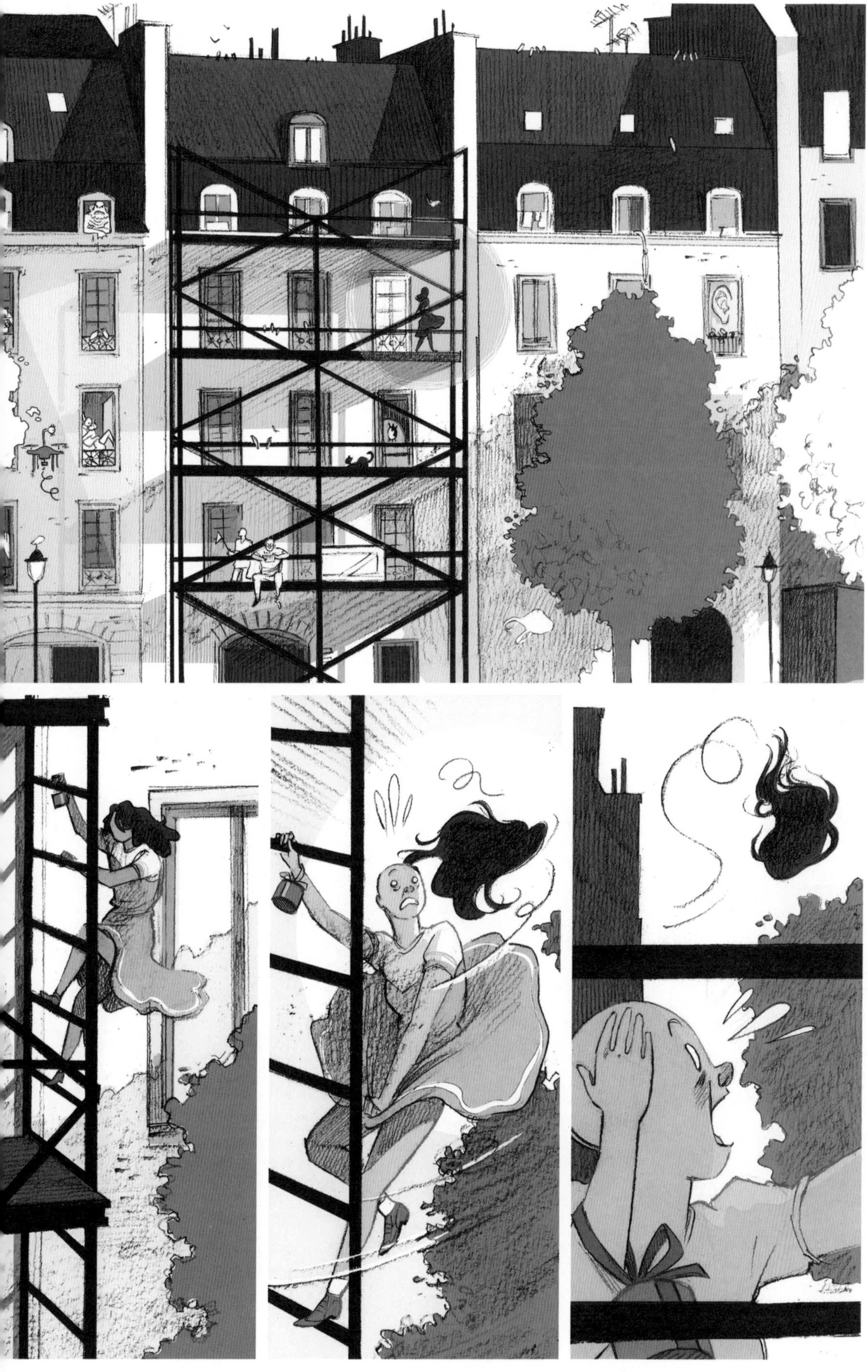

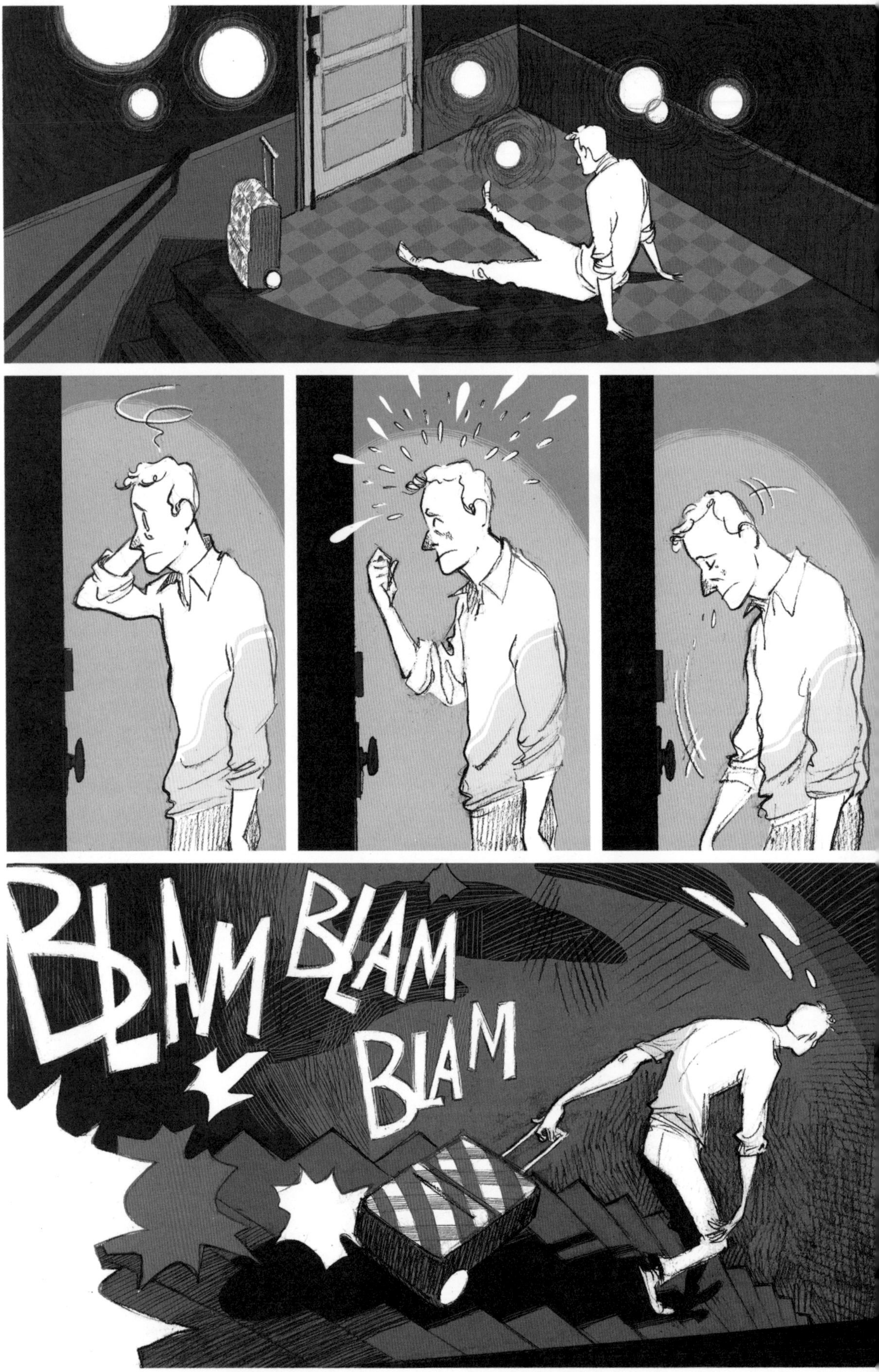
BLAM
BLAM
BLAM

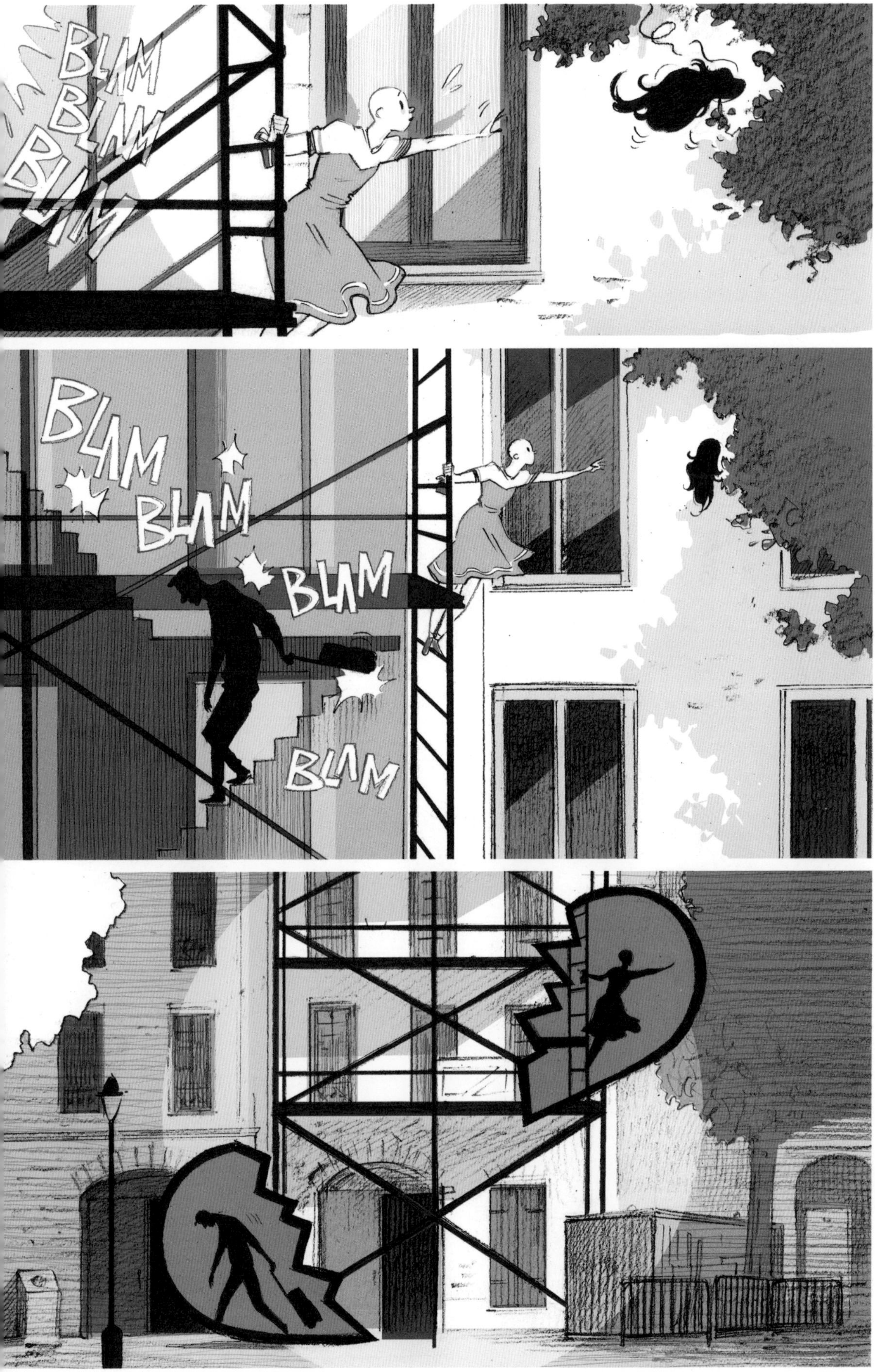
BLAM
BLAM
BLAM
BLAM
BLAM
BLAM
BLAM

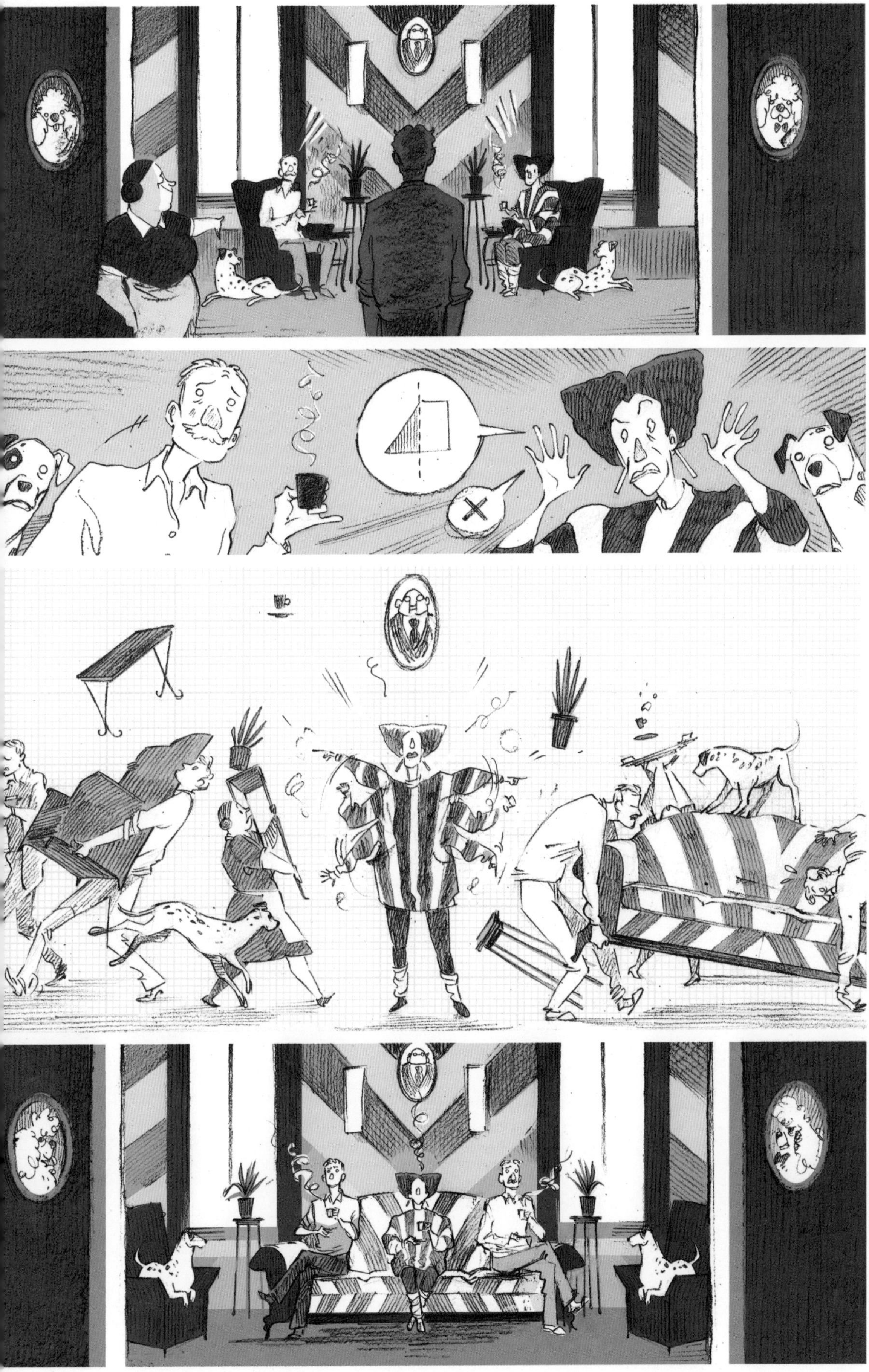

-Gadzooks! This wig is just a head!

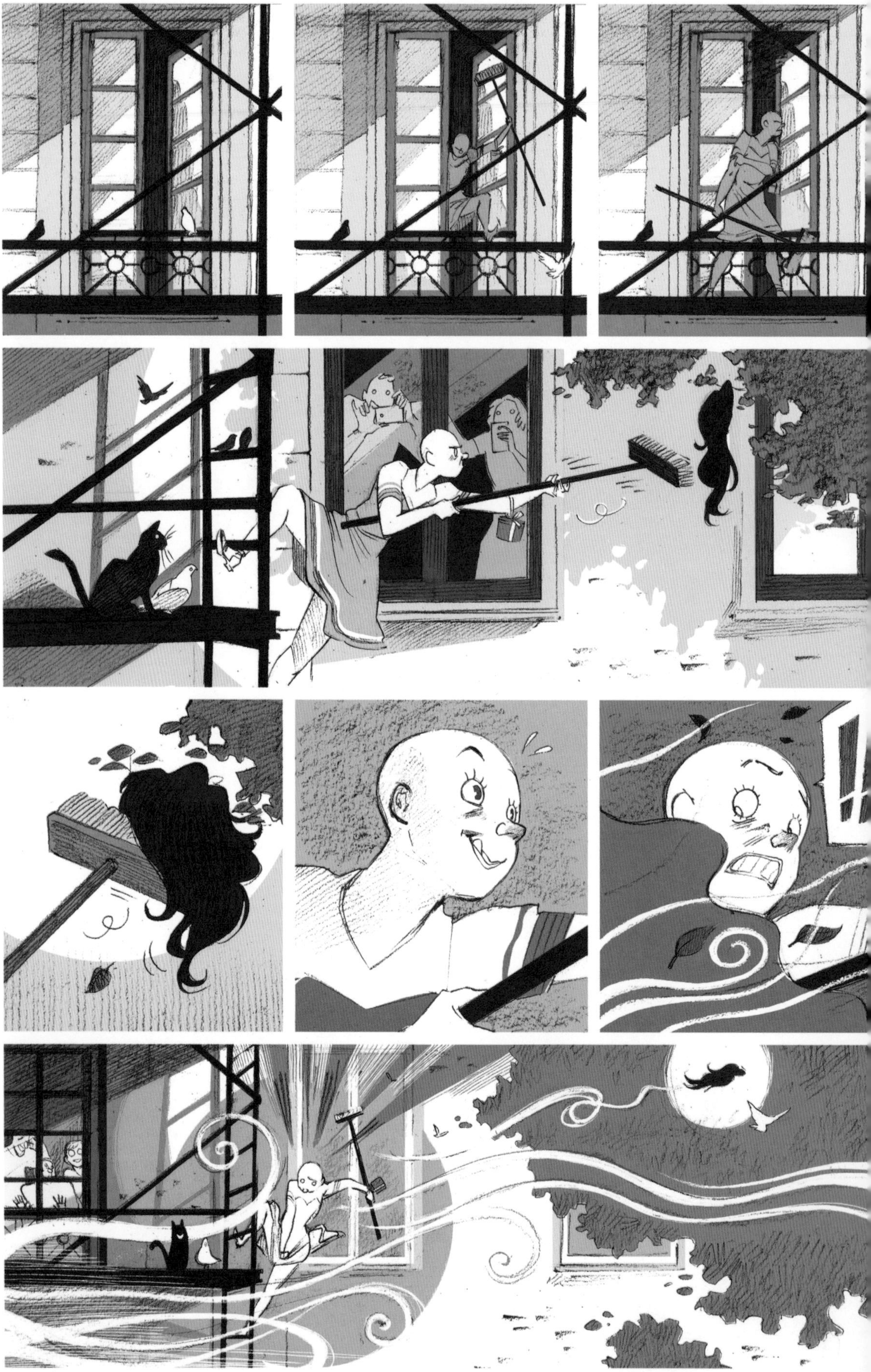

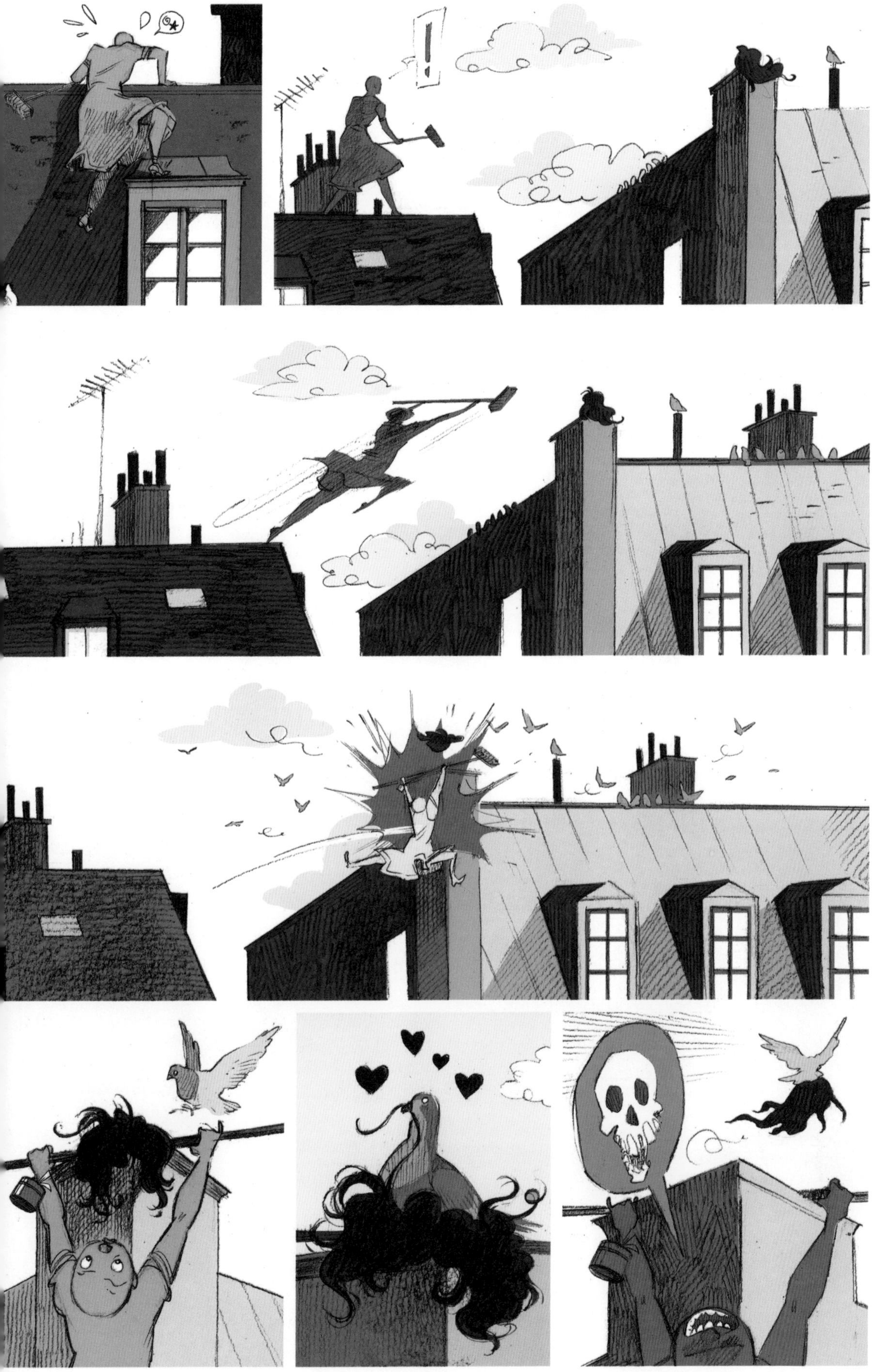
!

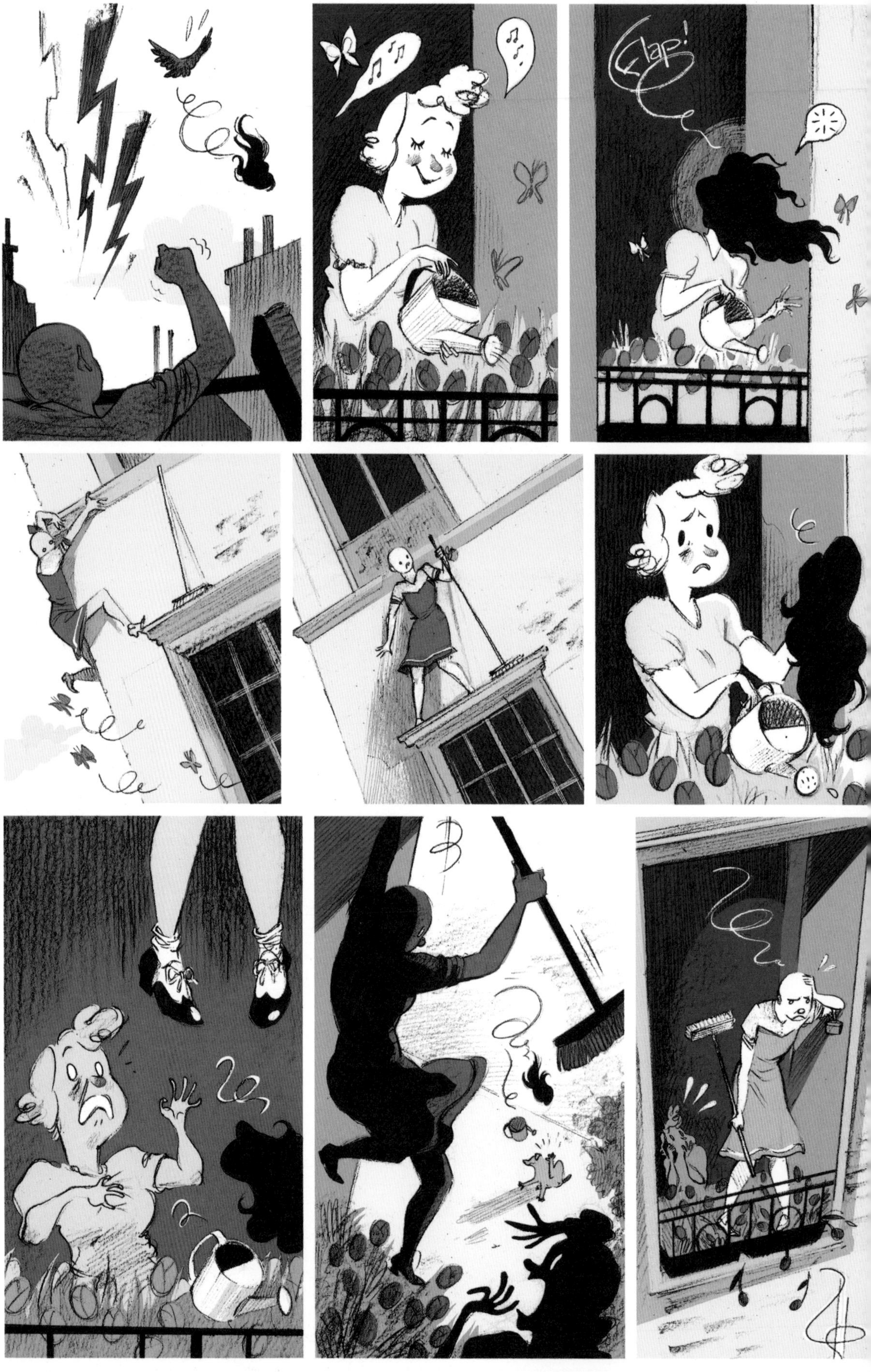
Clap!

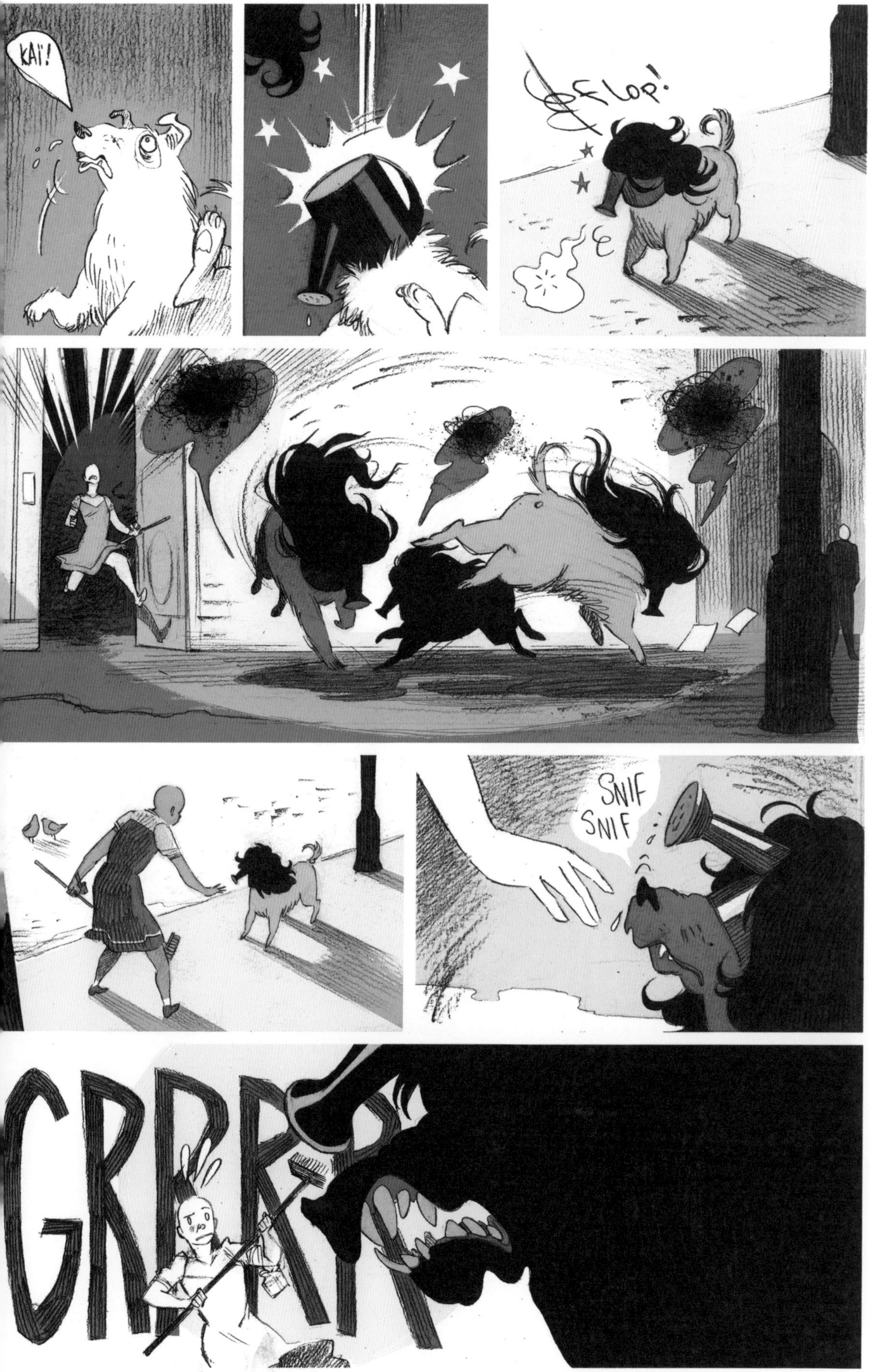
KAÏ!
FLOP!
SNIF
SNIF
GRRR

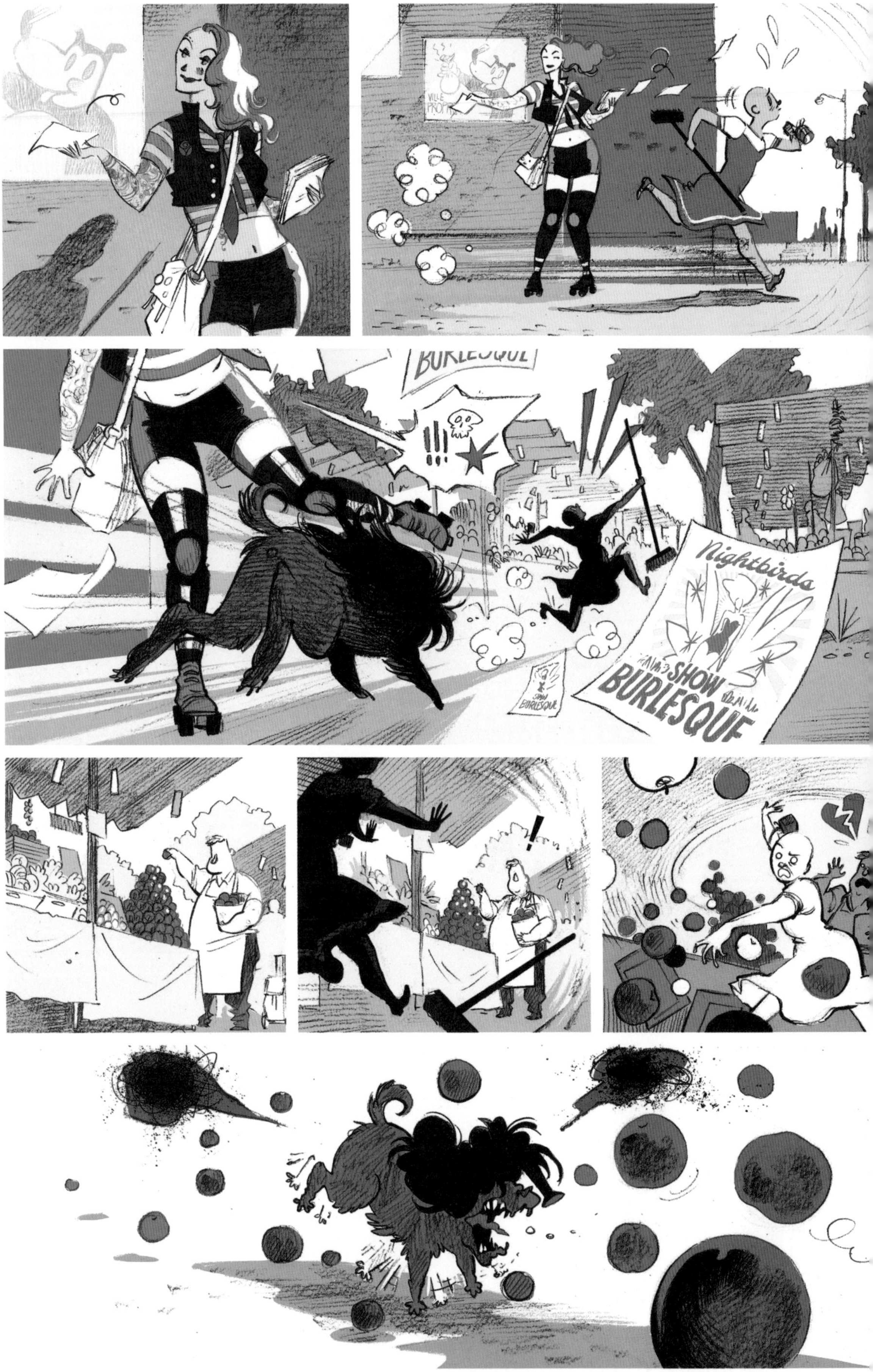

BURLESQUE
Nightbirds
SHOW
BURLESQUE

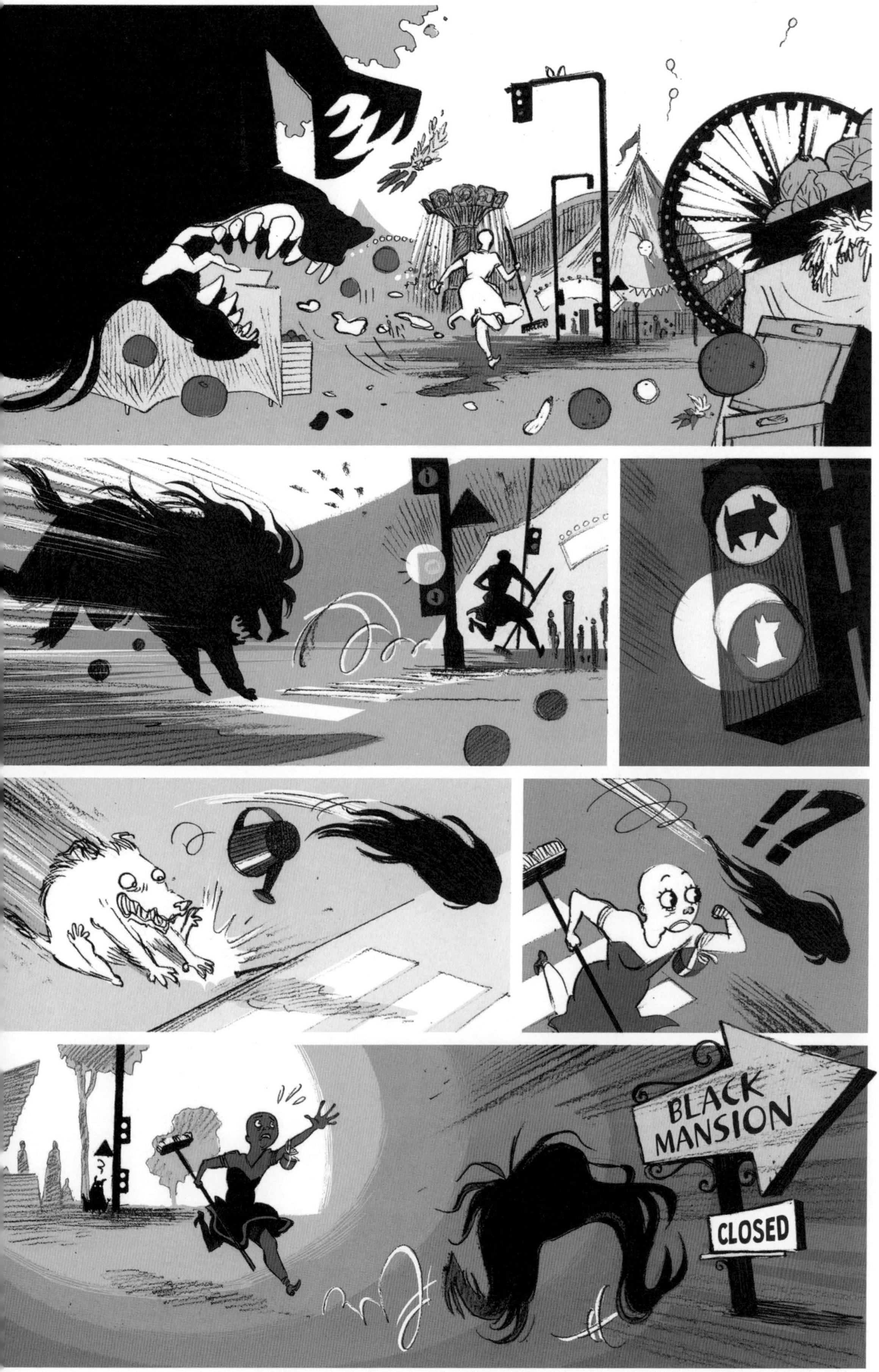
!?
BLACK MANSION
CLOSED

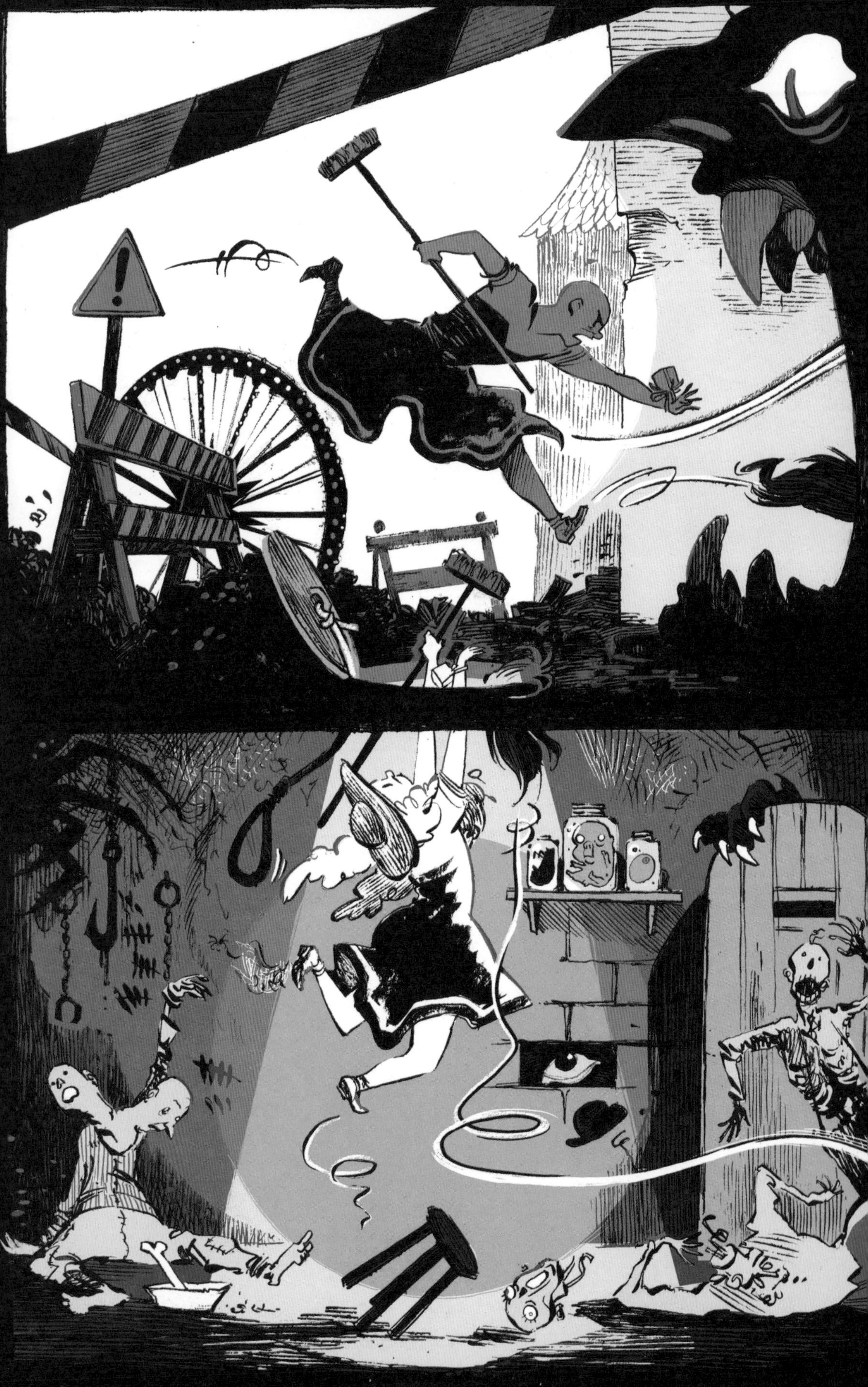

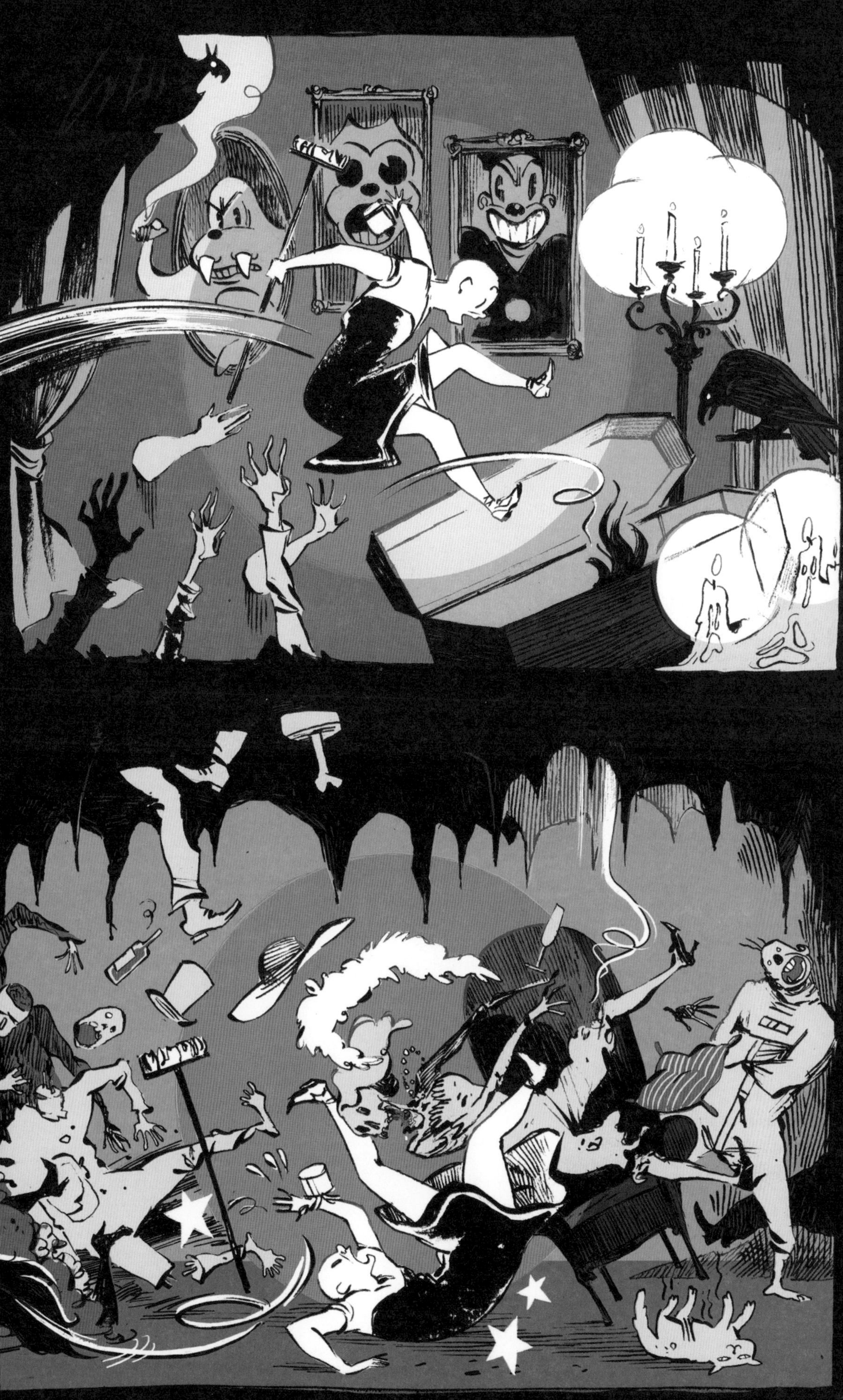

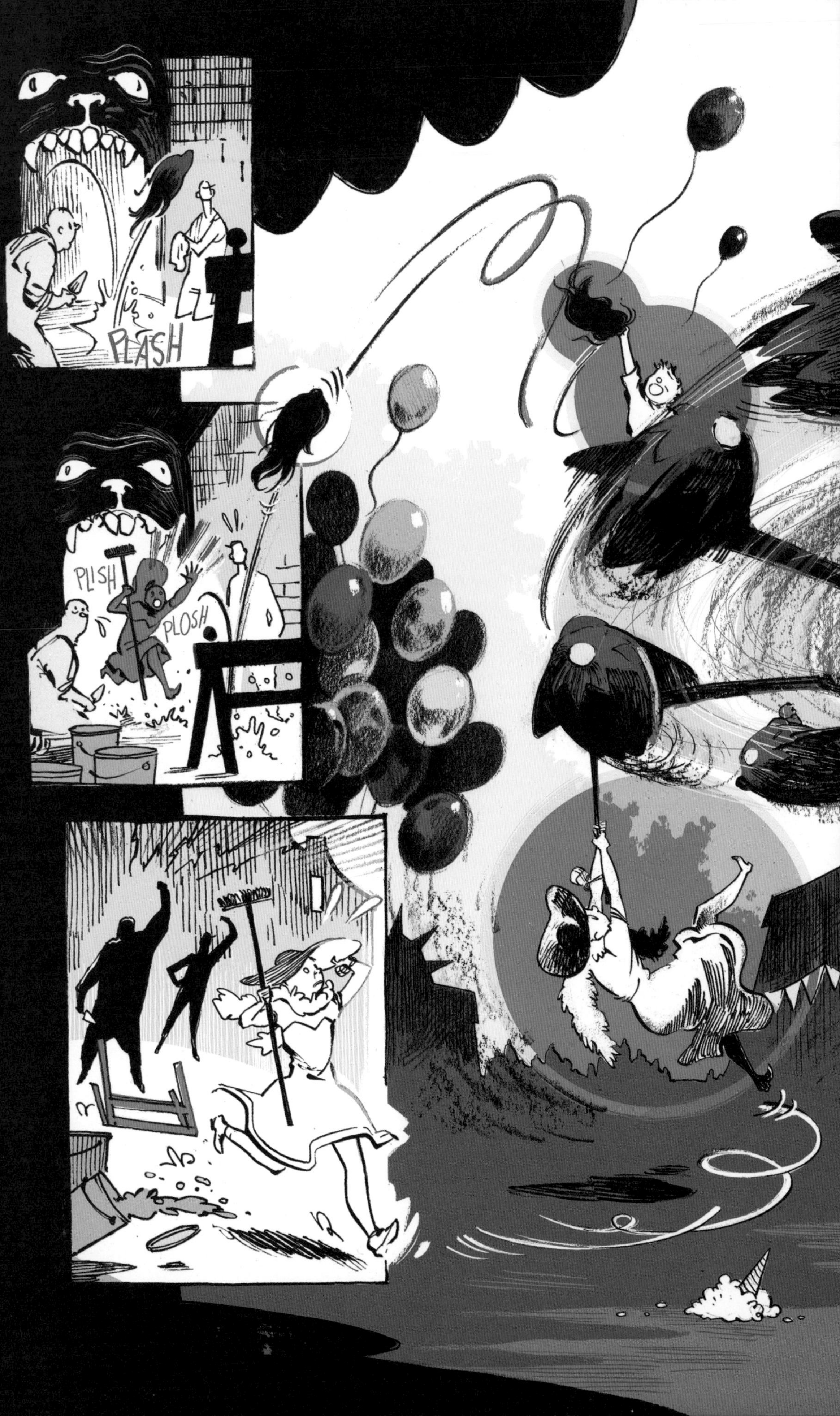
PLASH
PLISH
PLOSH

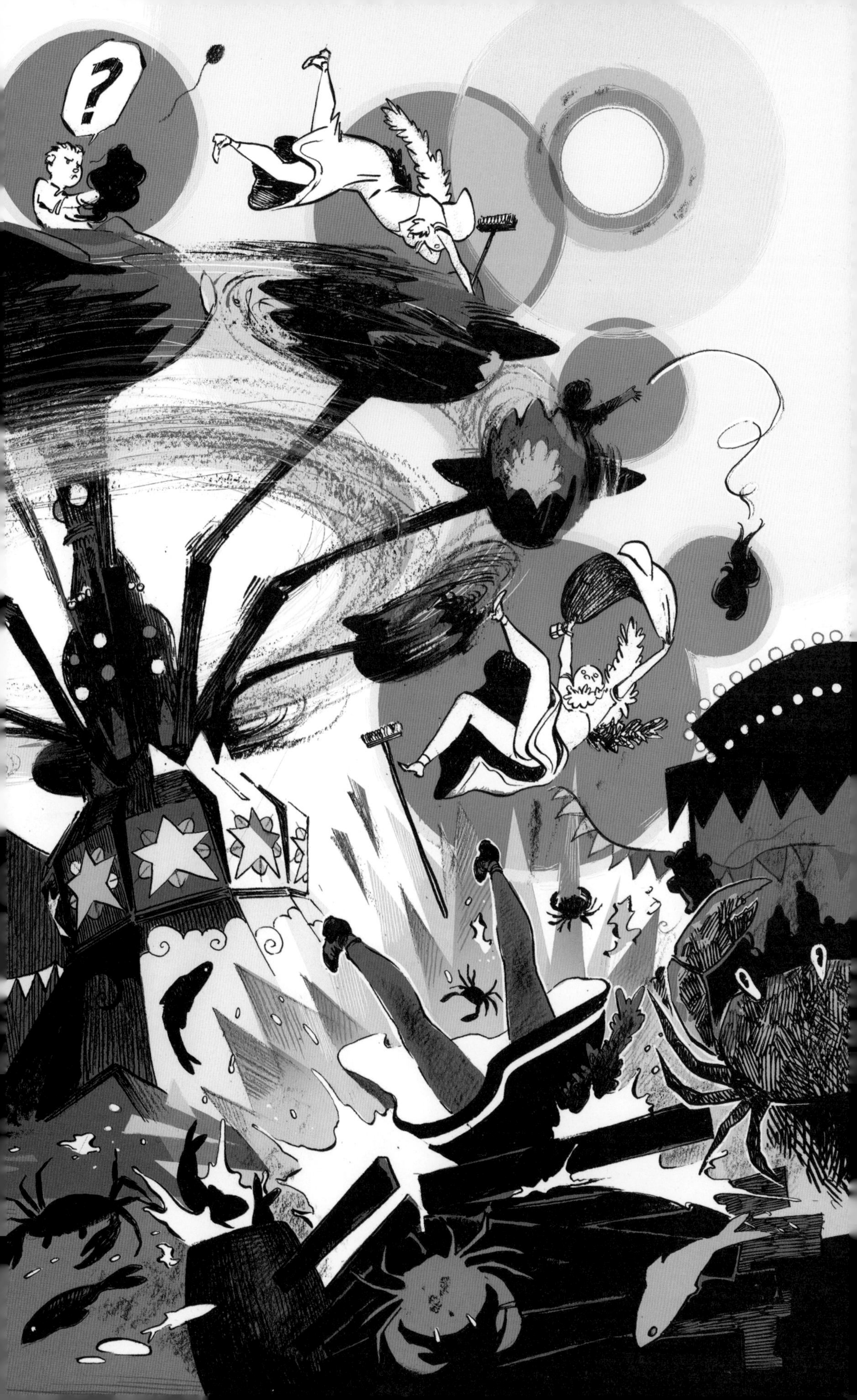
?

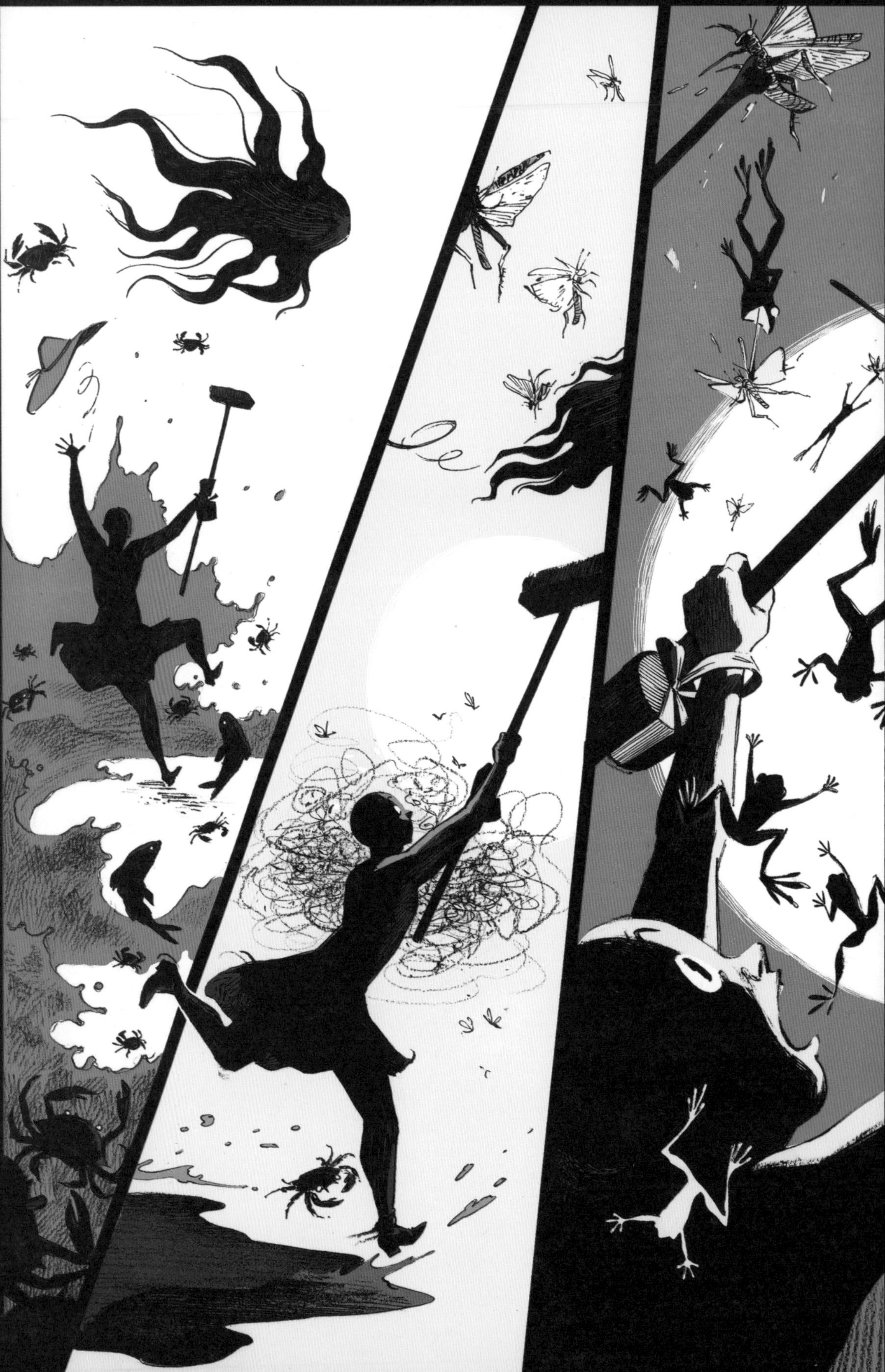

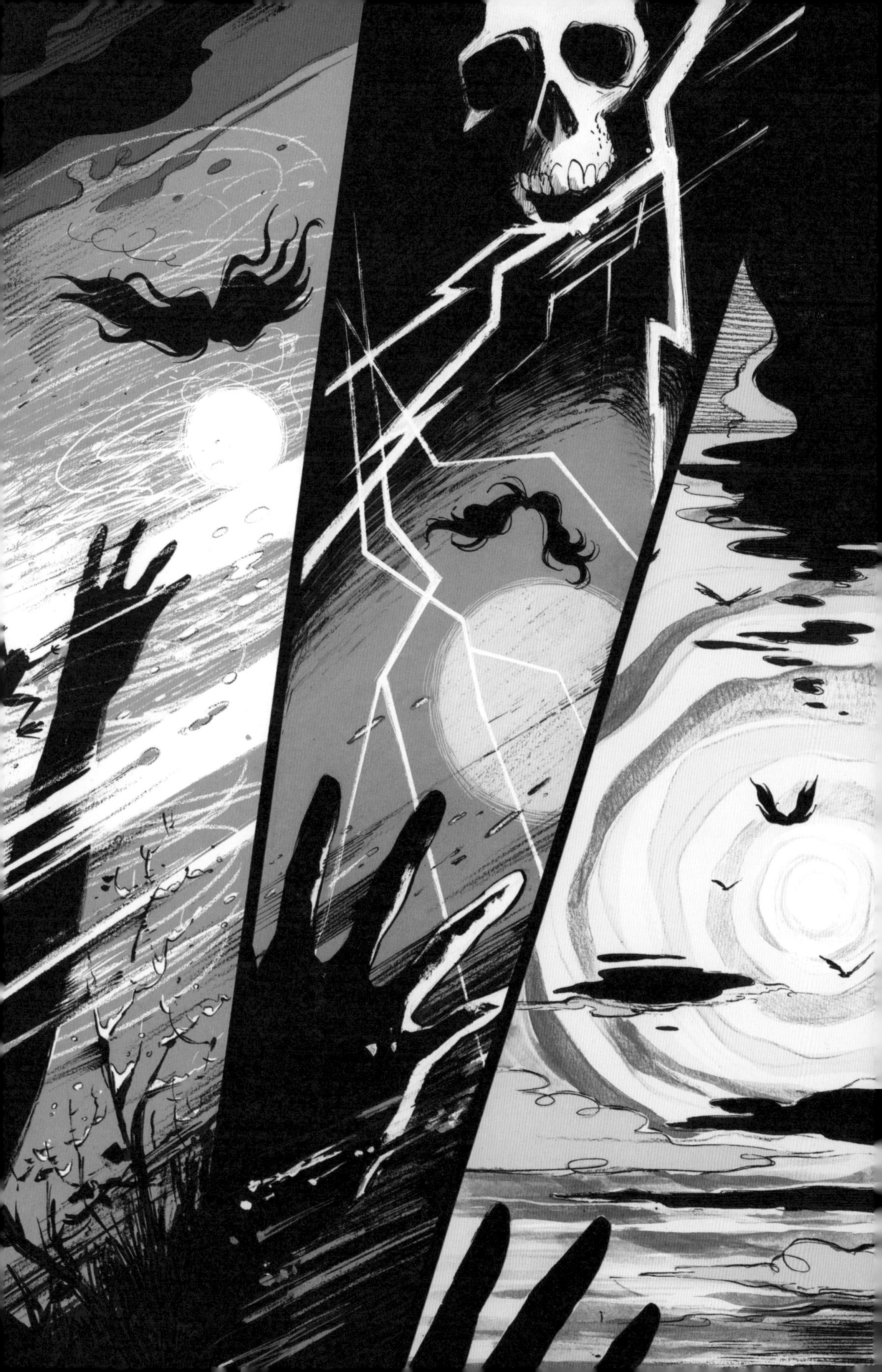

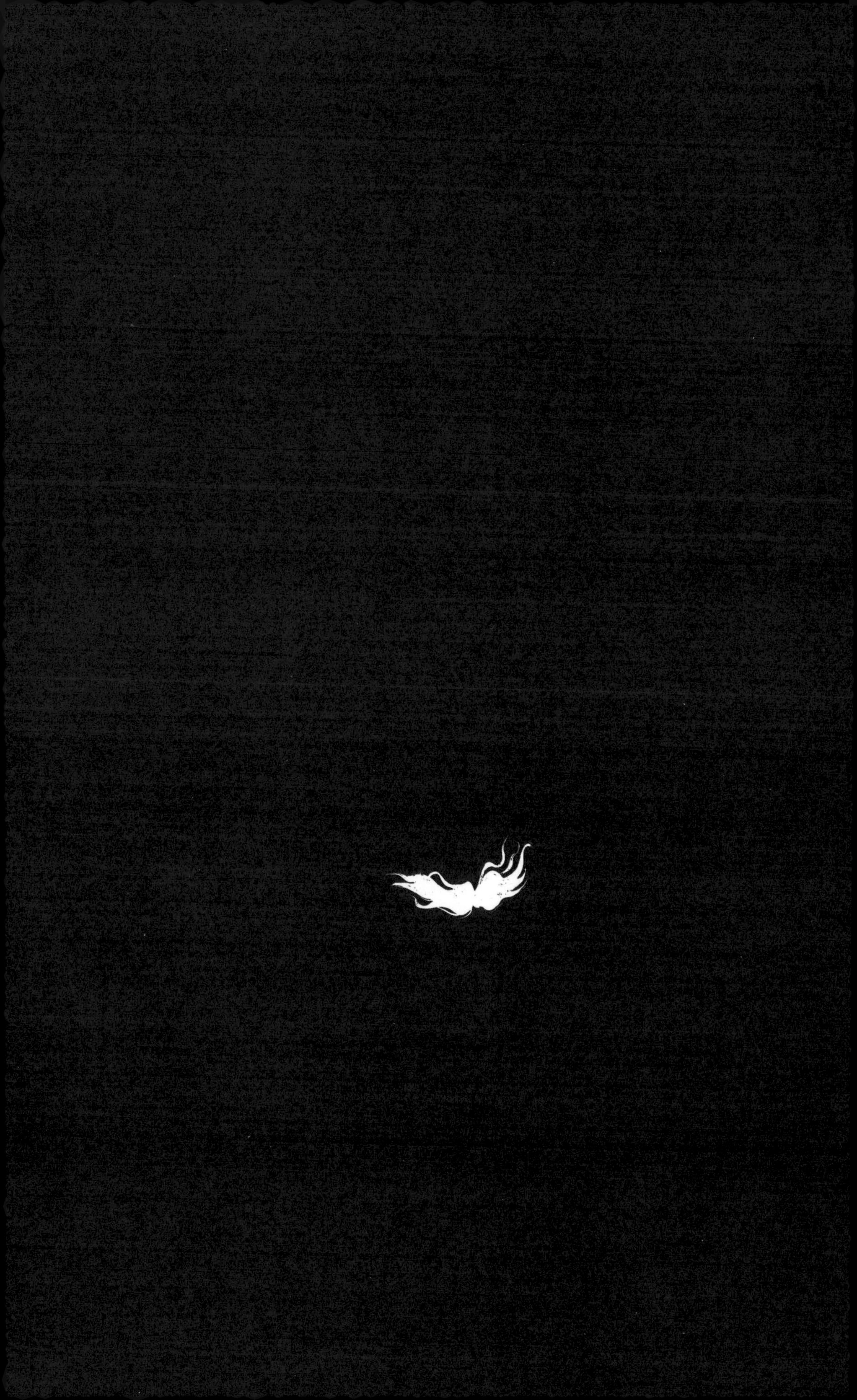

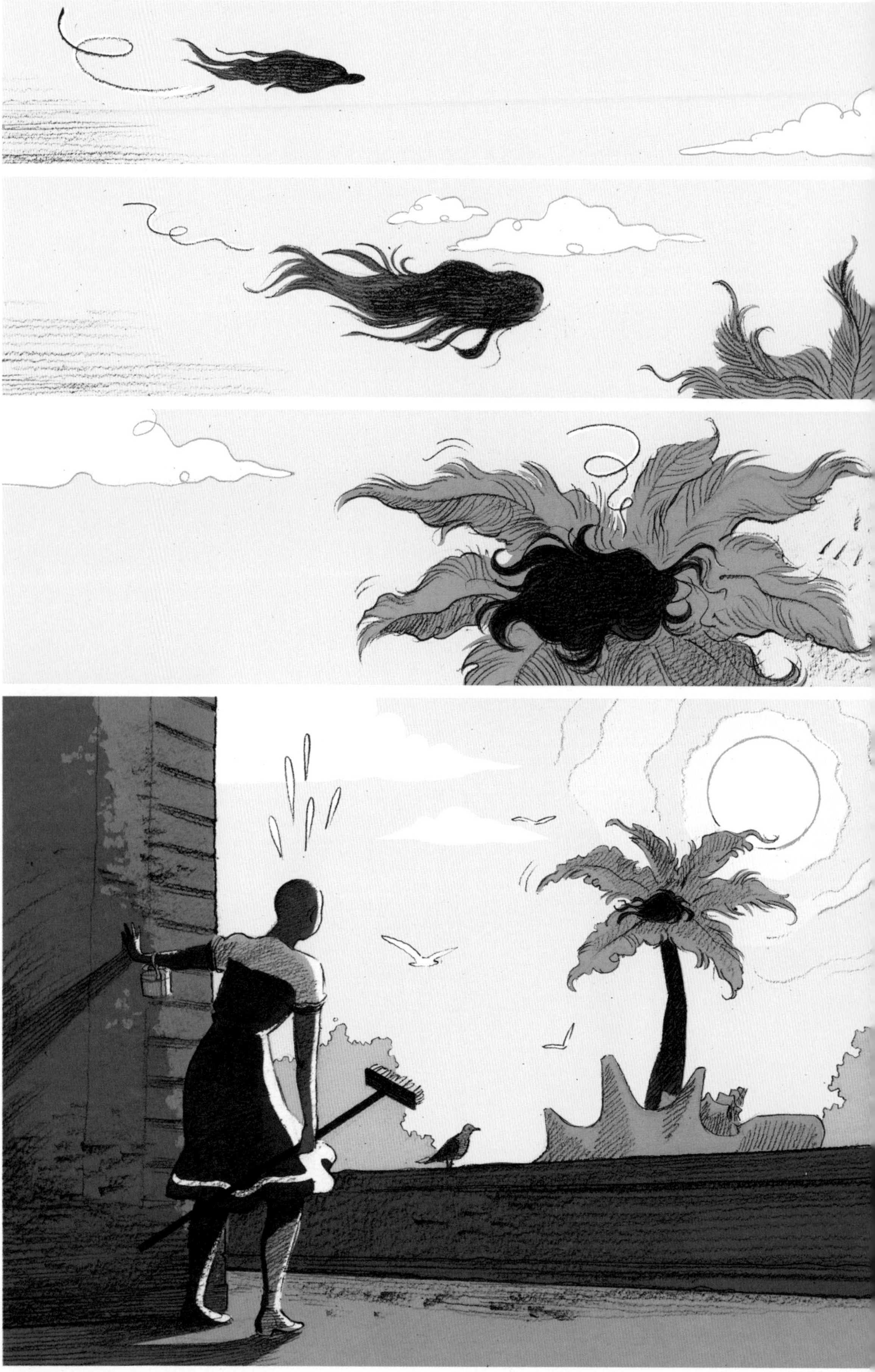

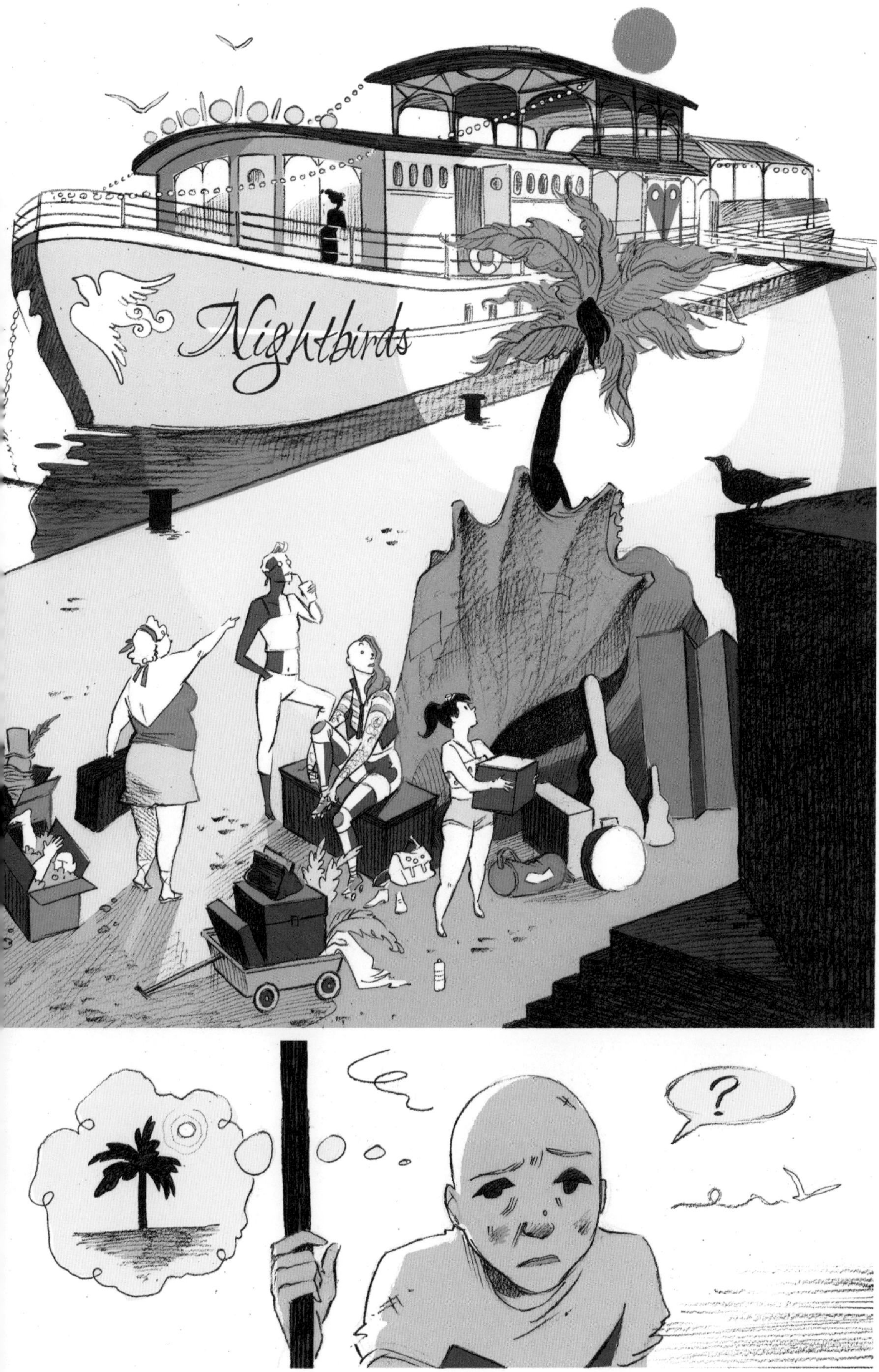
Nightbirds
?

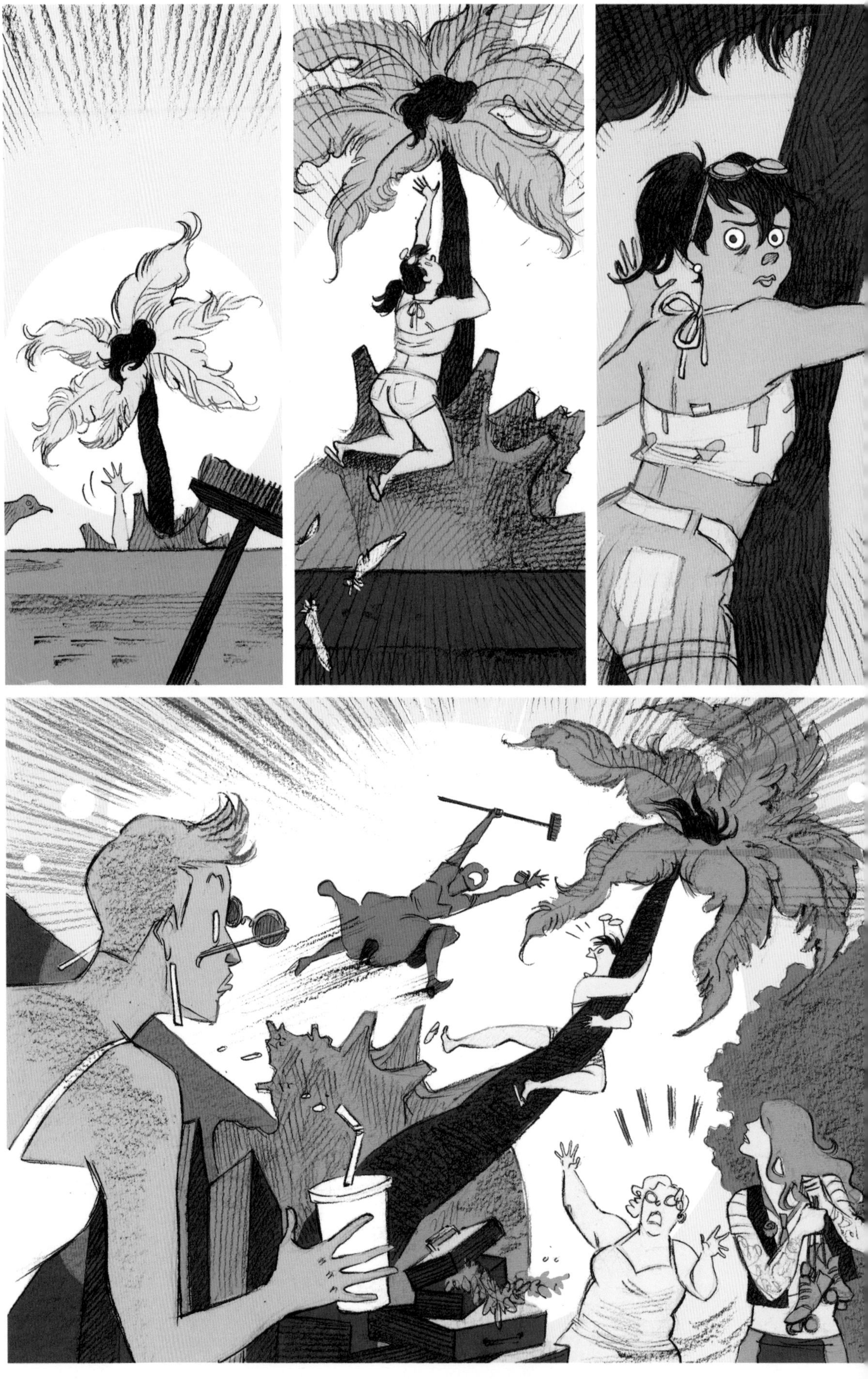

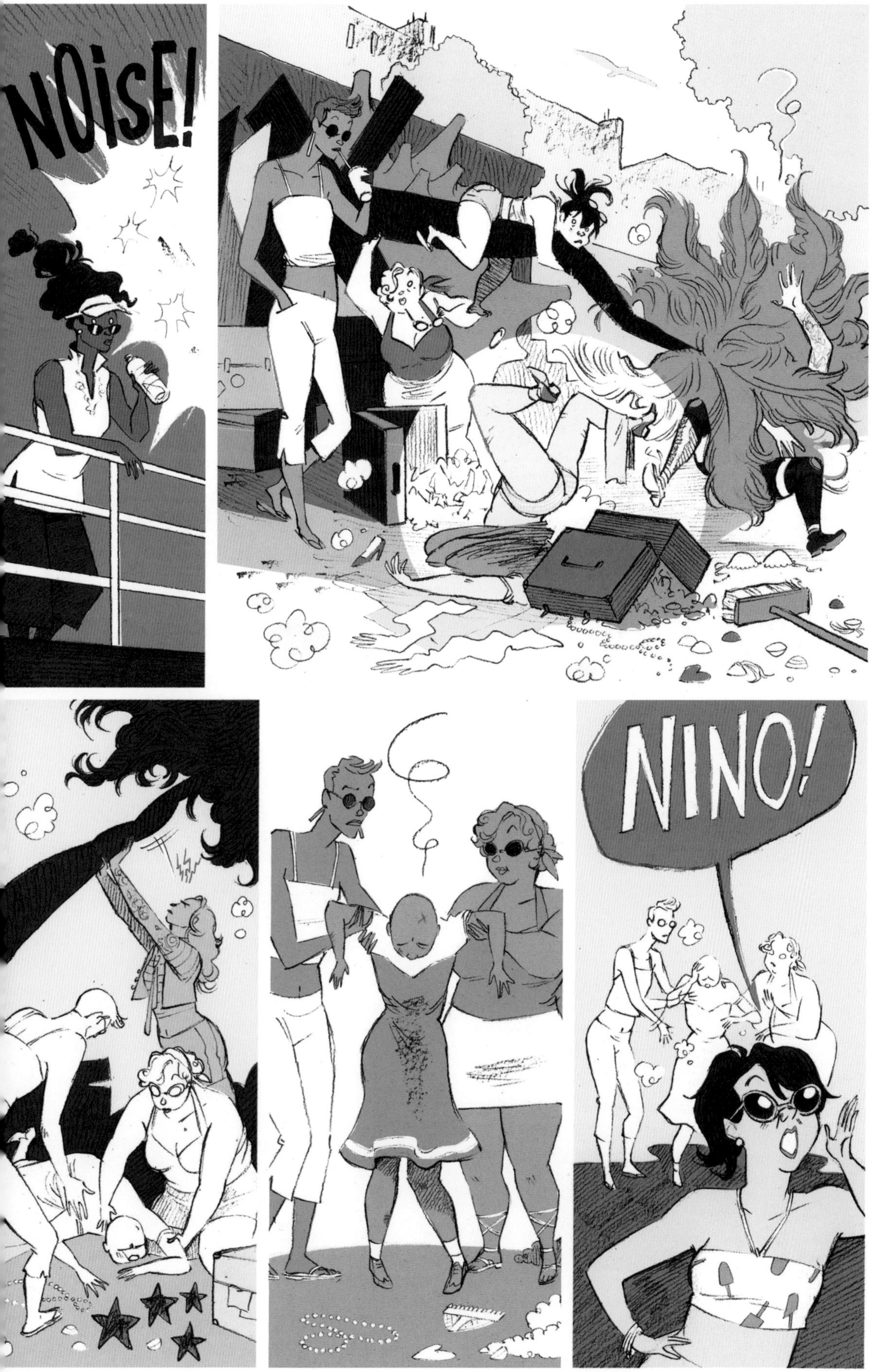
NOiSE!
NINO!

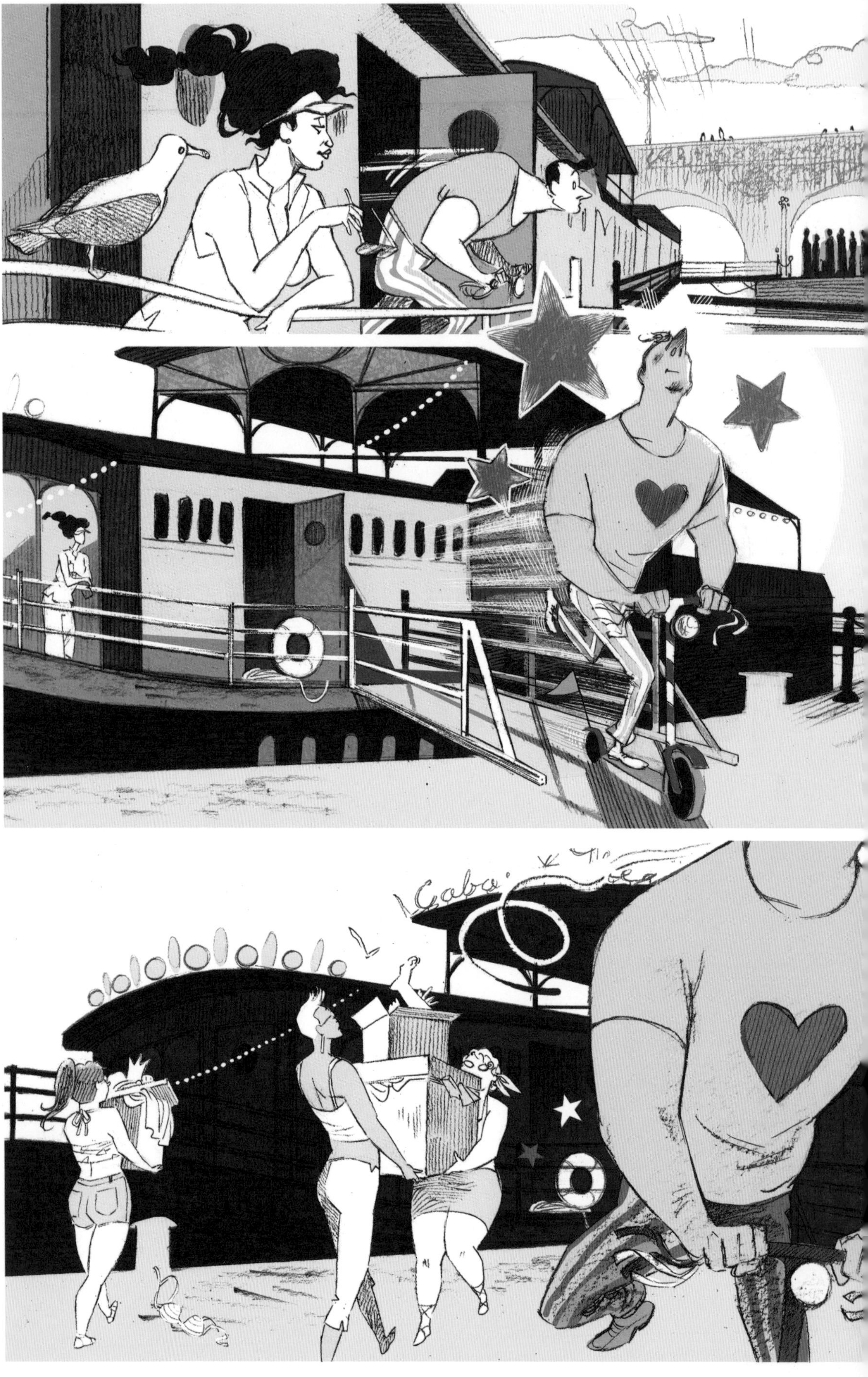

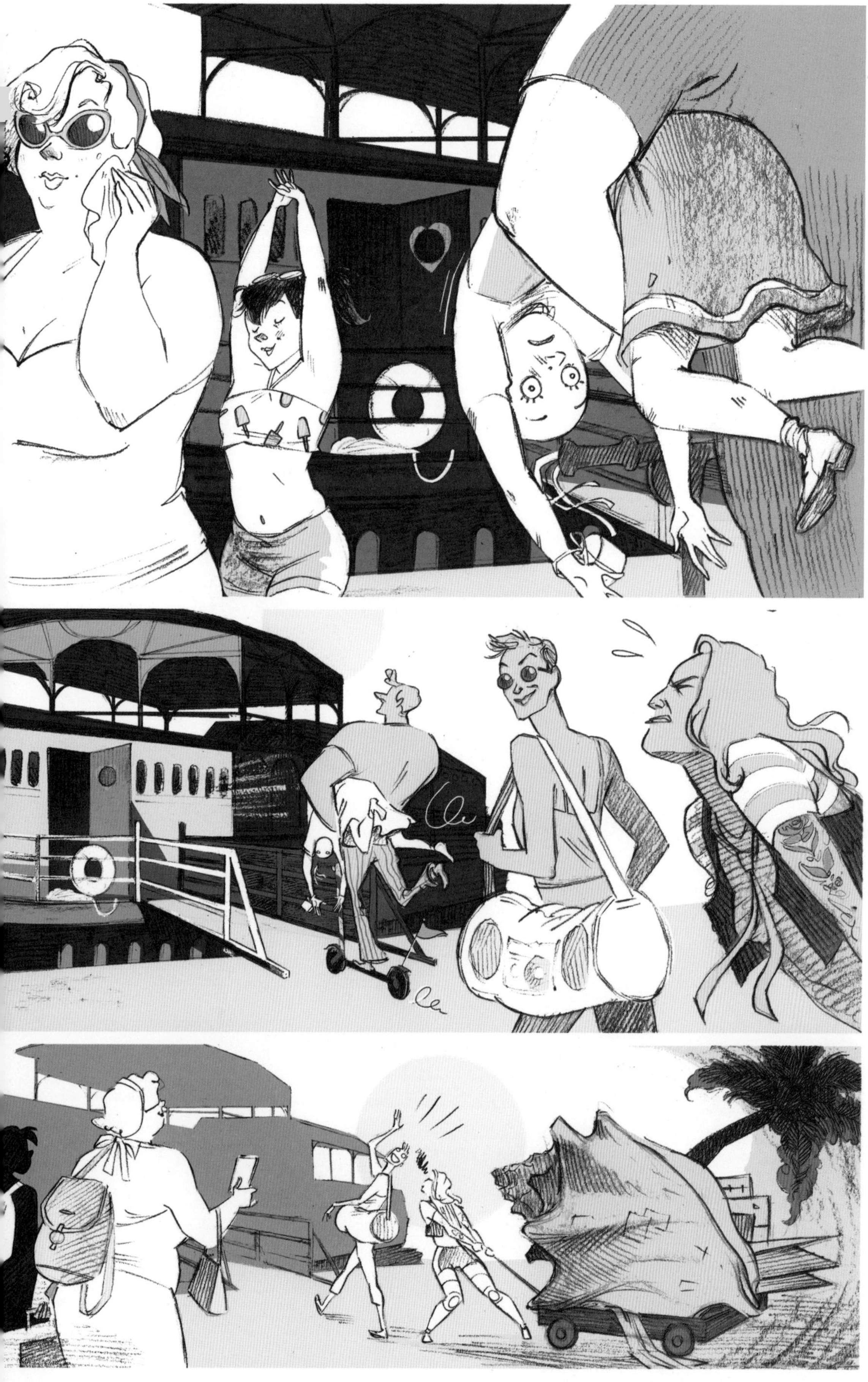

-No body is perfect, Elisabeth.

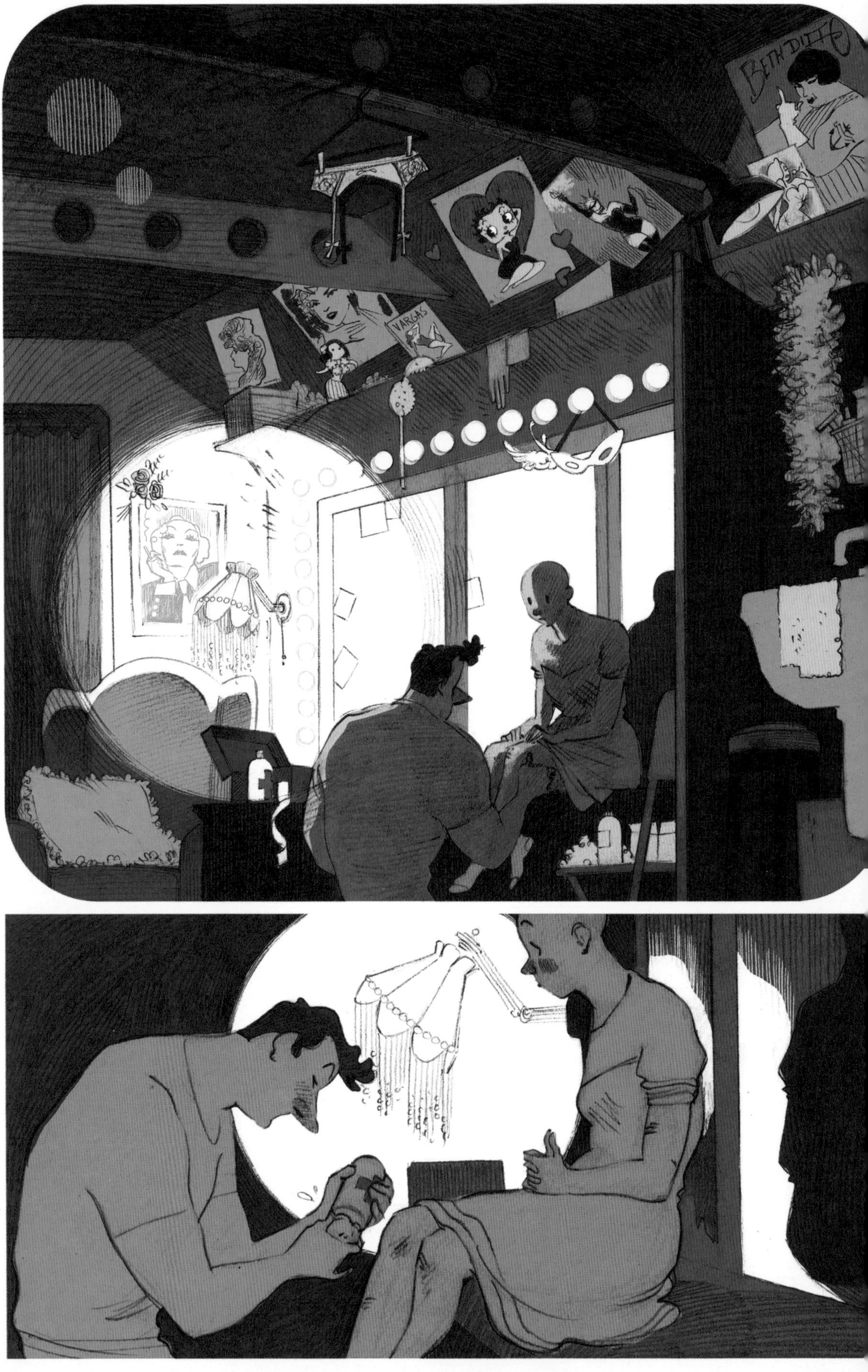
VARGAS

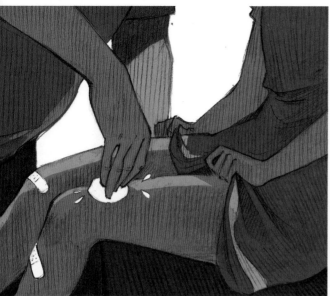

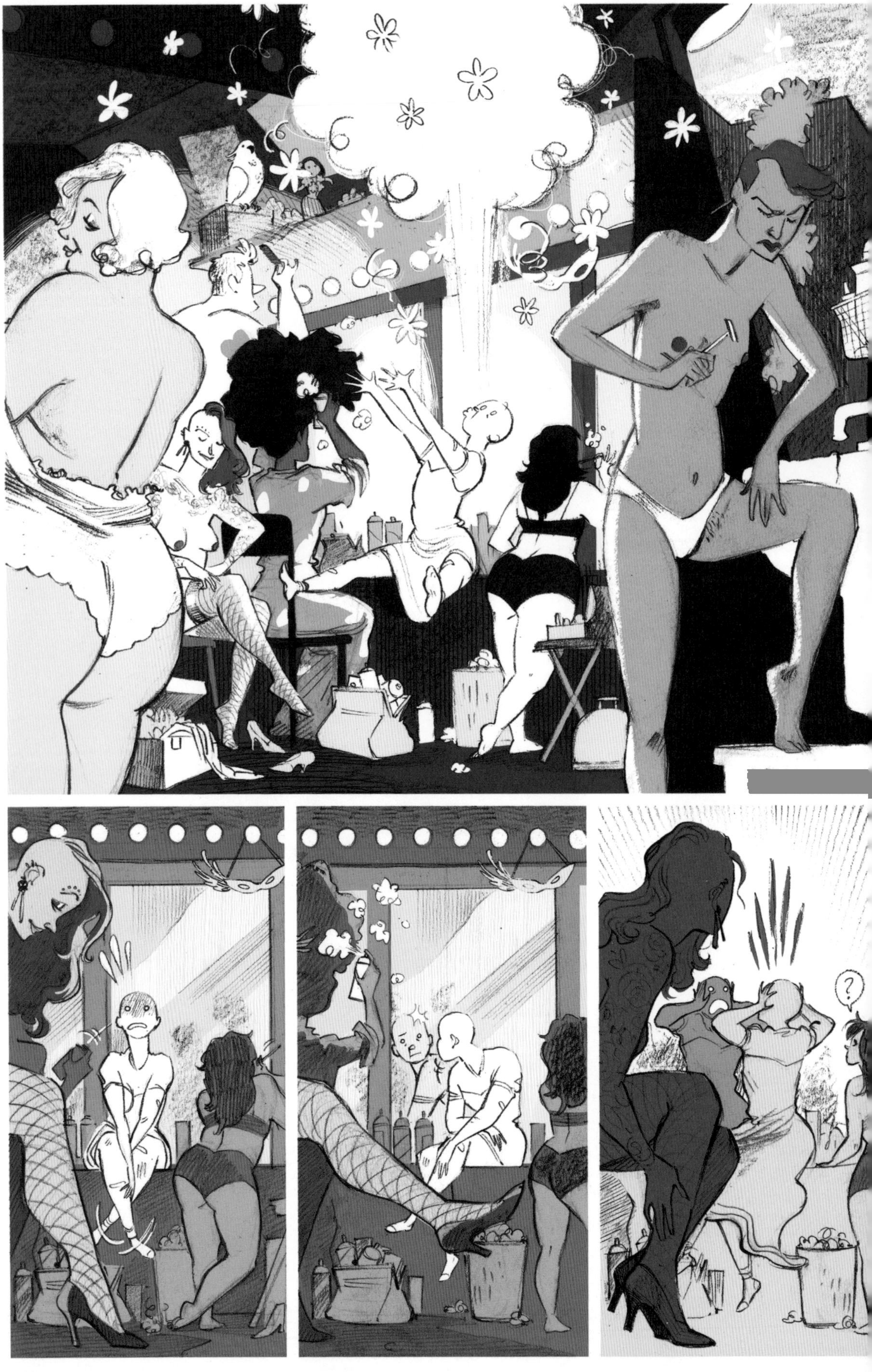
?

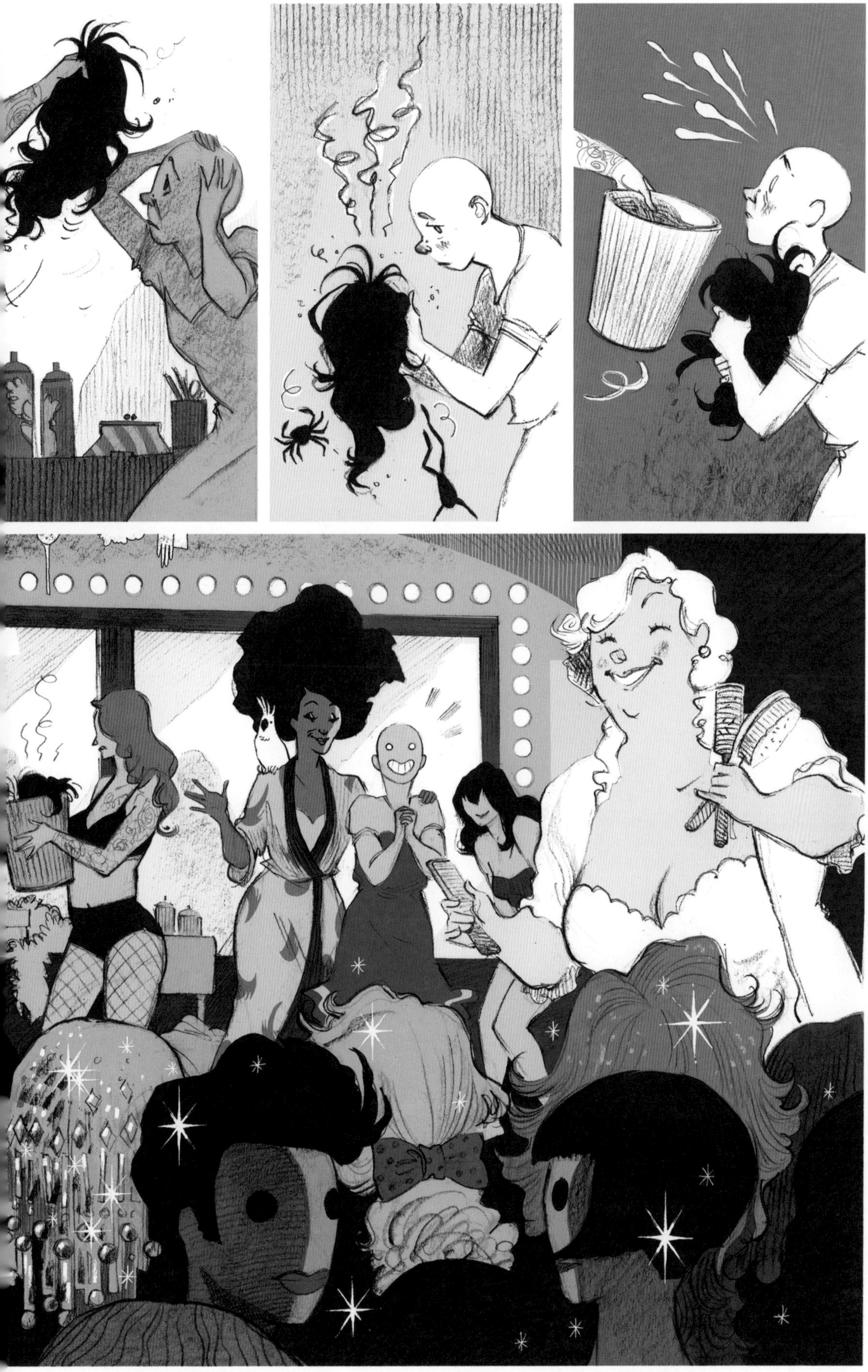

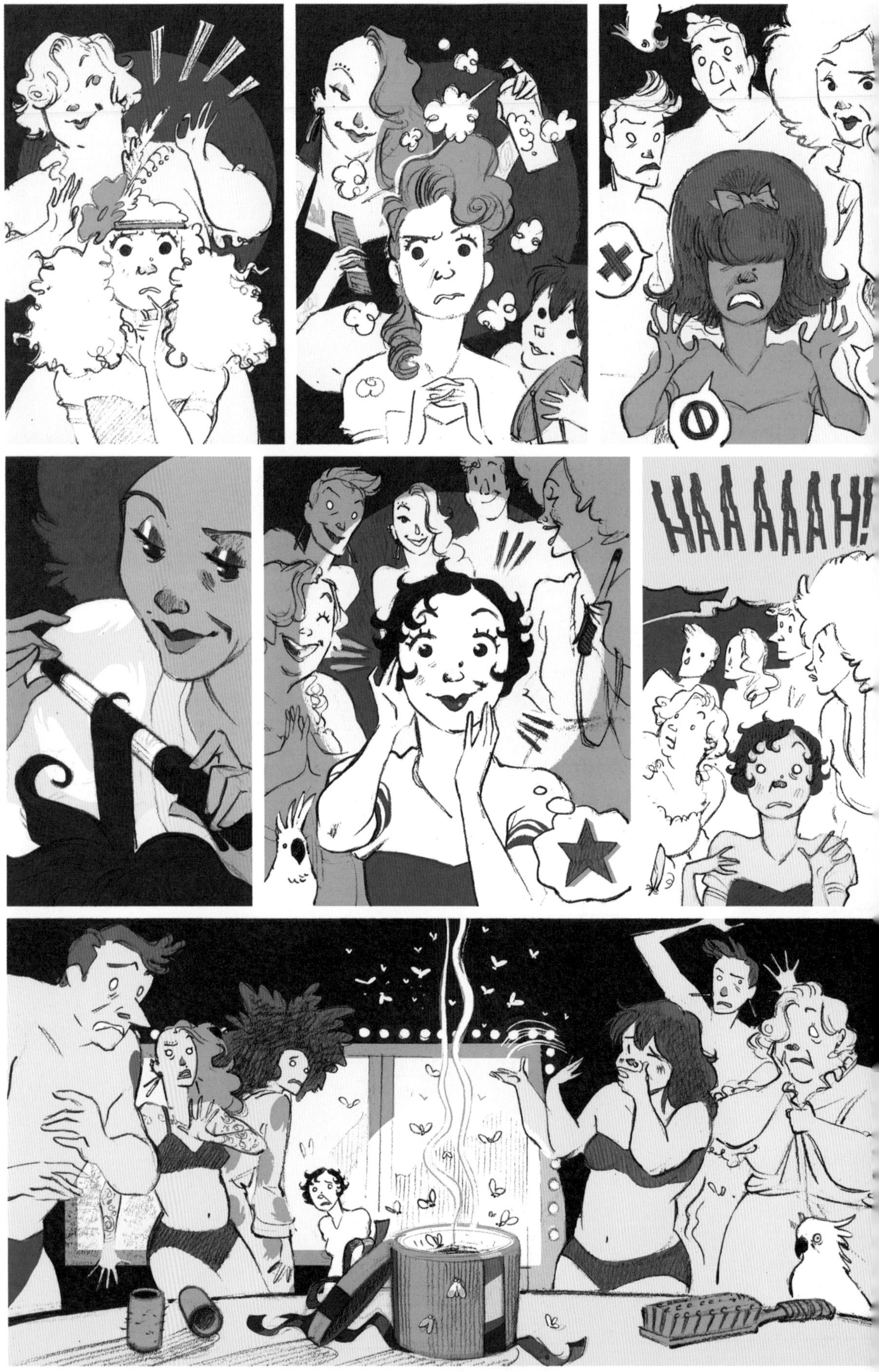
HAAAAAH!

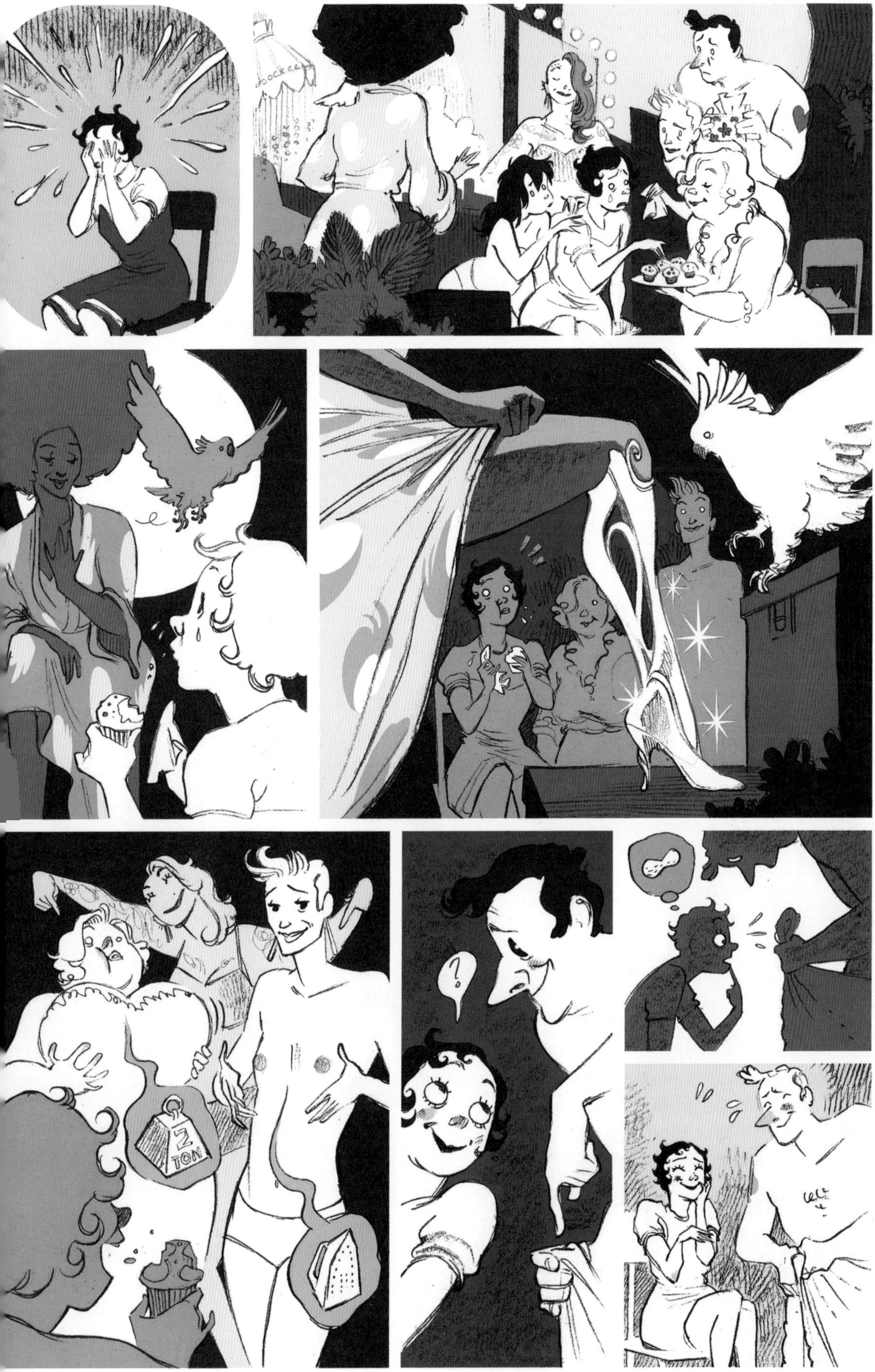
2 TON
?

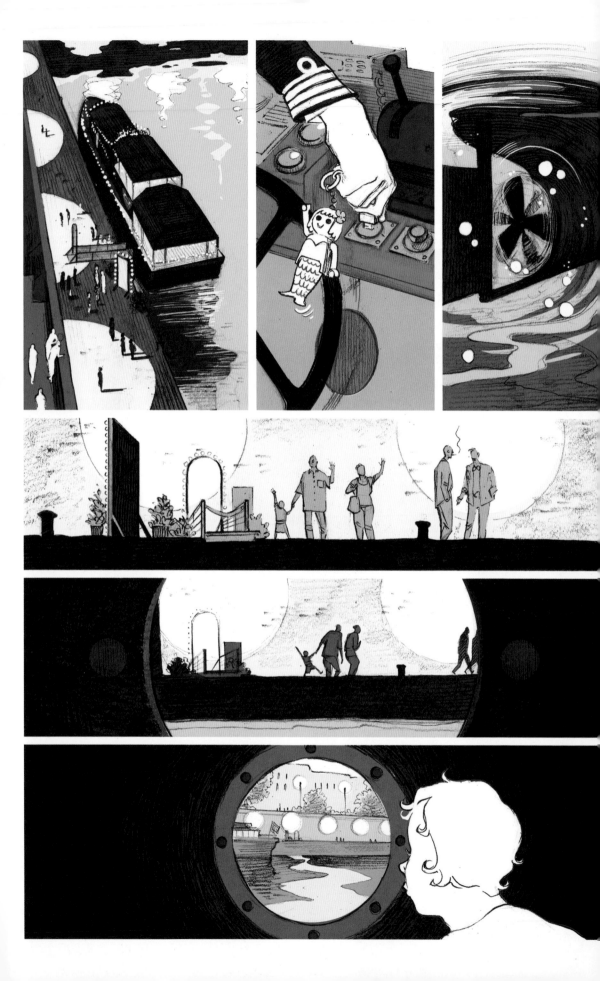

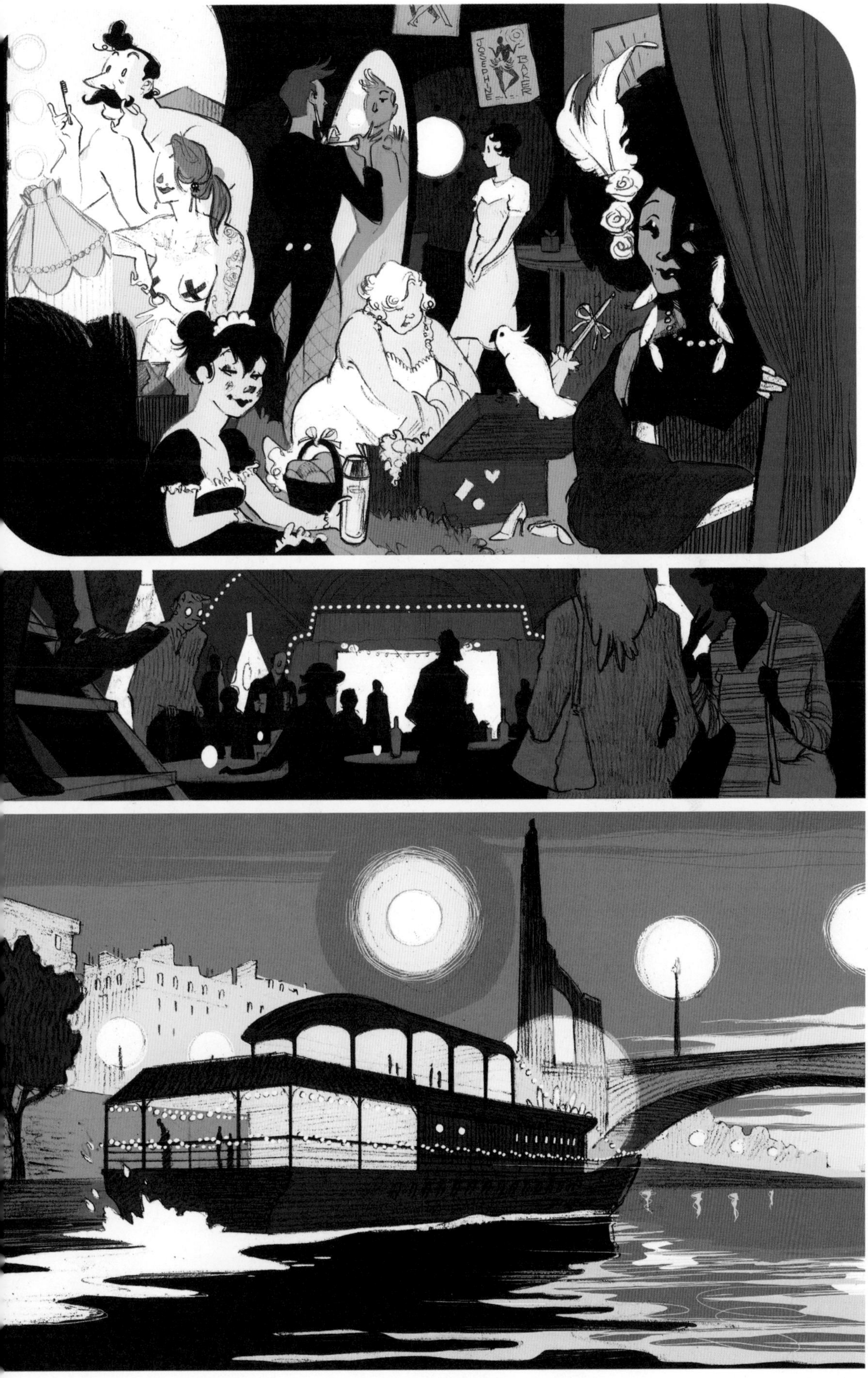
JOSEPHINE BAKER

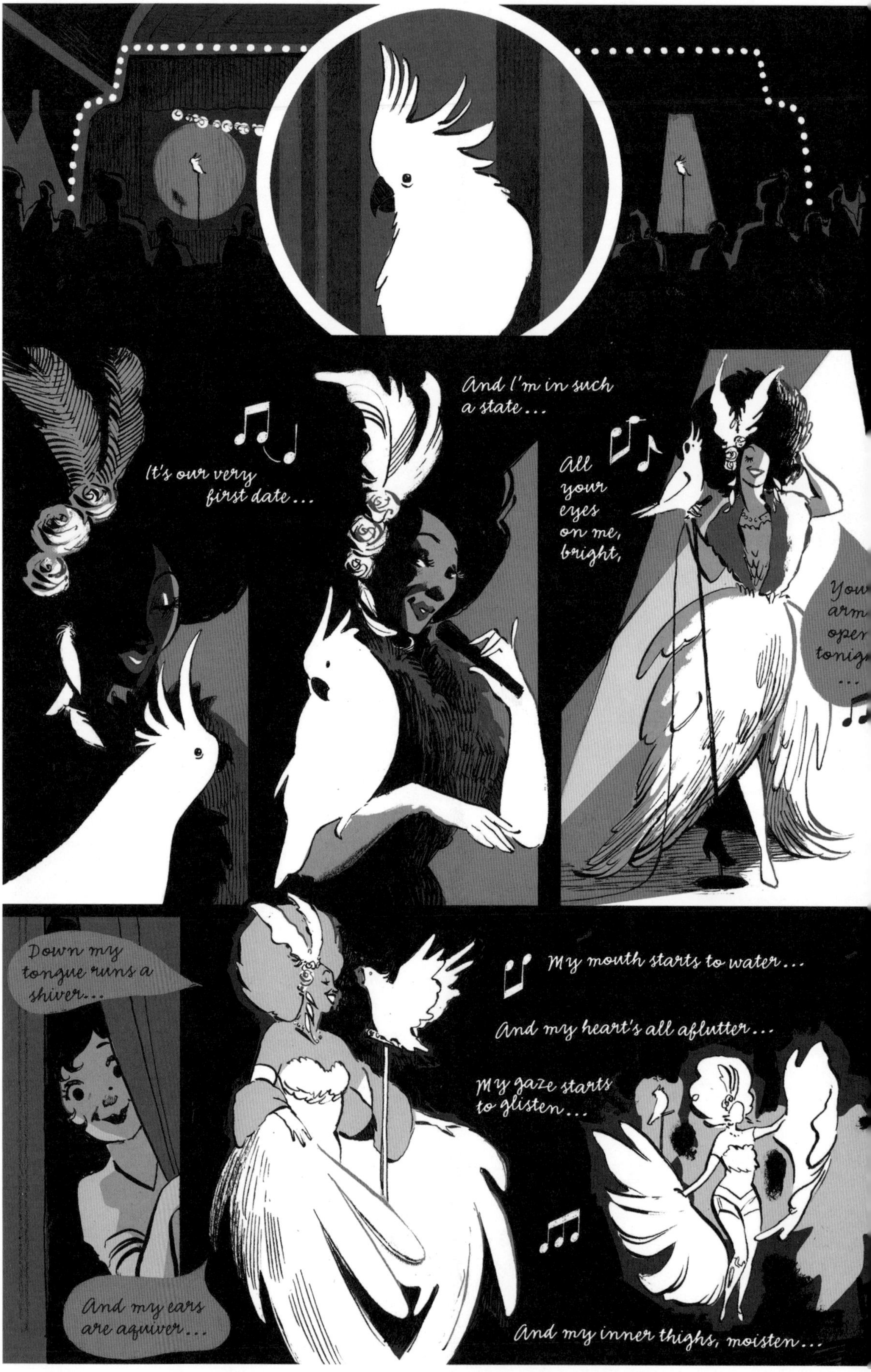

It's our very first date...
And I'm in such a state...
All your eyes on me, bright,
Down my tongue runs a shiver...
And my ears are aquiver...
My mouth starts to water...
And my heart's all aflutter...
My gaze starts to glisten...
And my inner thighs, moisten...

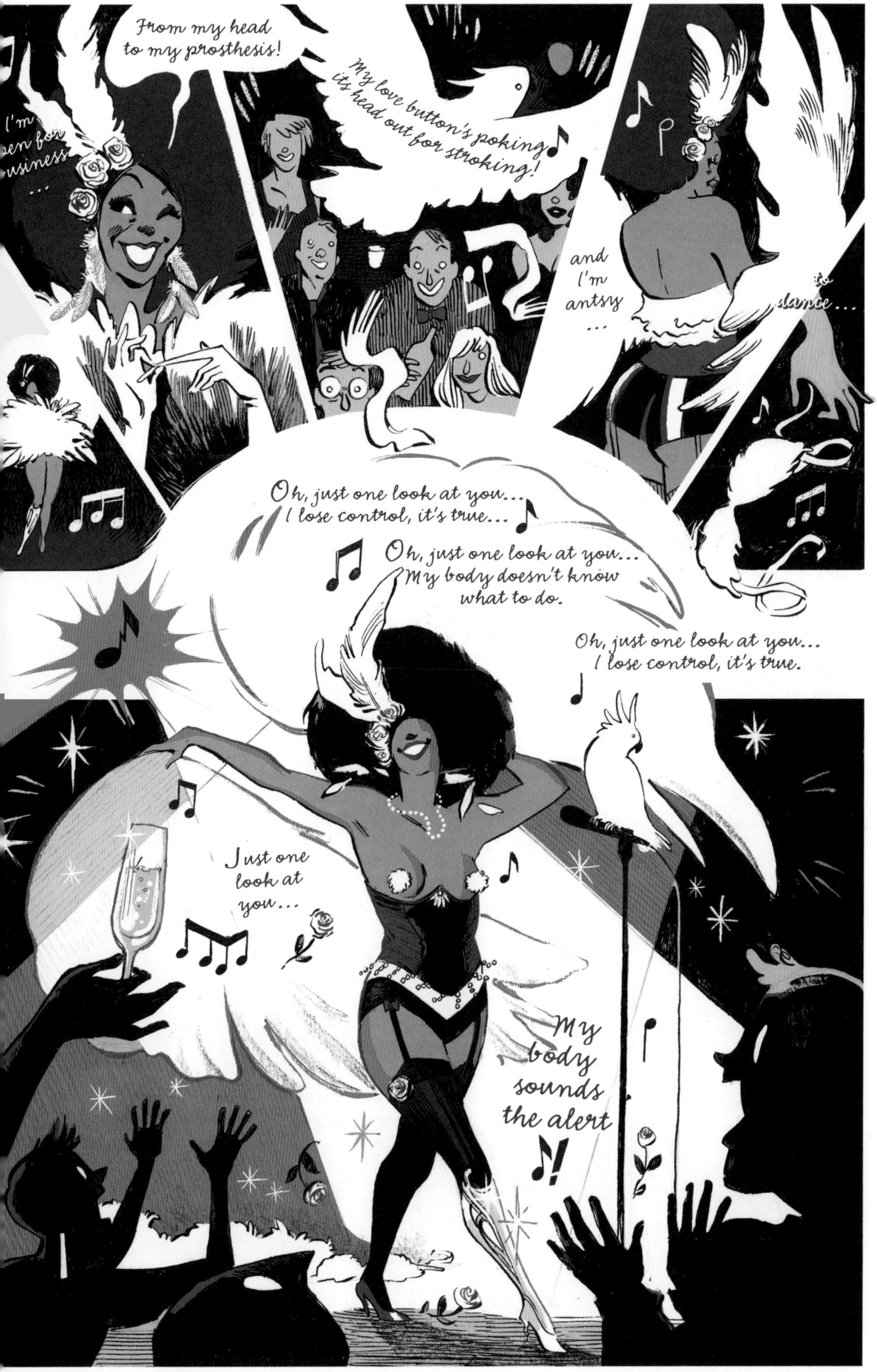

From my head to my prosthesis!
I'm
en for
usiness
...
My love button's poking its head out for stroking!
and I'm antsy ...
to
dance...
Oh, just one look at you... I lose control, it's true...
Oh, just one look at you... My body doesn't know what to do.
Oh, just one look at you... I lose control, it's true.
Just one look at you...
My body sounds the alert!

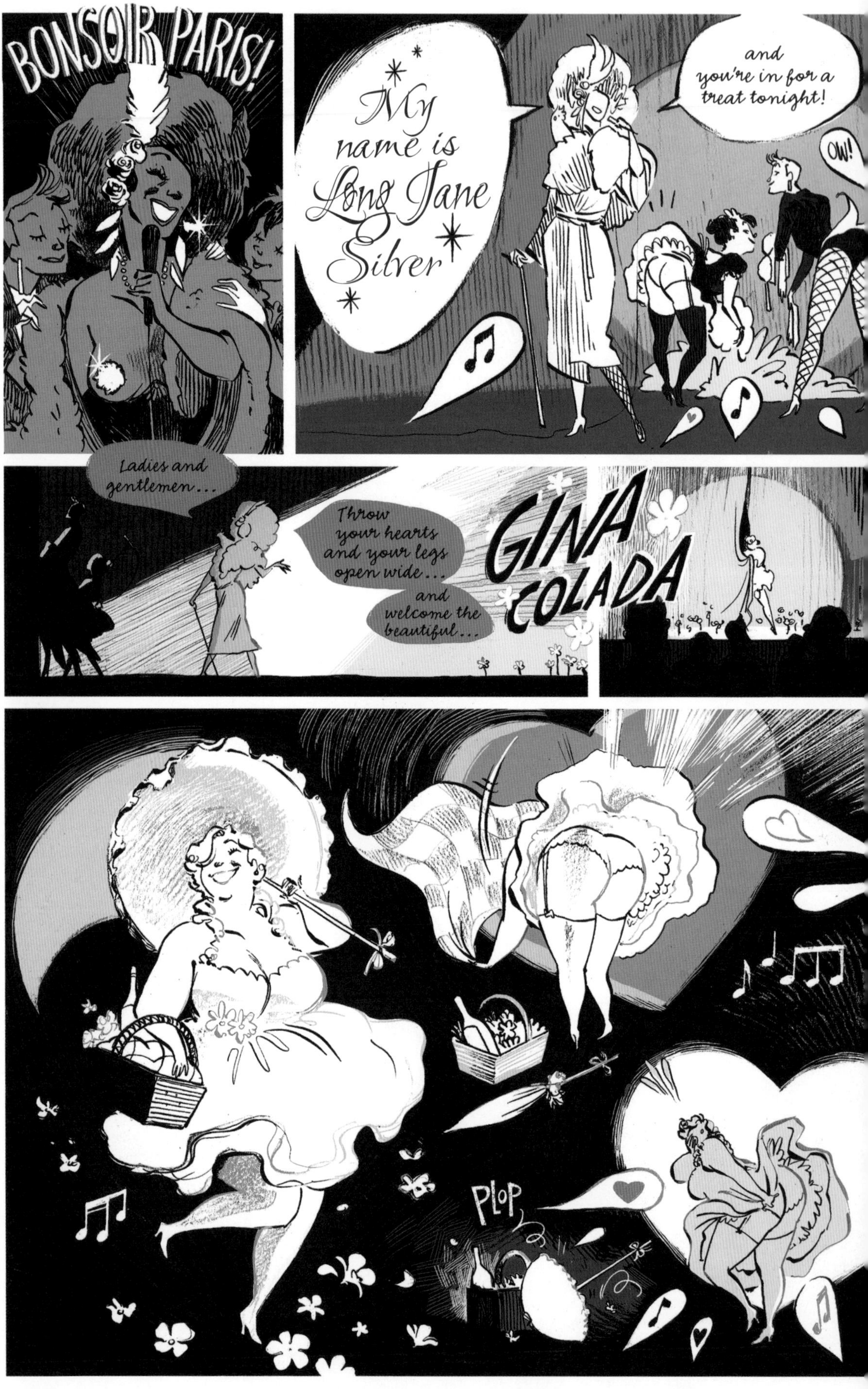
BONSOIR PARIS!
My name is Long Jane Silver
and you're in for a treat tonight!
OW!
Ladies and gentlemen...
Throw your hearts and your legs open wide...
and welcome the beautiful...
GINA COLADA
PLOP

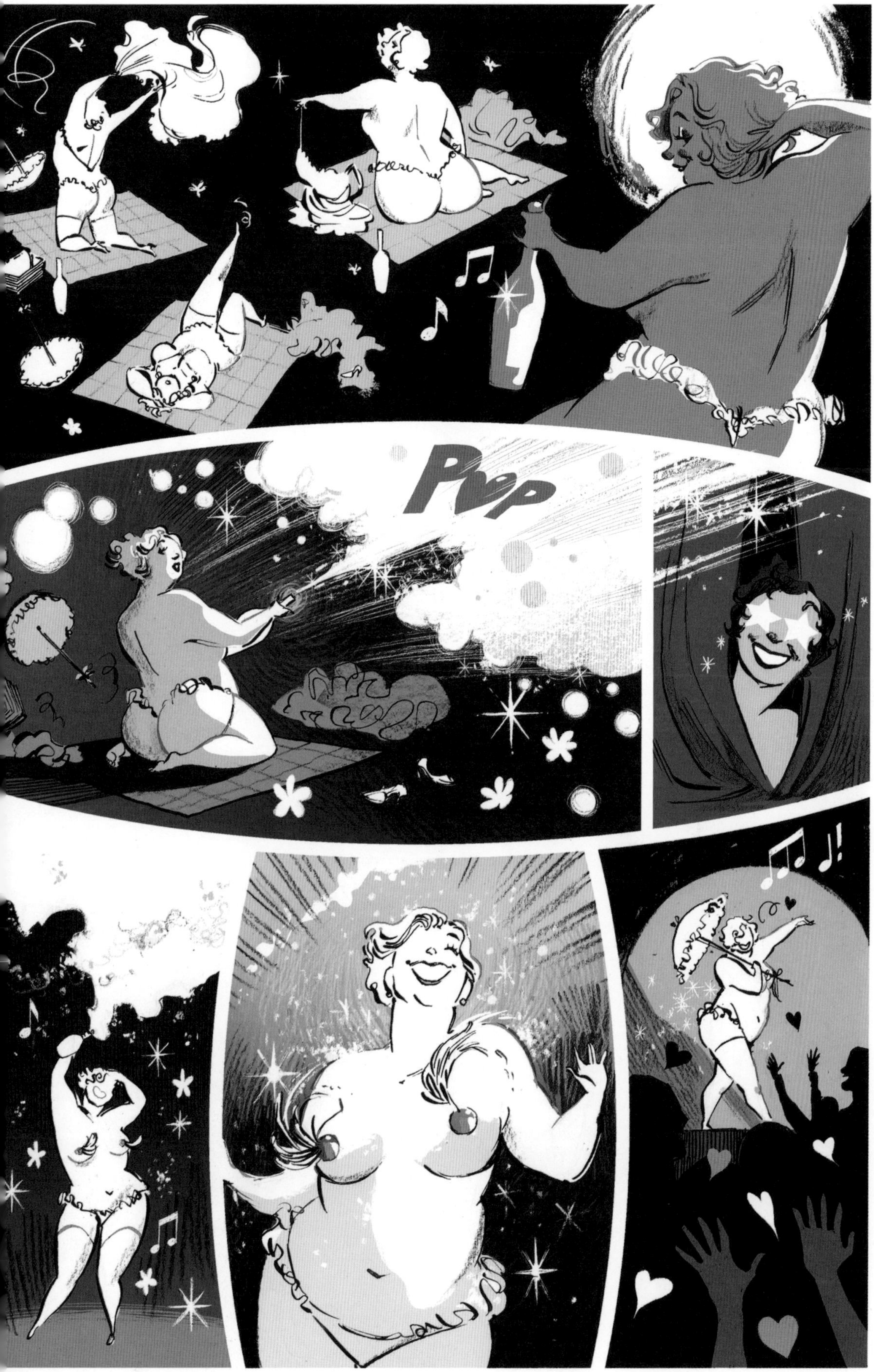
POP

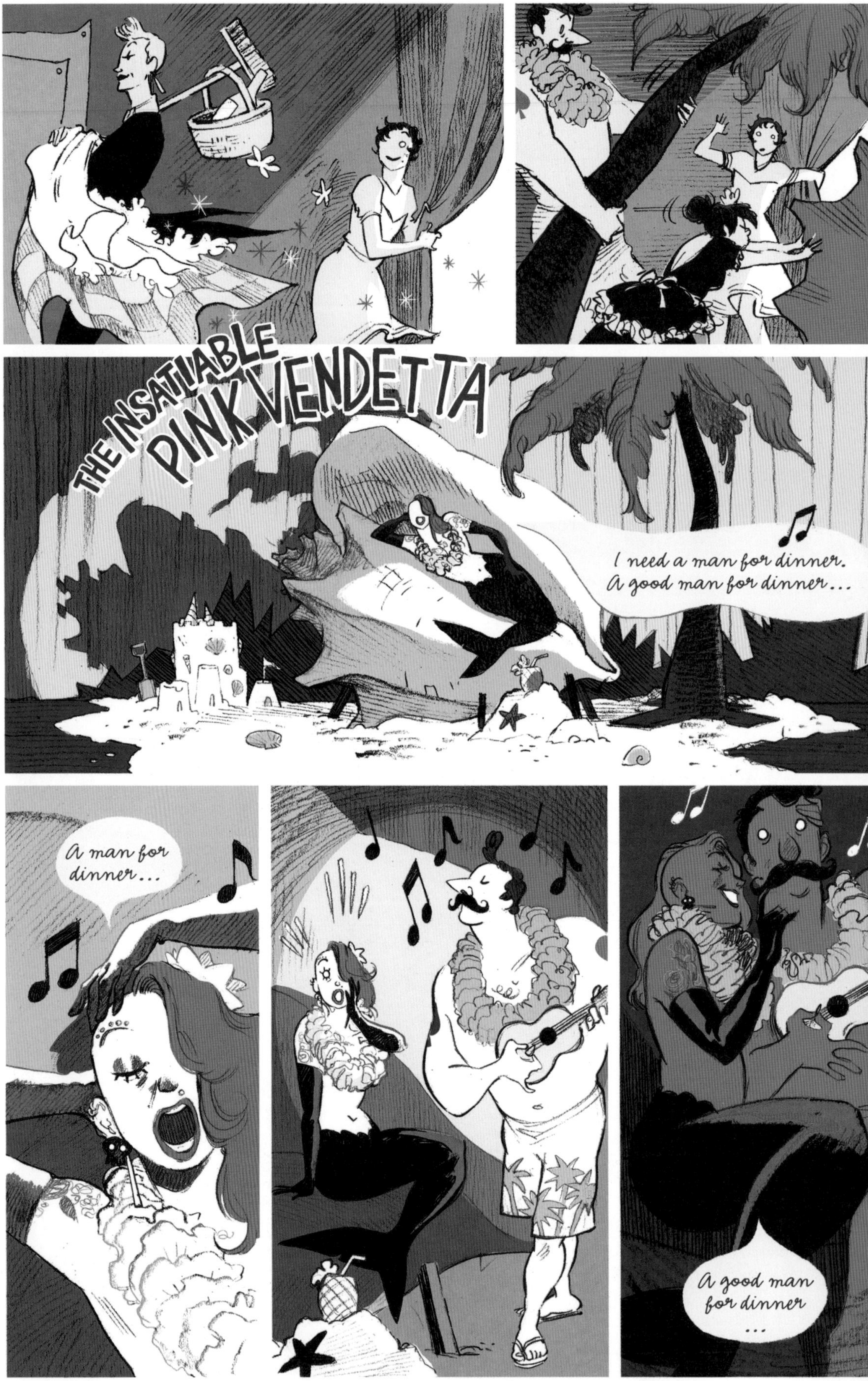
THE INSATIABLE PINK VENDETTA
I need a man for dinner.
A good man for dinner...
A man for dinner...
A good man for dinner
...

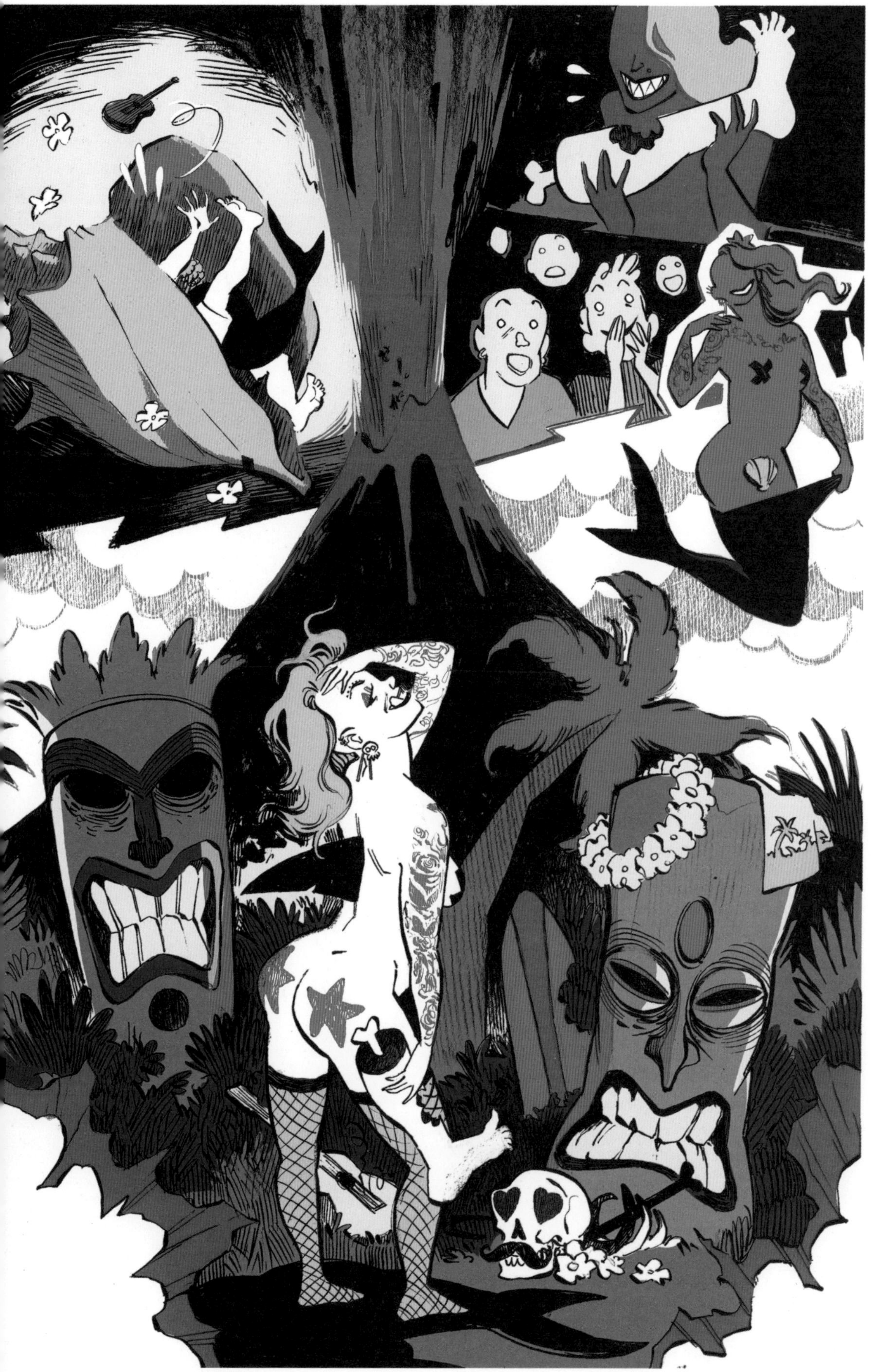

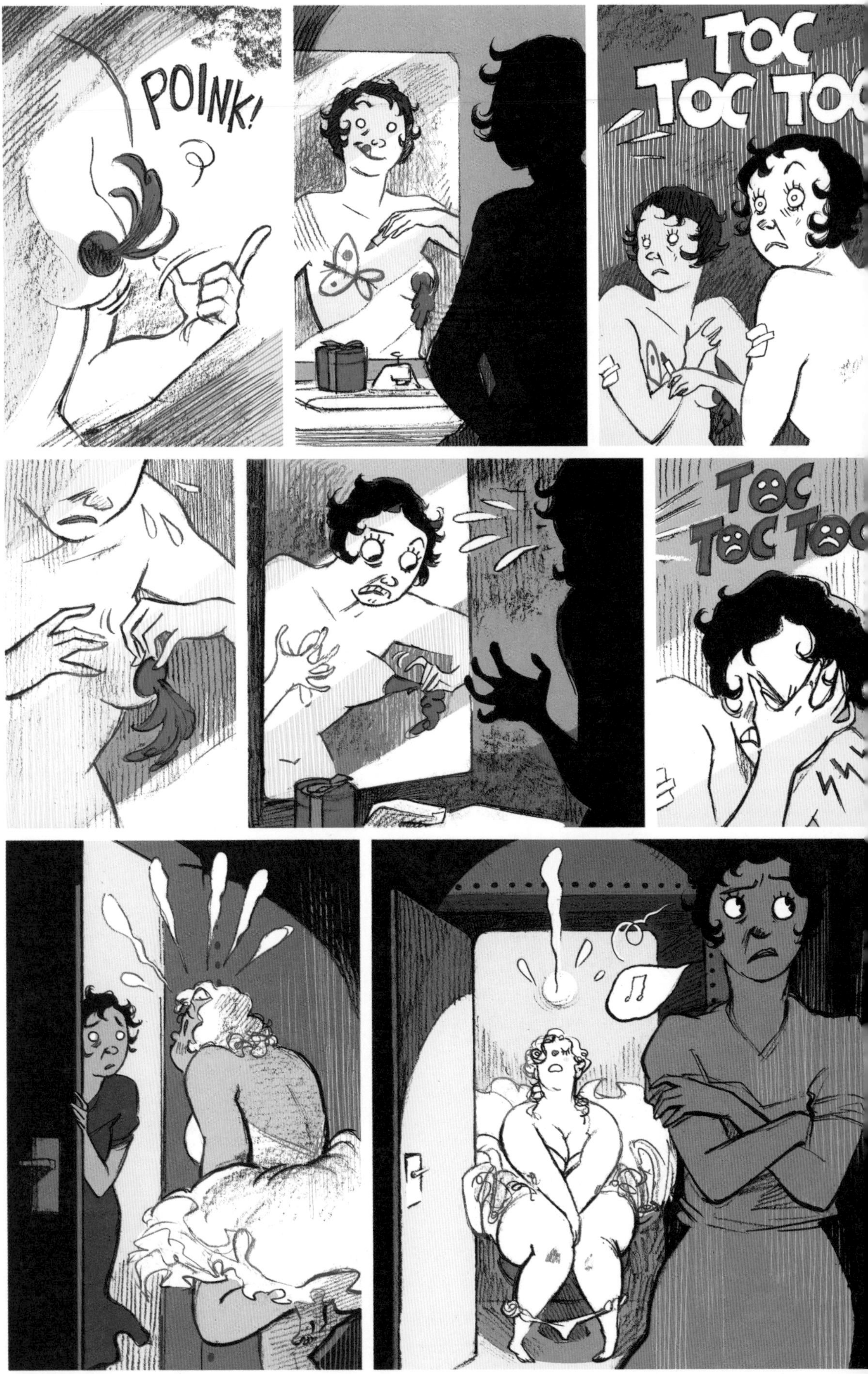
POINK!
TOC
TOC TOC
TOC
TOC TOC

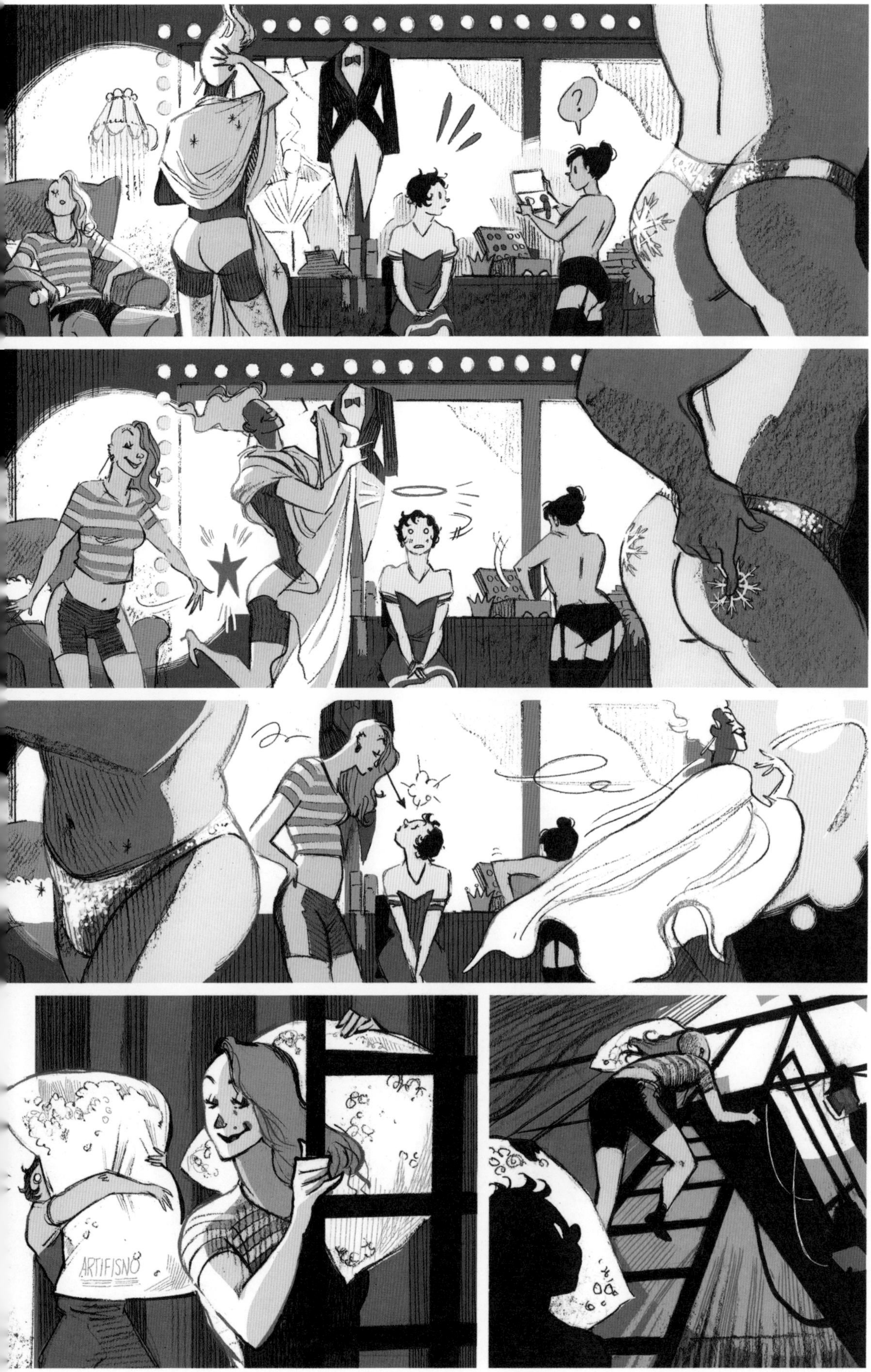
?
ARTIFISNO

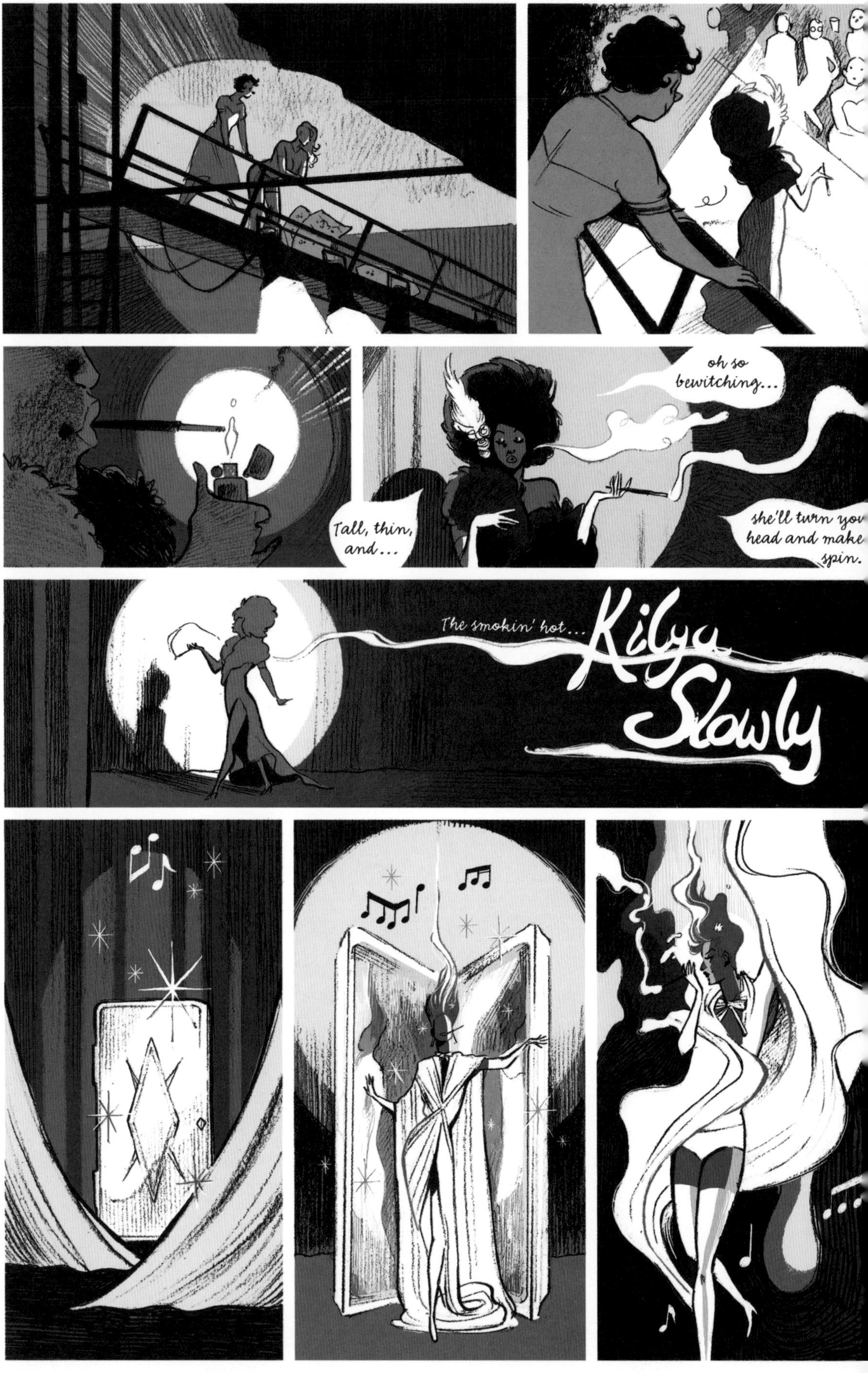

Tall, thin, and...
oh so bewitching...
she'll turn you head and make spin.
The smokin' hot...
Kilya Slowly

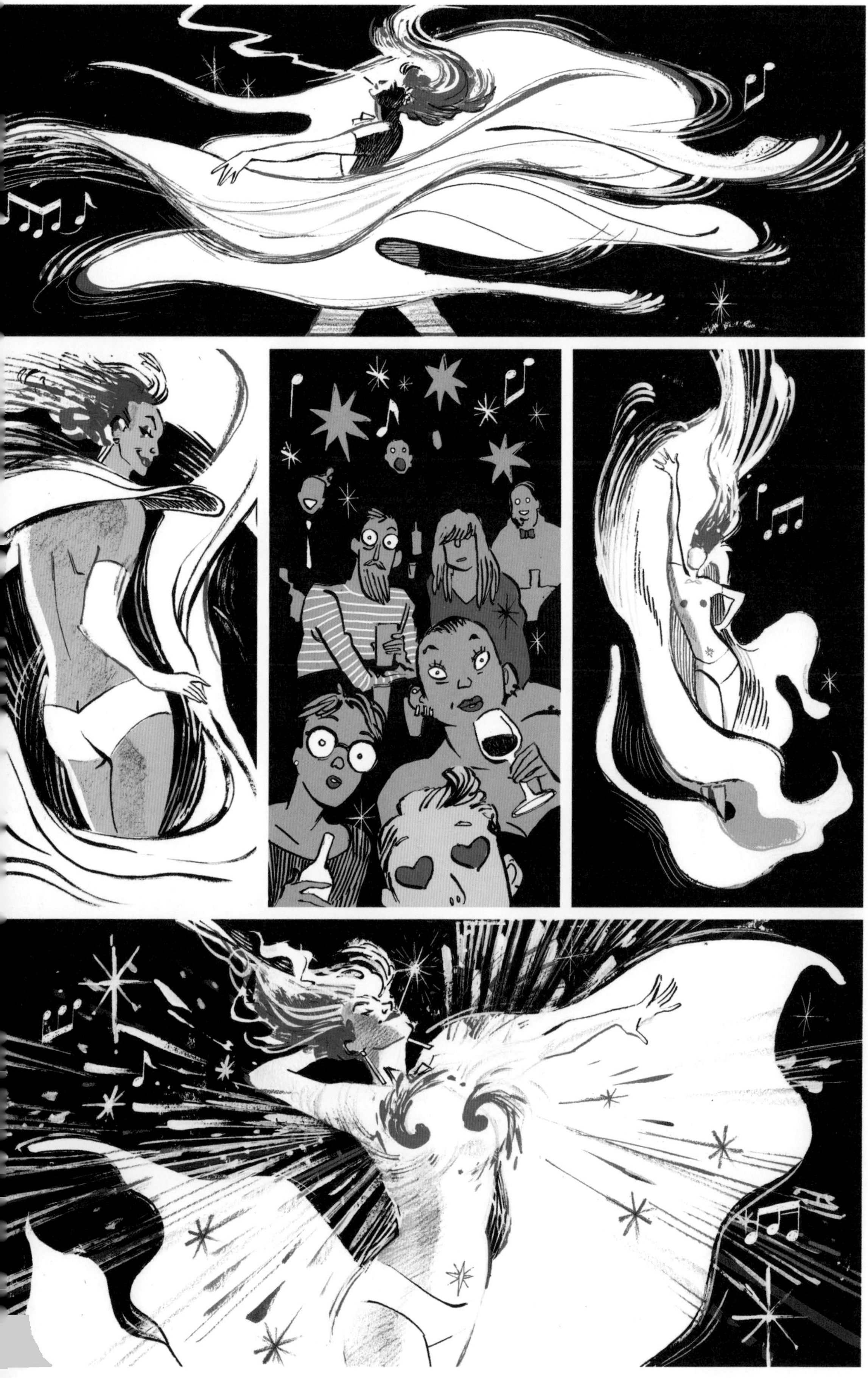

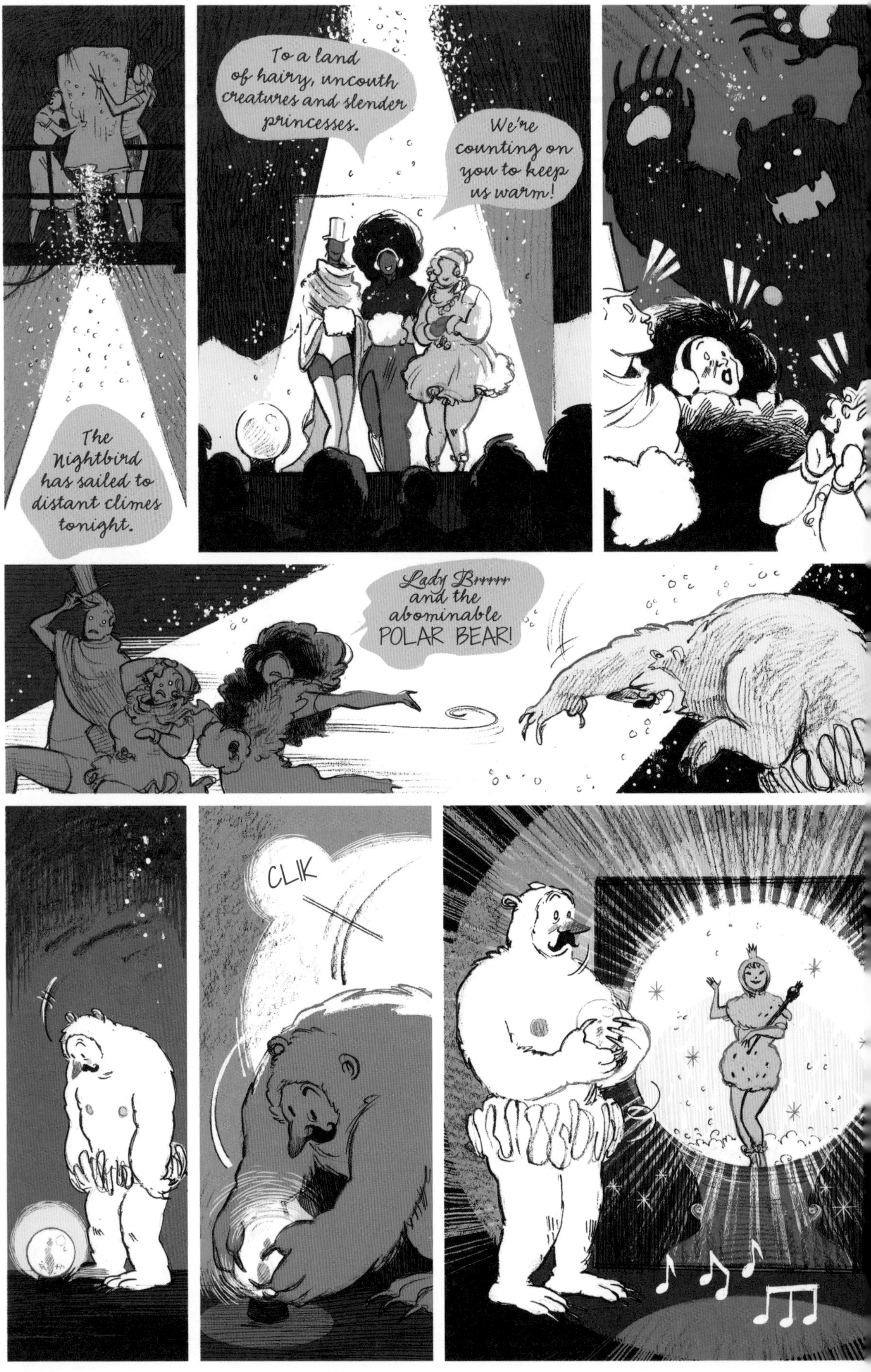
The Nightbird has sailed to distant climes tonight.
To a land of hairy, uncouth creatures and slender princesses.
We're counting on you to keep us warm!
Lady Brrrrr and the abominable POLAR BEAR!
CLIK

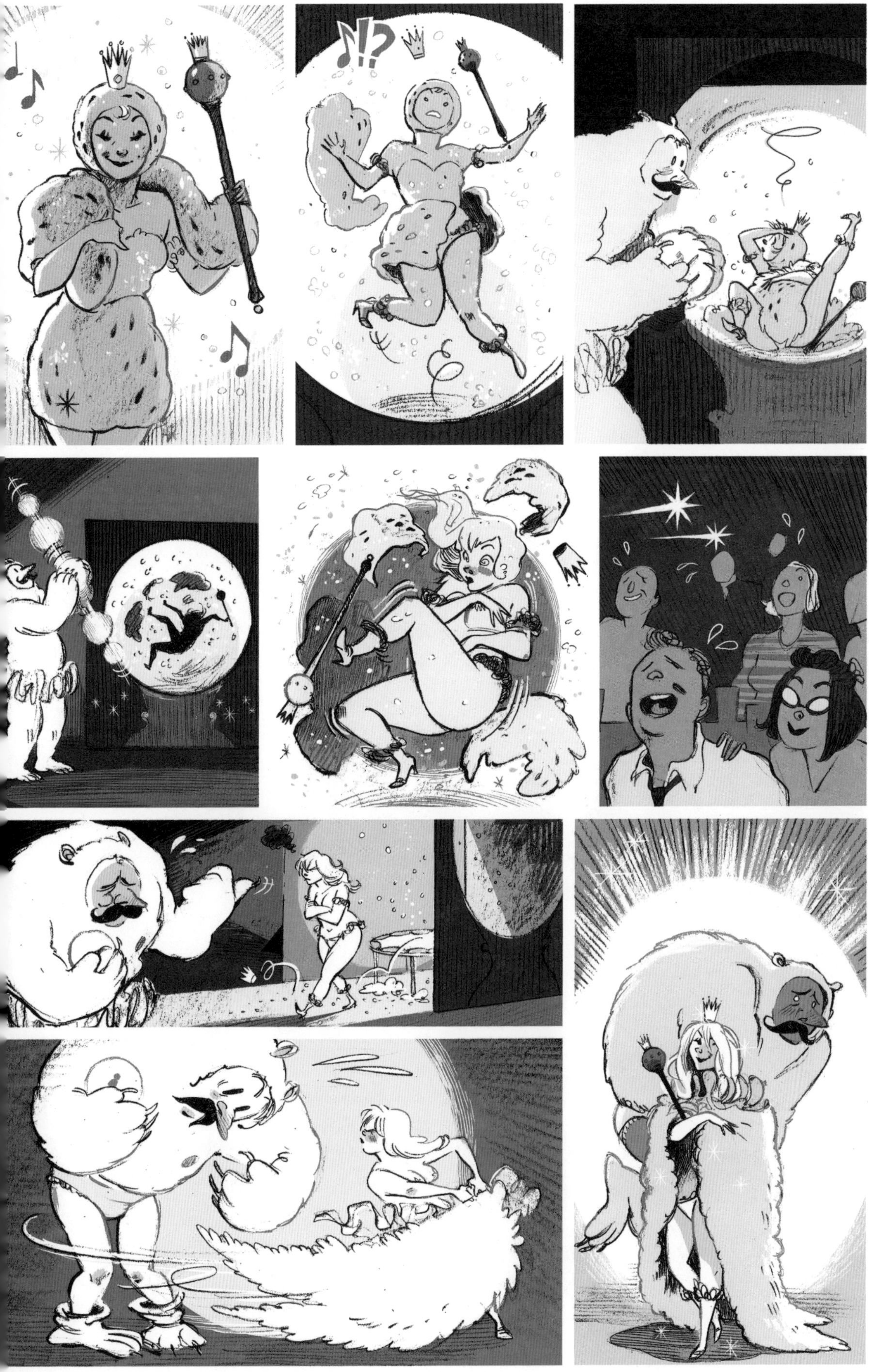
!?

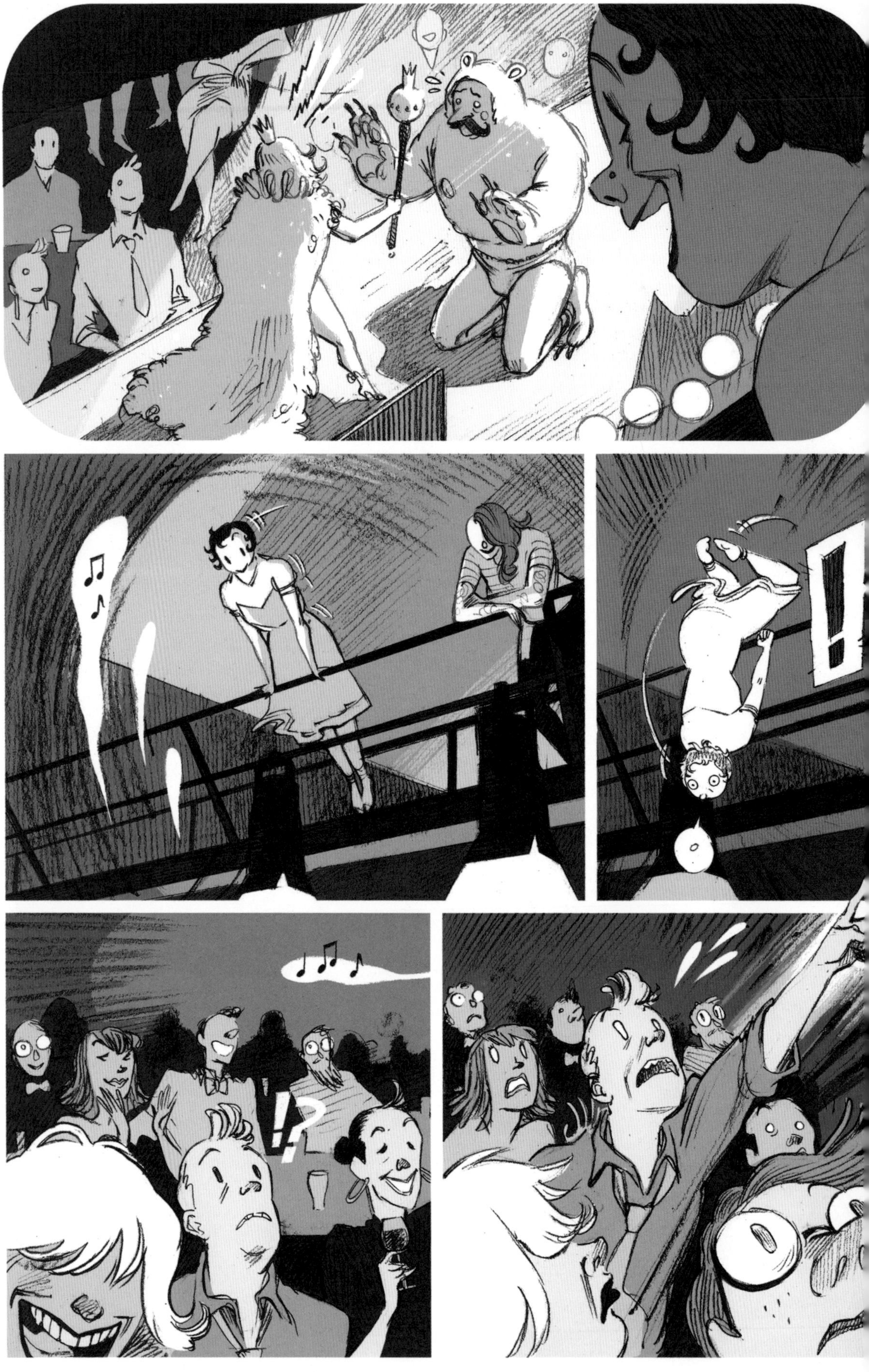
!
!?

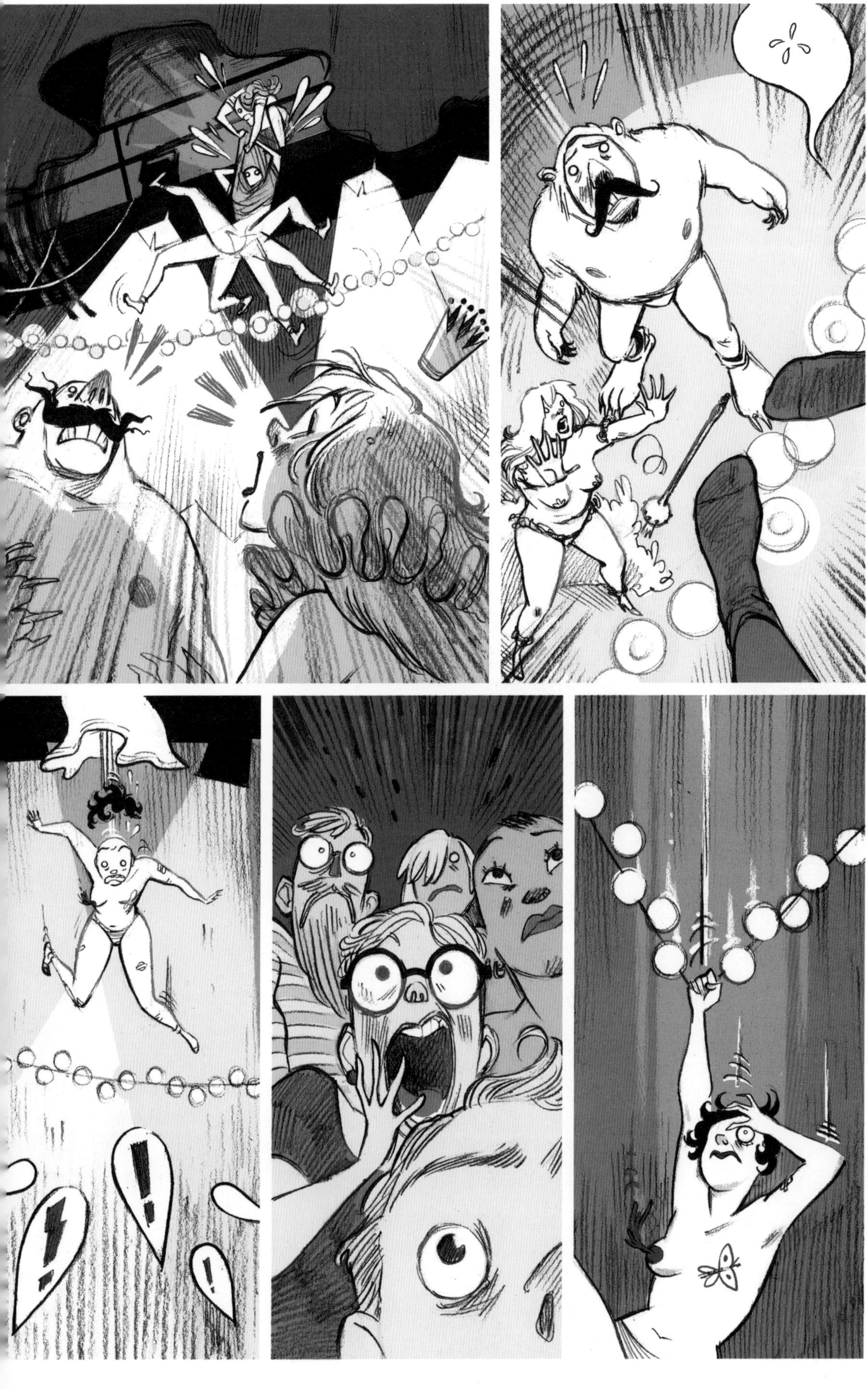
!
!

CLIC!

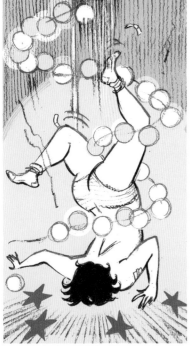

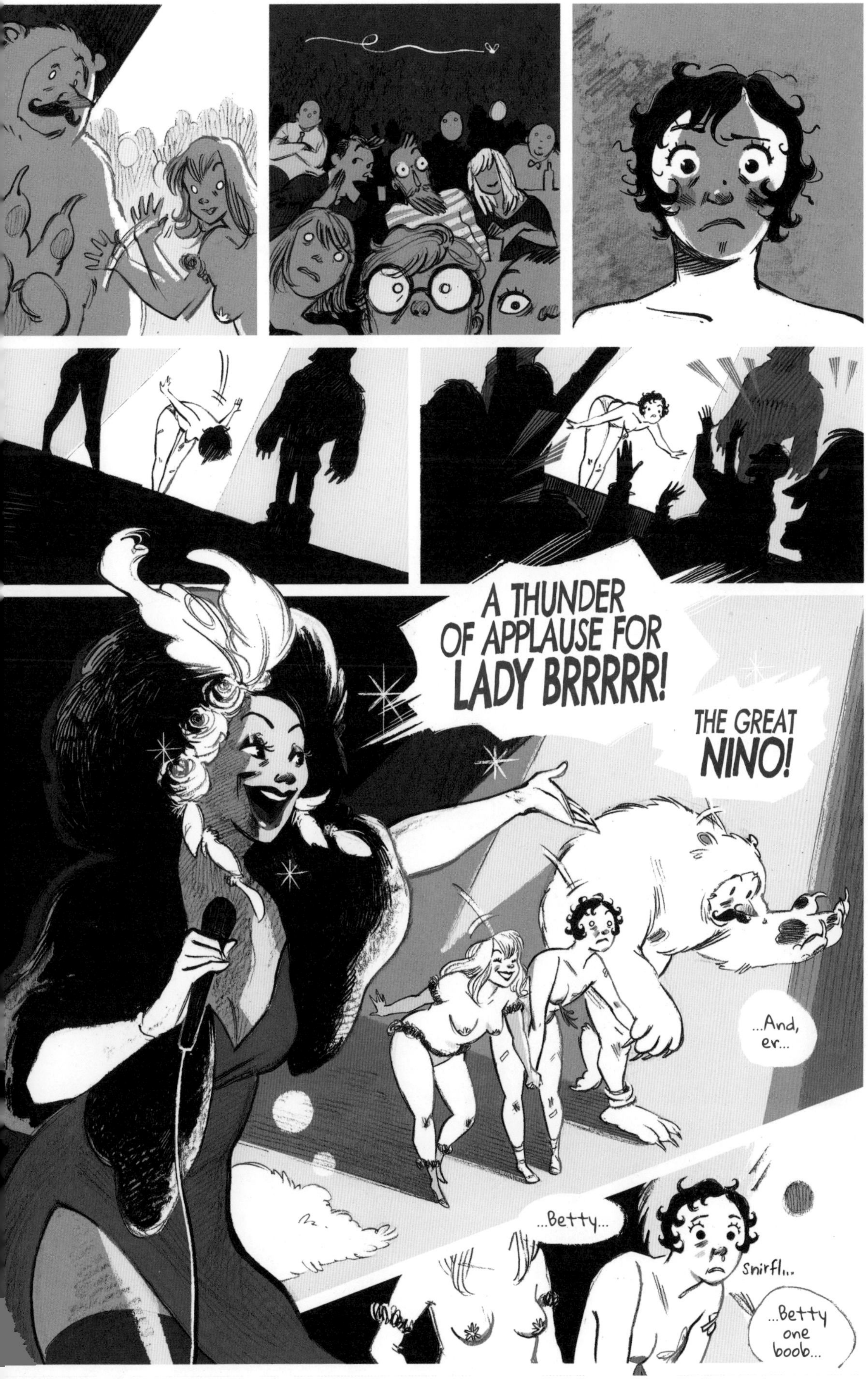
A THUNDER OF APPLAUSE FOR LADY BRRRRR!
THE GREAT NINO!
...And, er...
...Betty...
snirfl...
...Betty one boob...

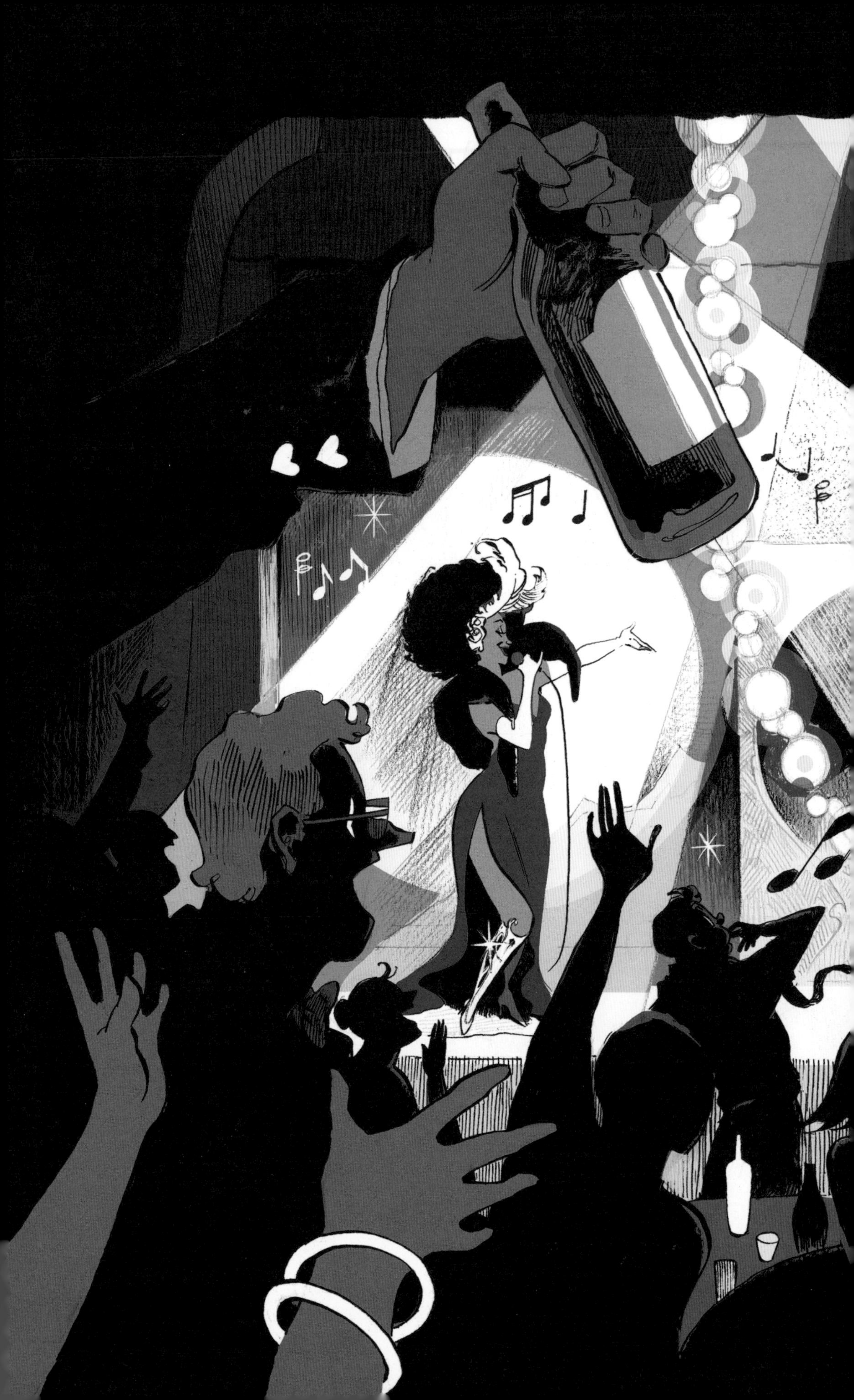

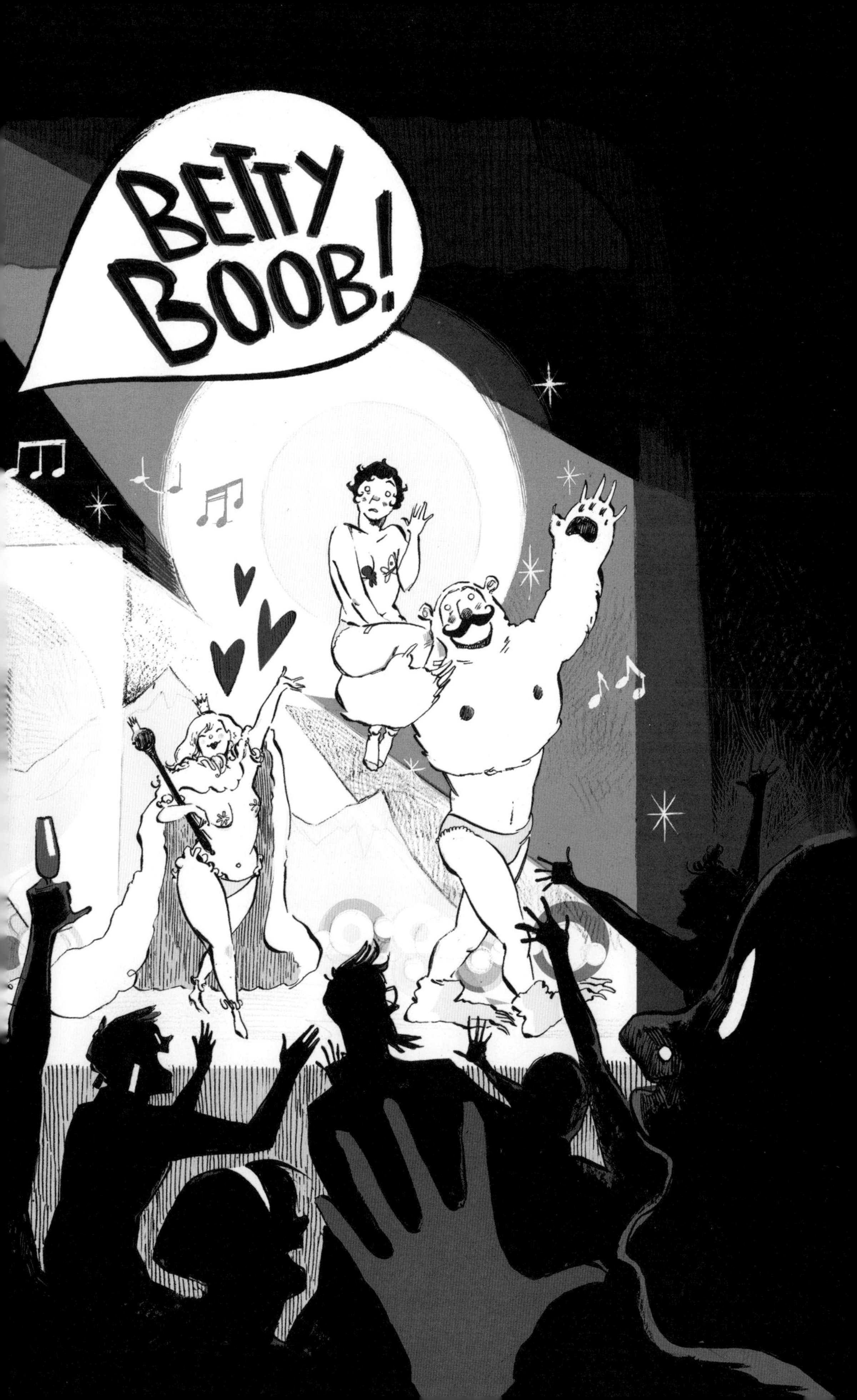
BETTY BOOB!

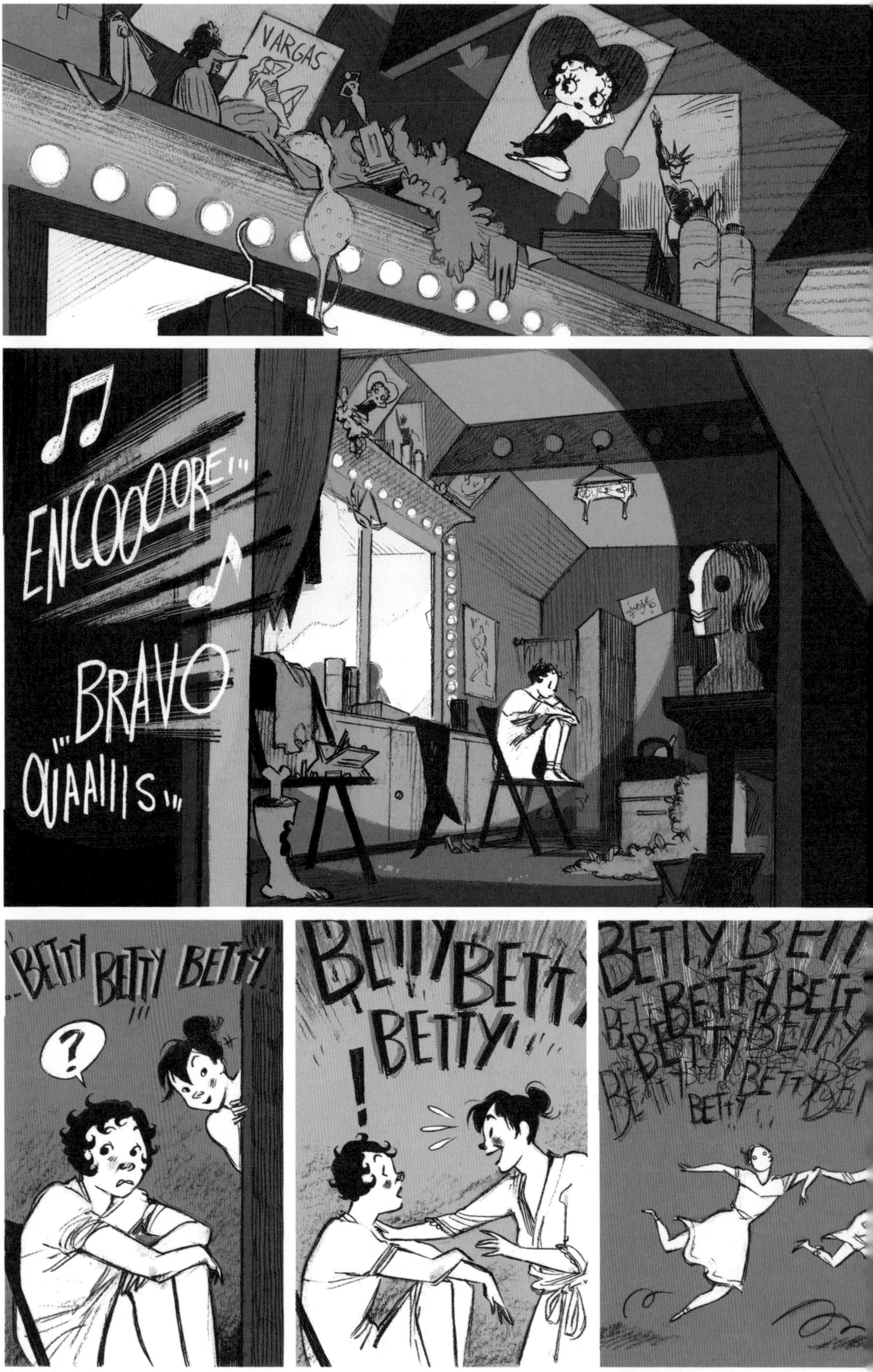
VARGAS
ENCOOOORE
BRAVO
OUAAIIIS
BETTY BETTY BETTY
?
BETTY BETTY
BETTY
!
BETTY BETTY BETTY
BETTY

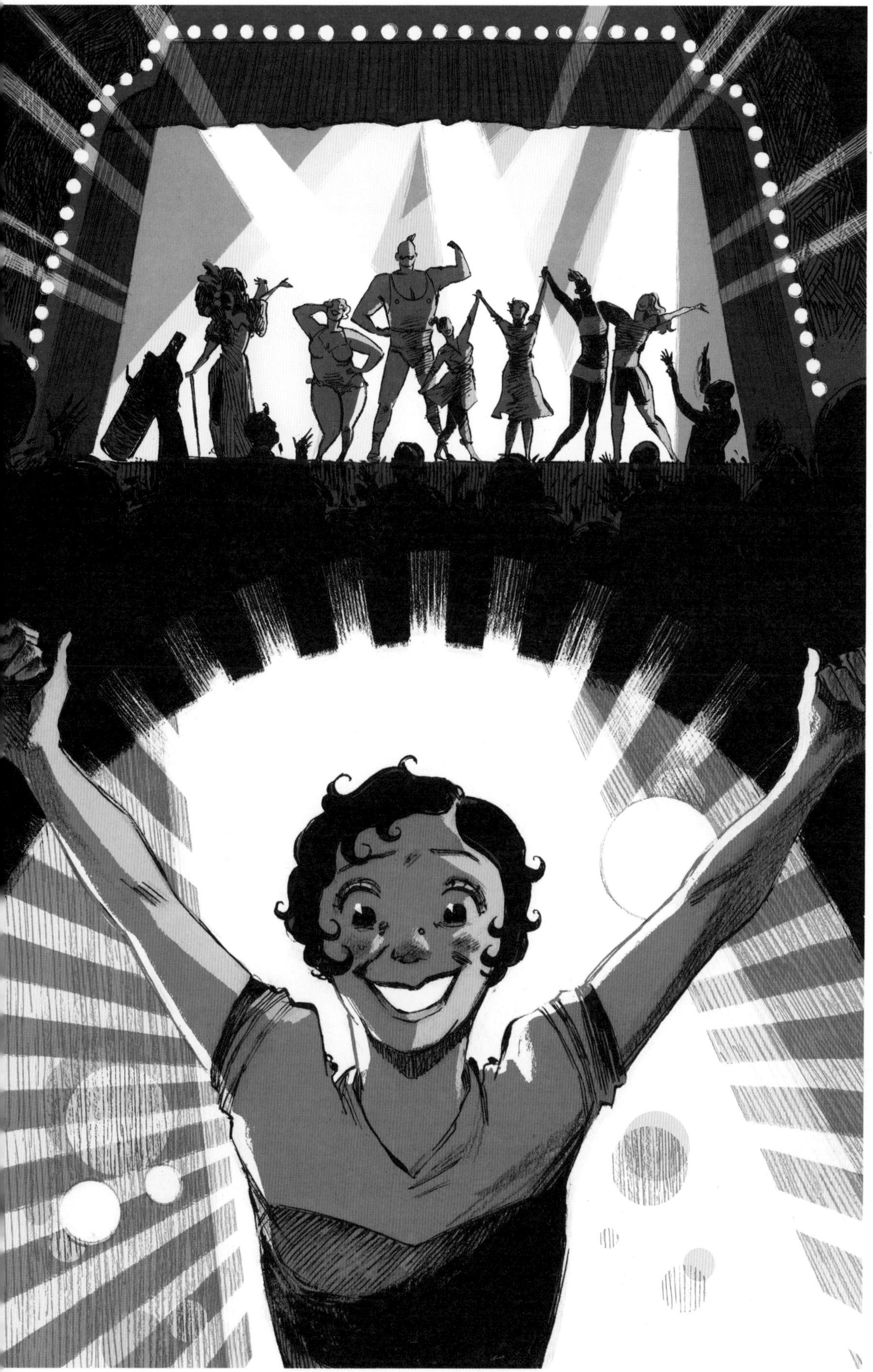

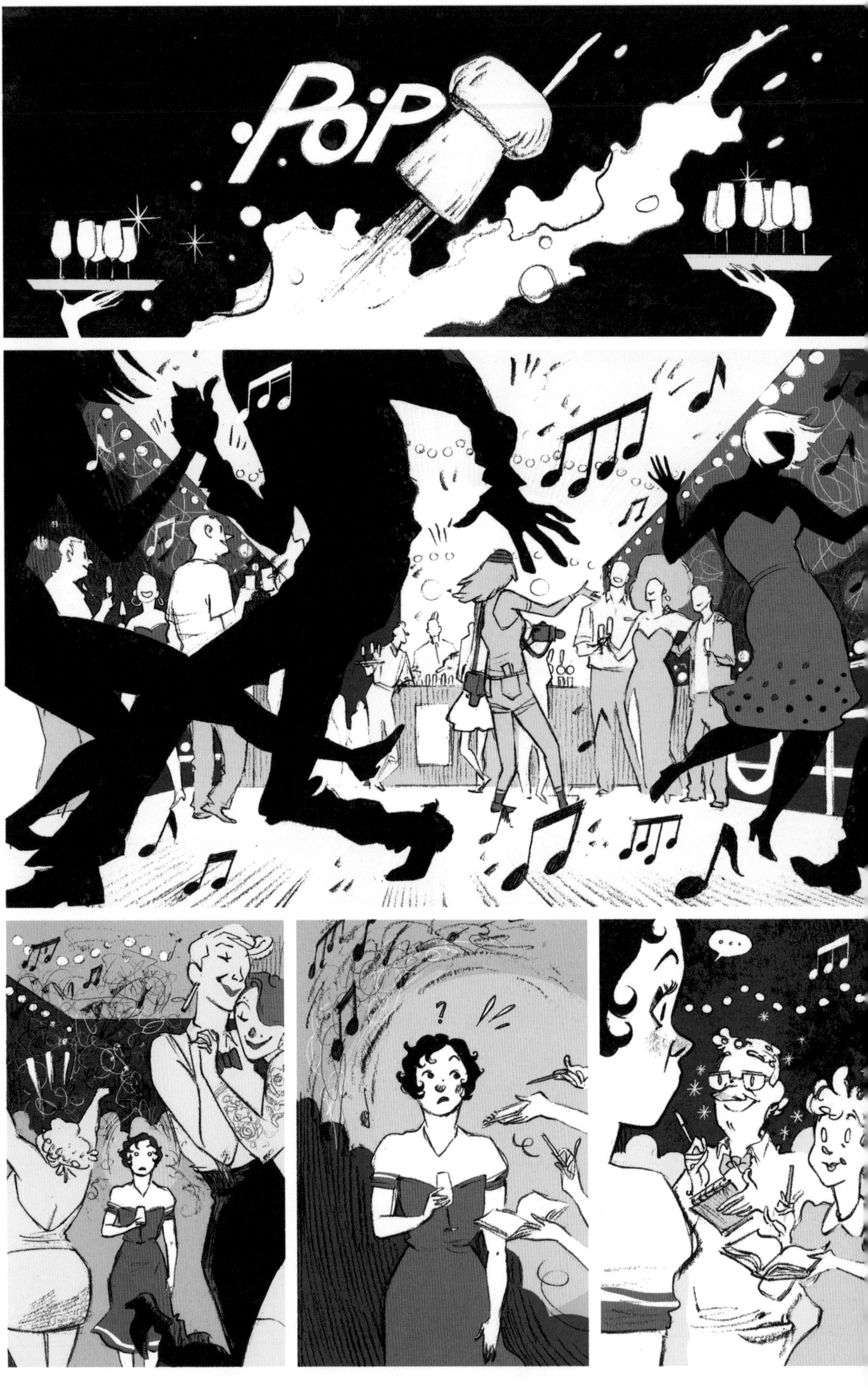
POP

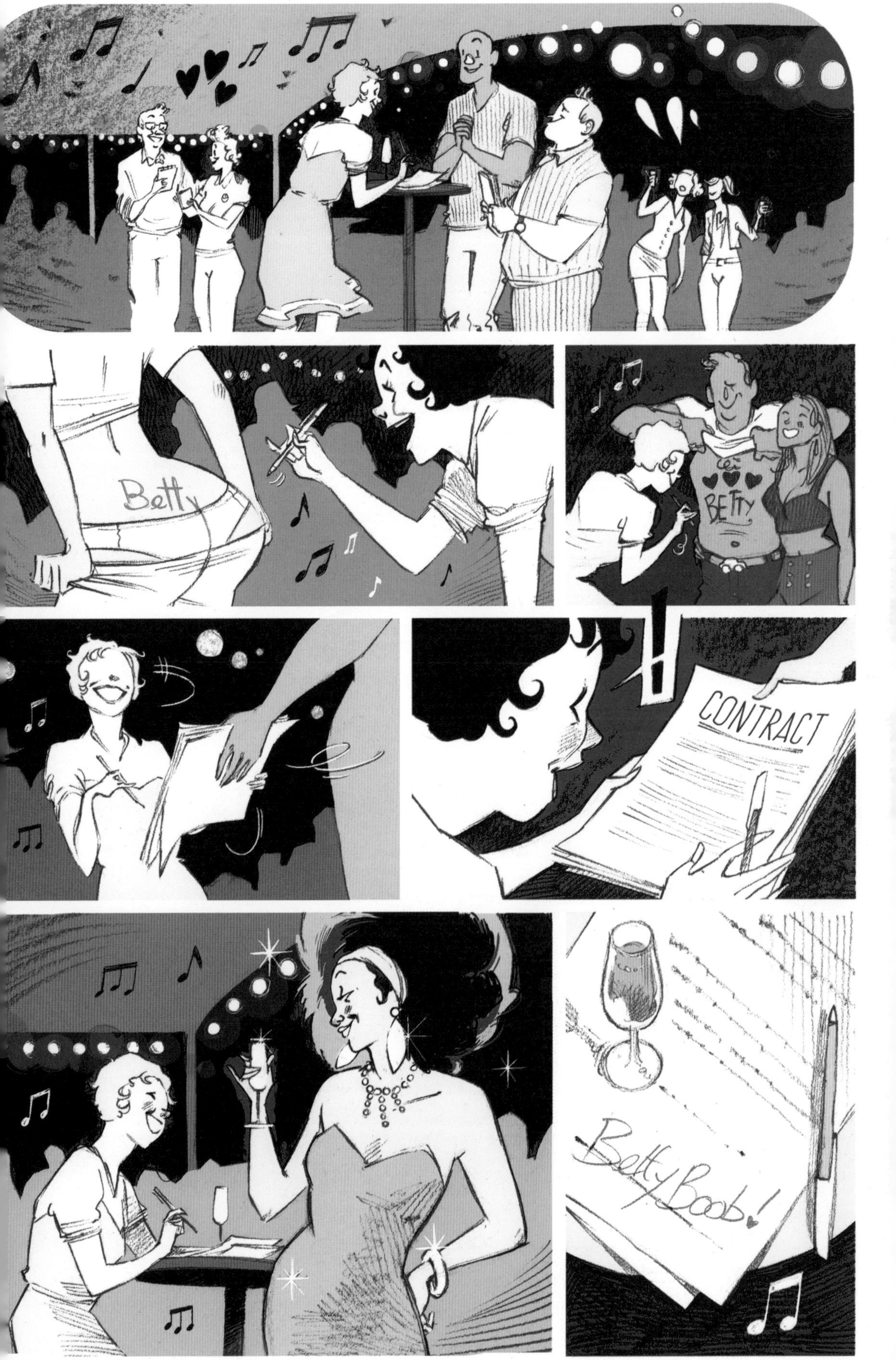
Betty
BETTY
CONTRACT
Betty Boob!

-I'm scared.
-Just let go.

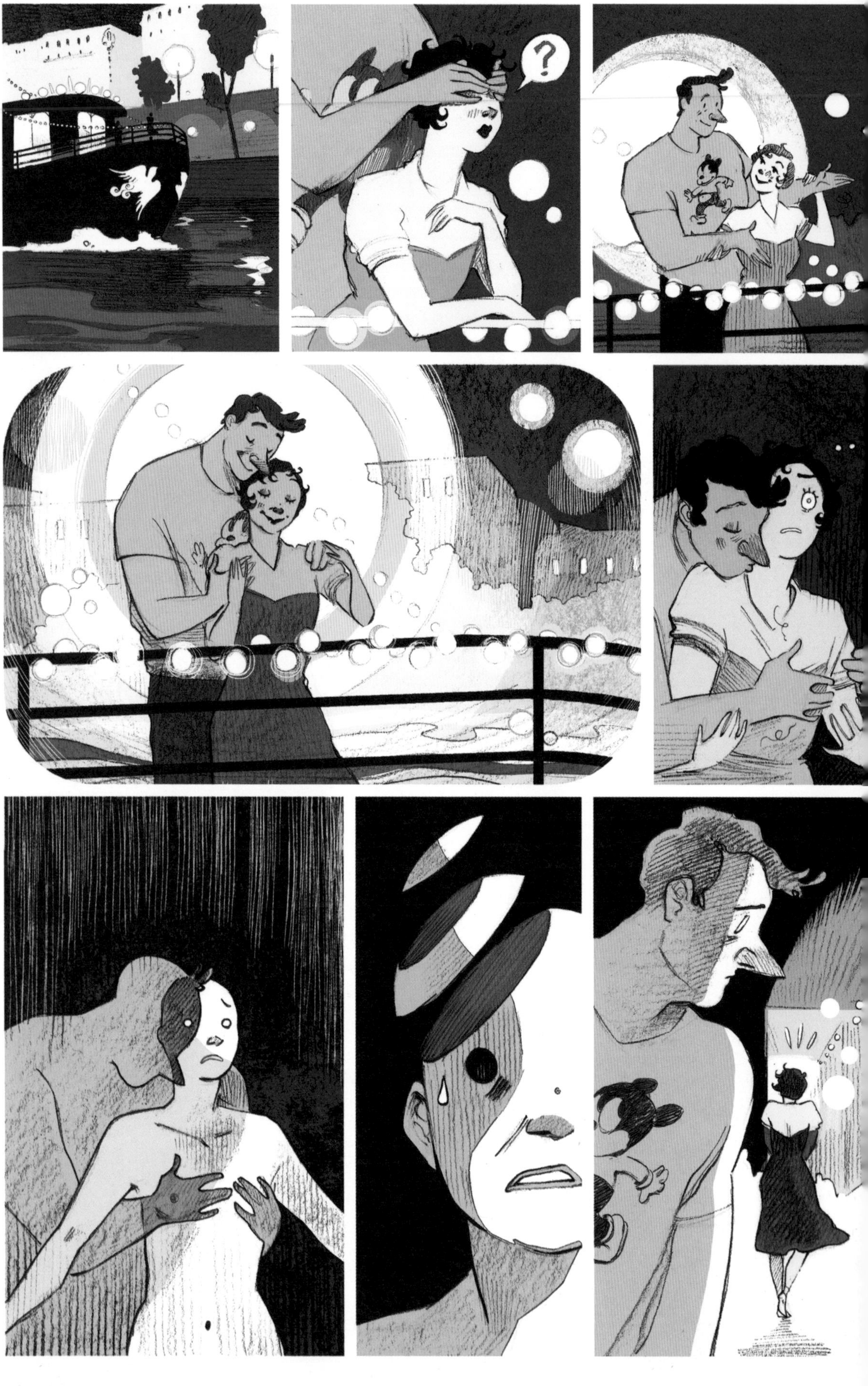
?

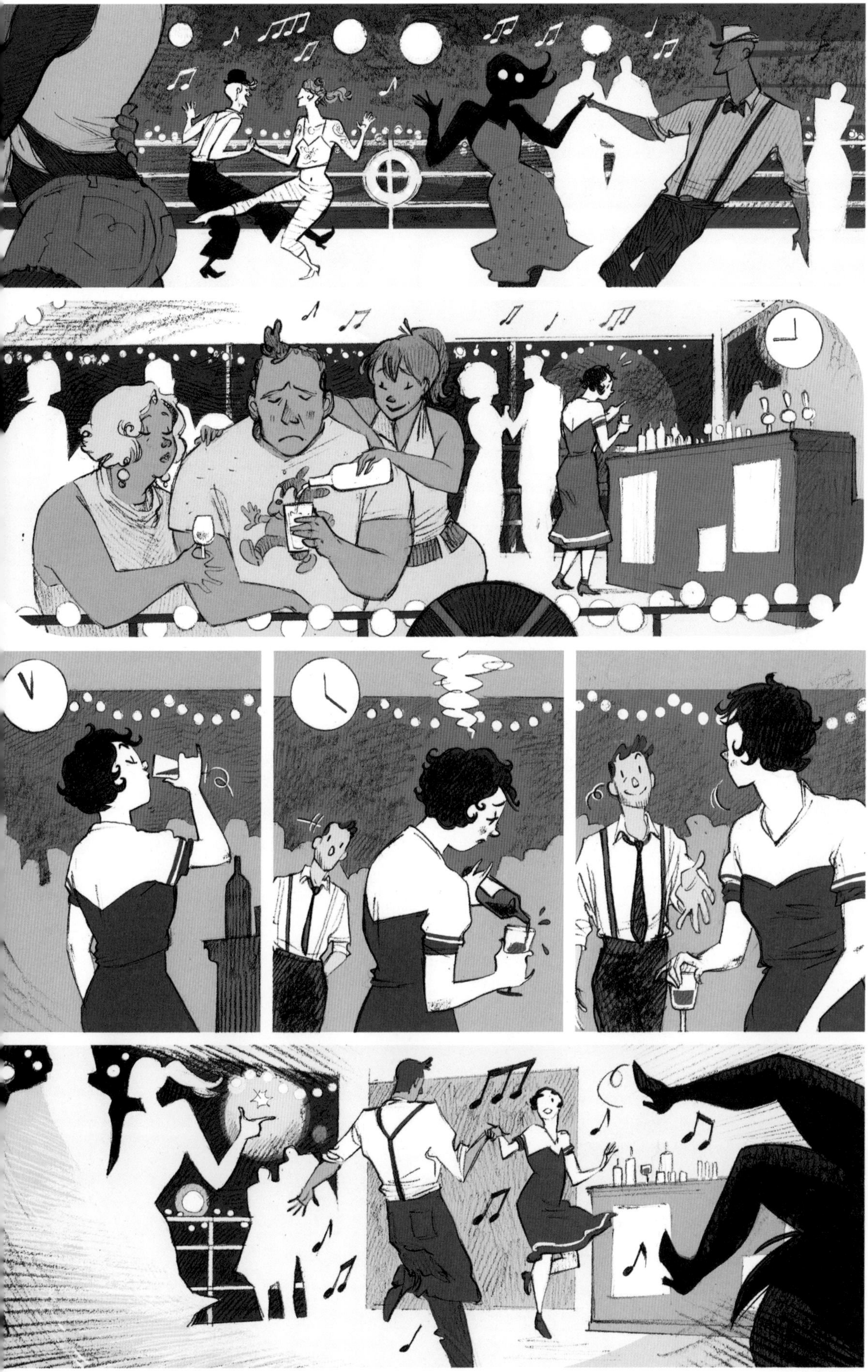

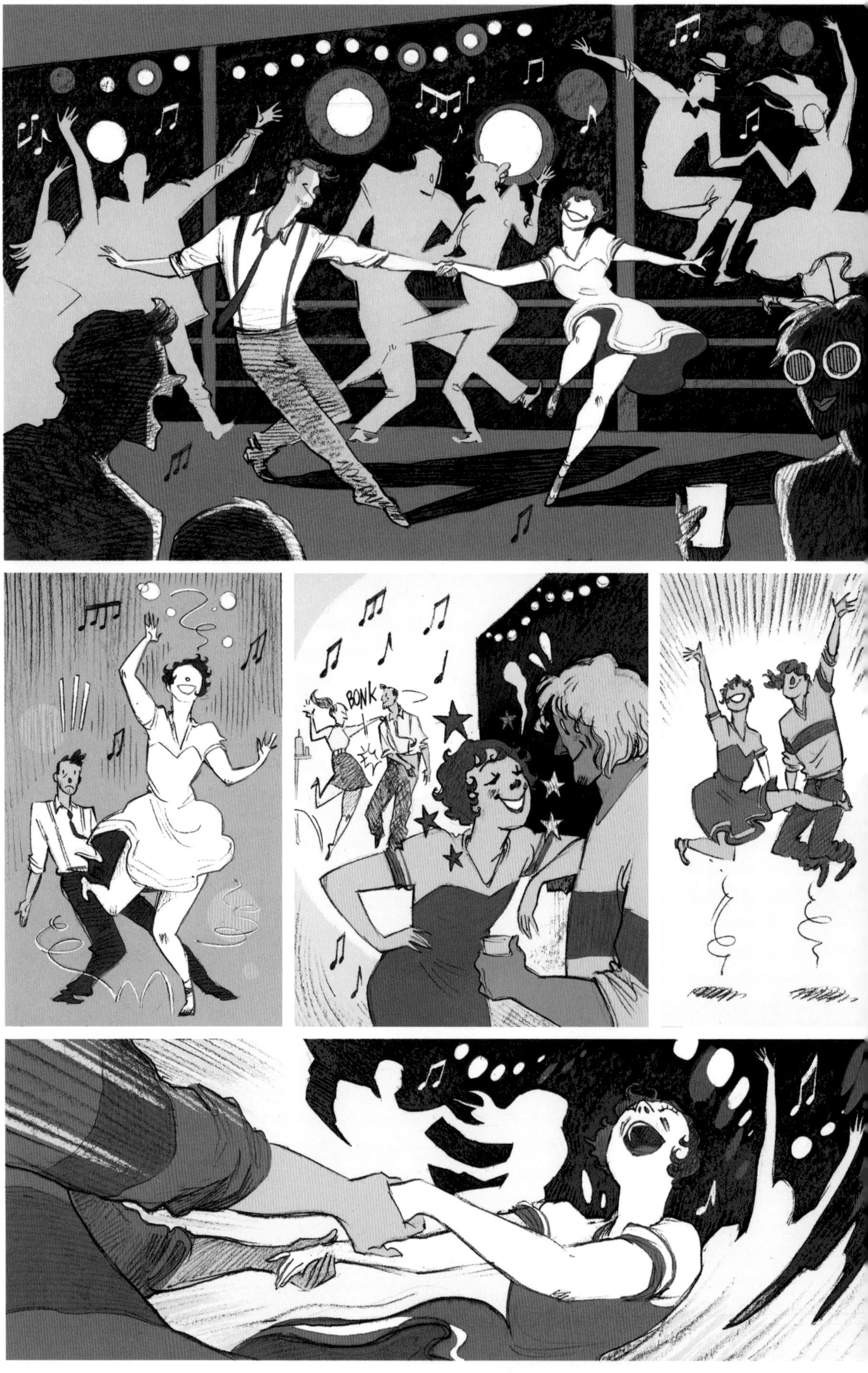
BONK

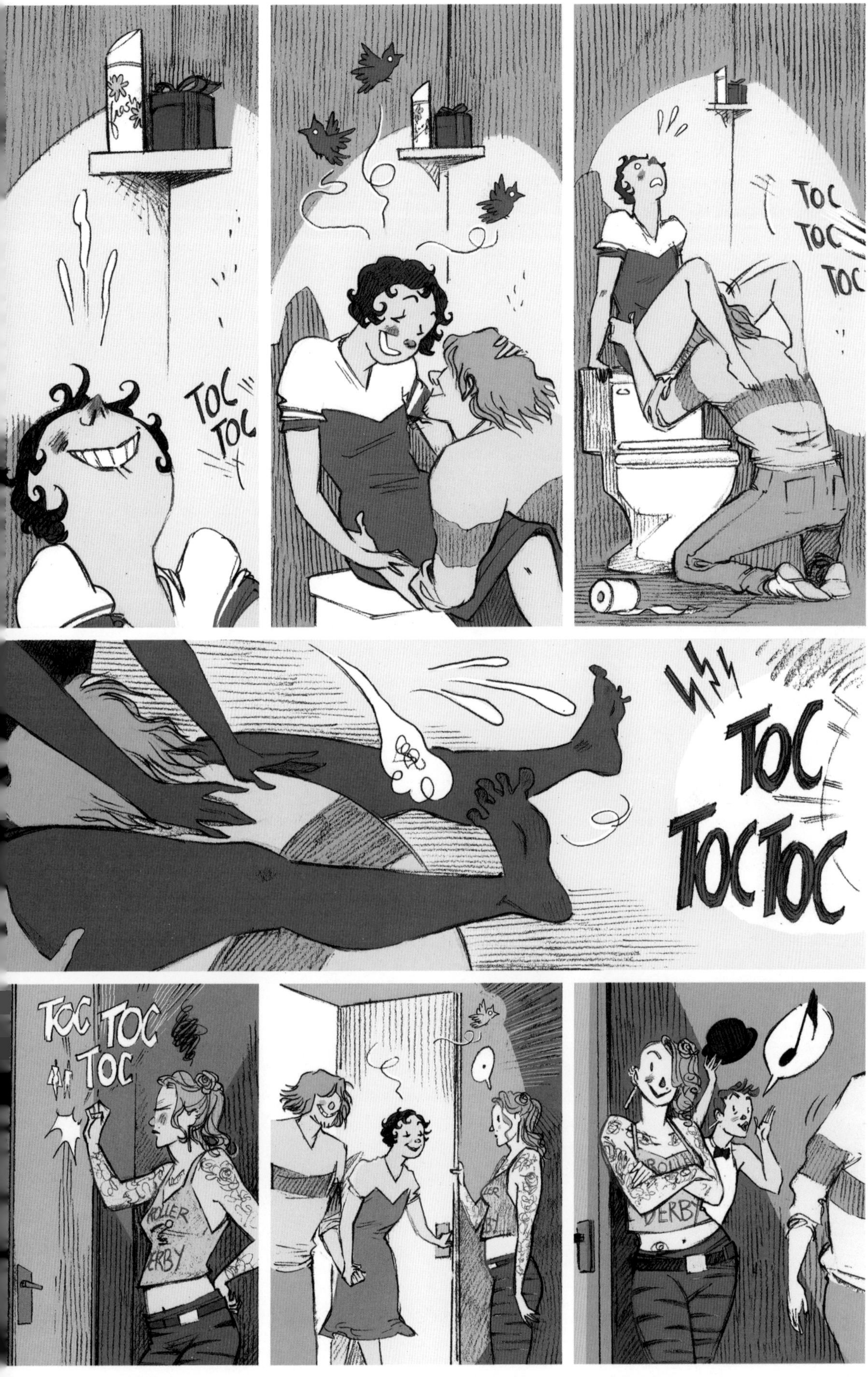
TOC
TOC
TOC
TOC
TOC
TOC
TOC
TOC TOC
TOC TOC
TOC
ROLLER
DERBY
DERBY

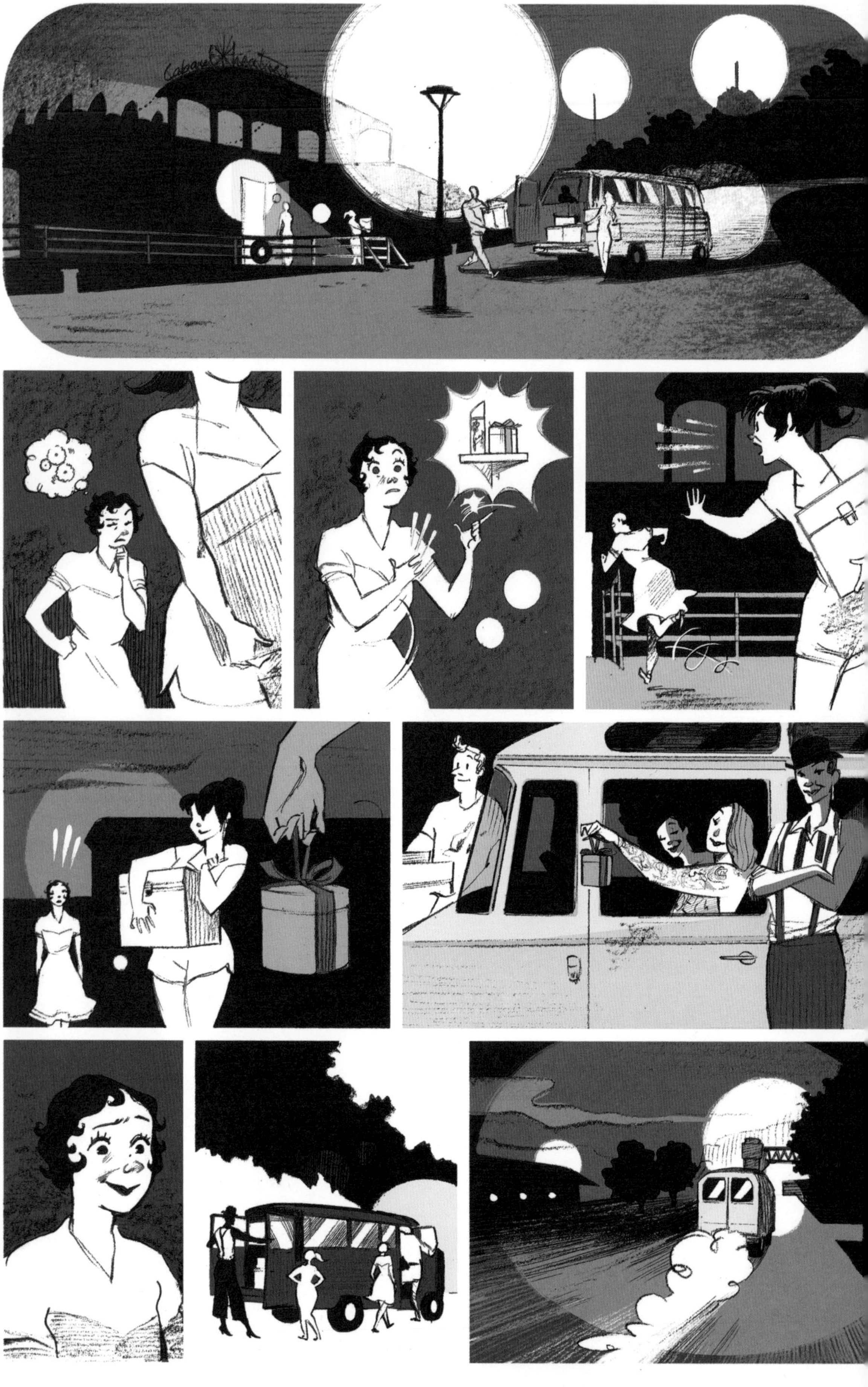

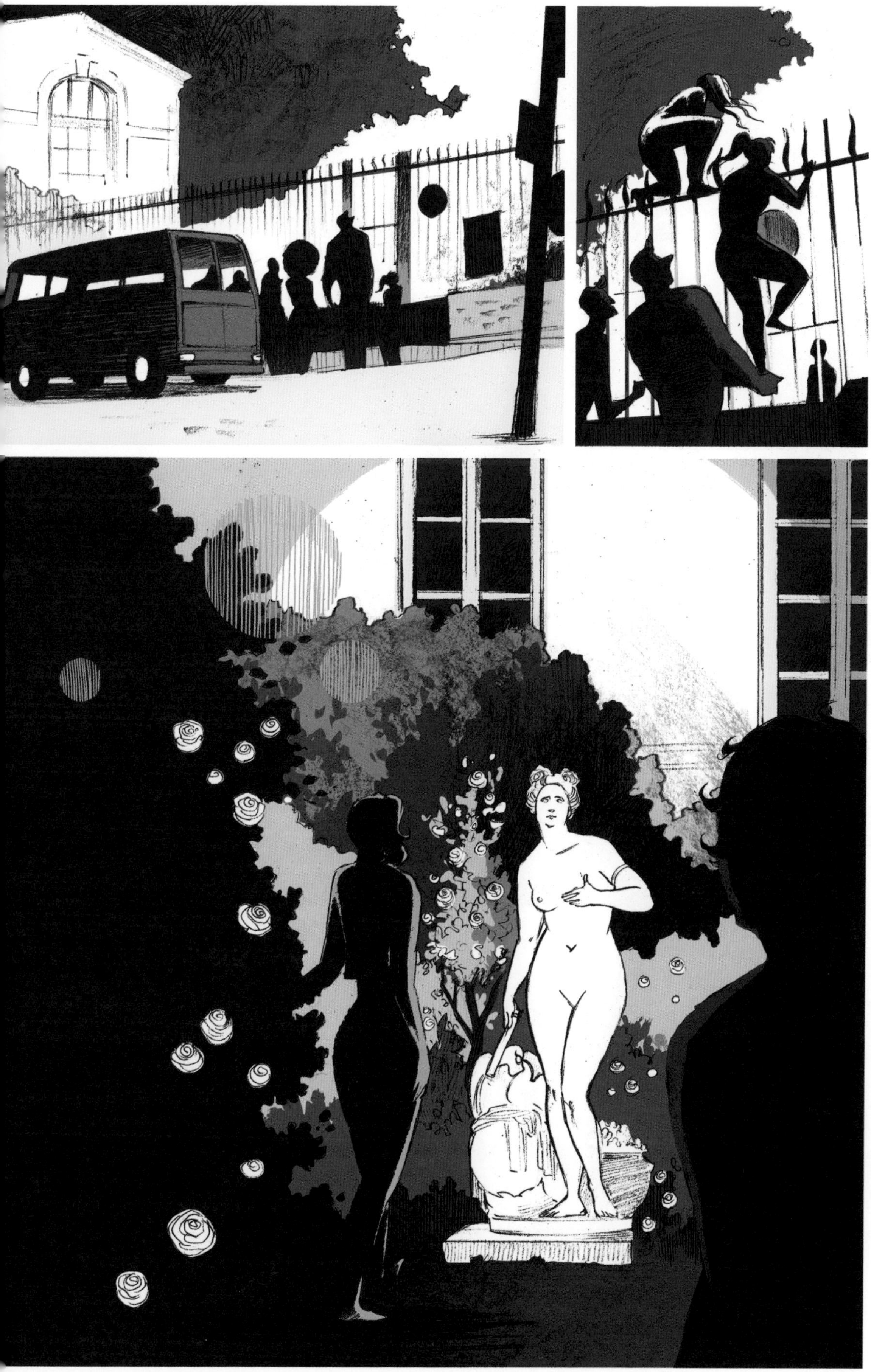

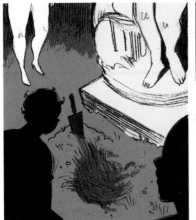

For auld lang syne, my dear,
For auld lang syne.

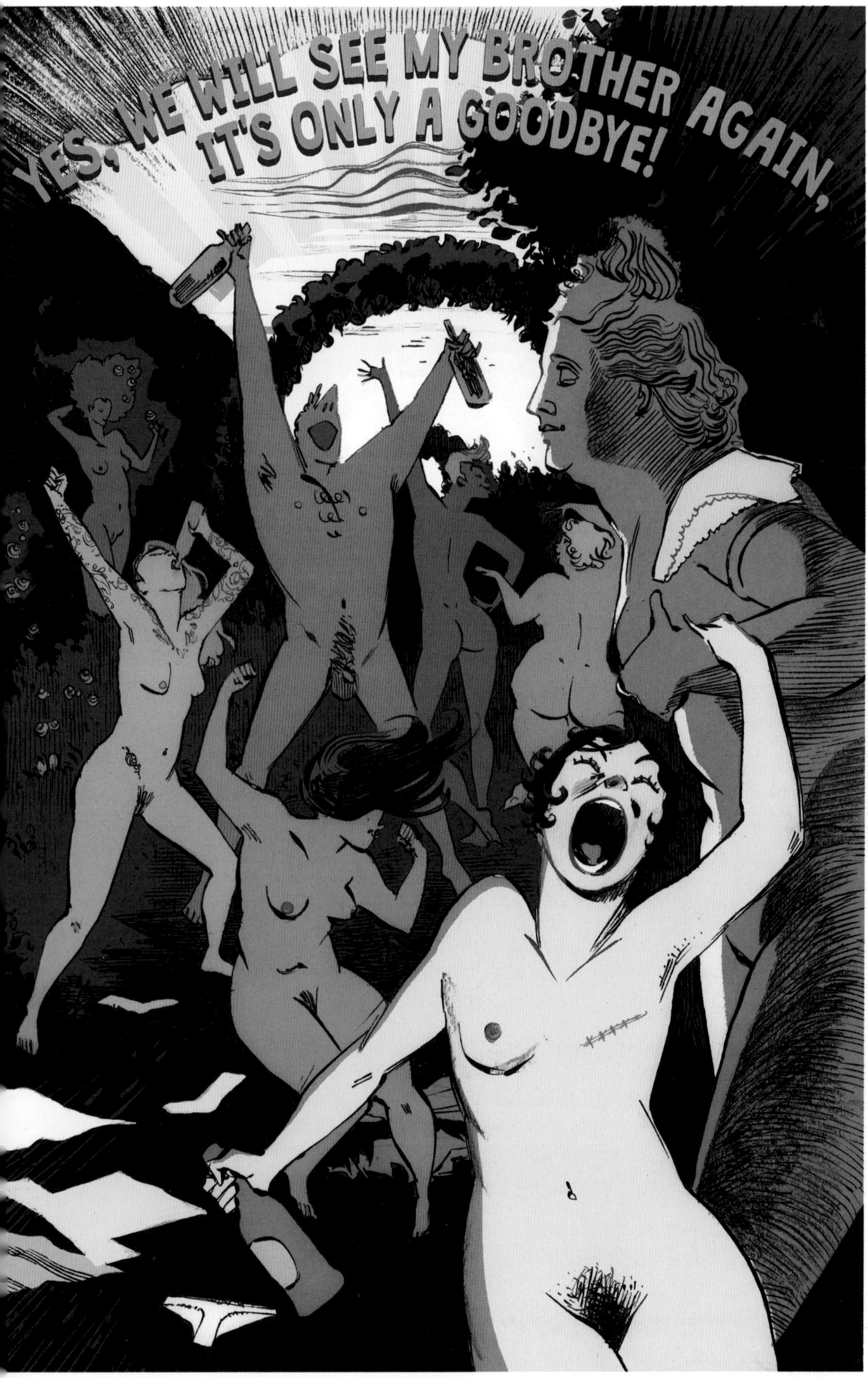
YES, WE WILL SEE MY BROTHER AGAIN, IT'S ONLY A GOODBYE!

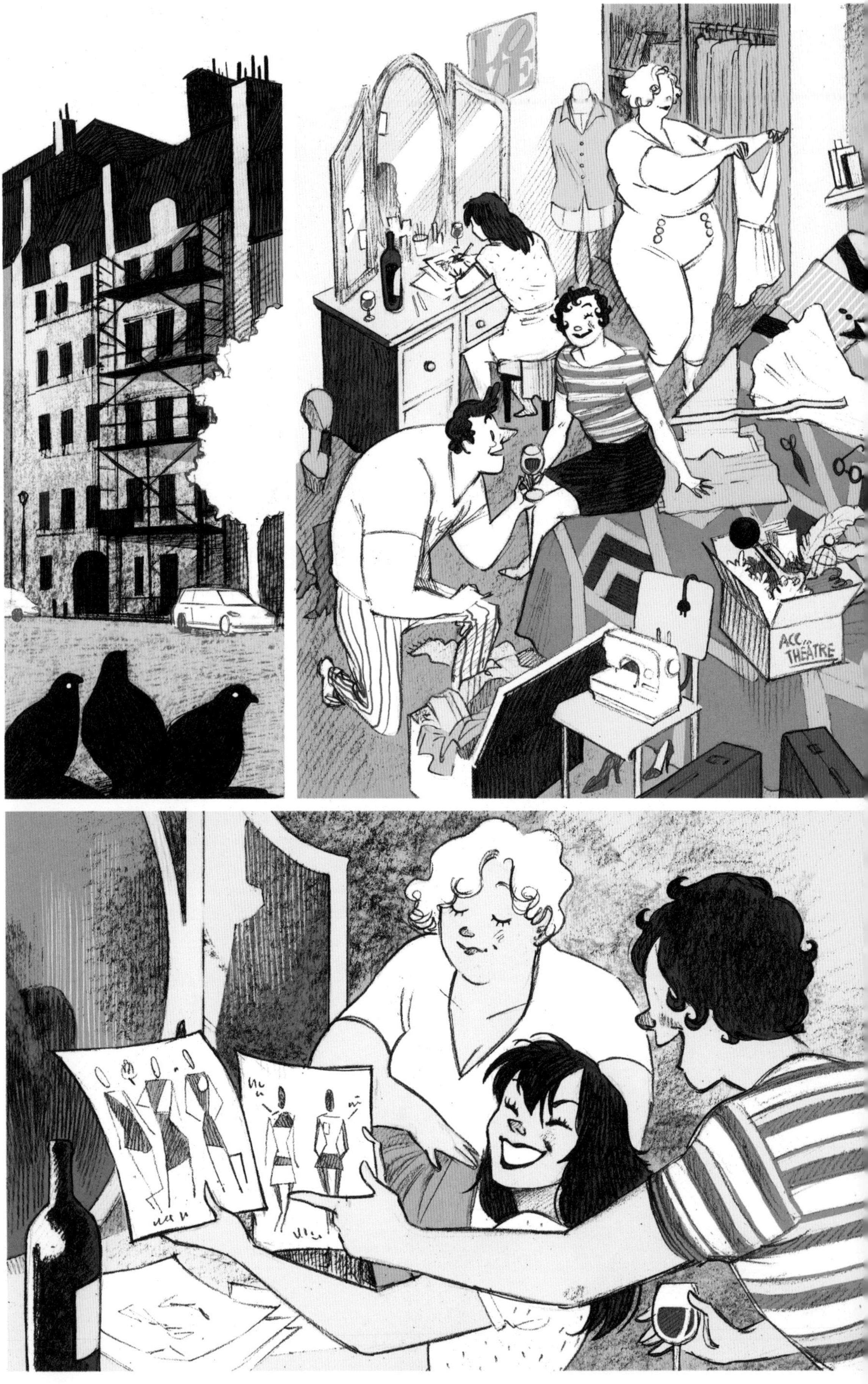
LOVE
ACC.
THÉÂTRE

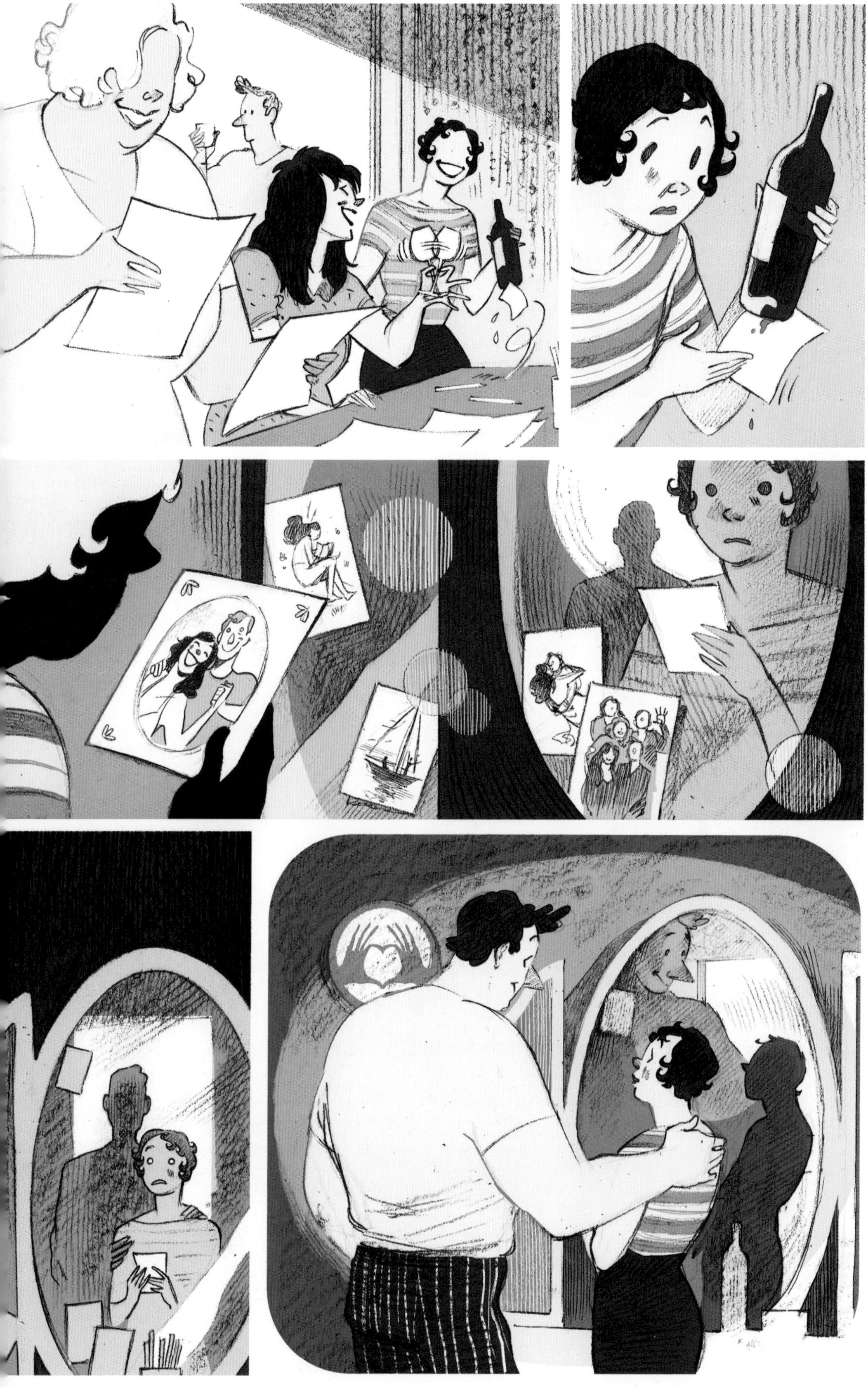

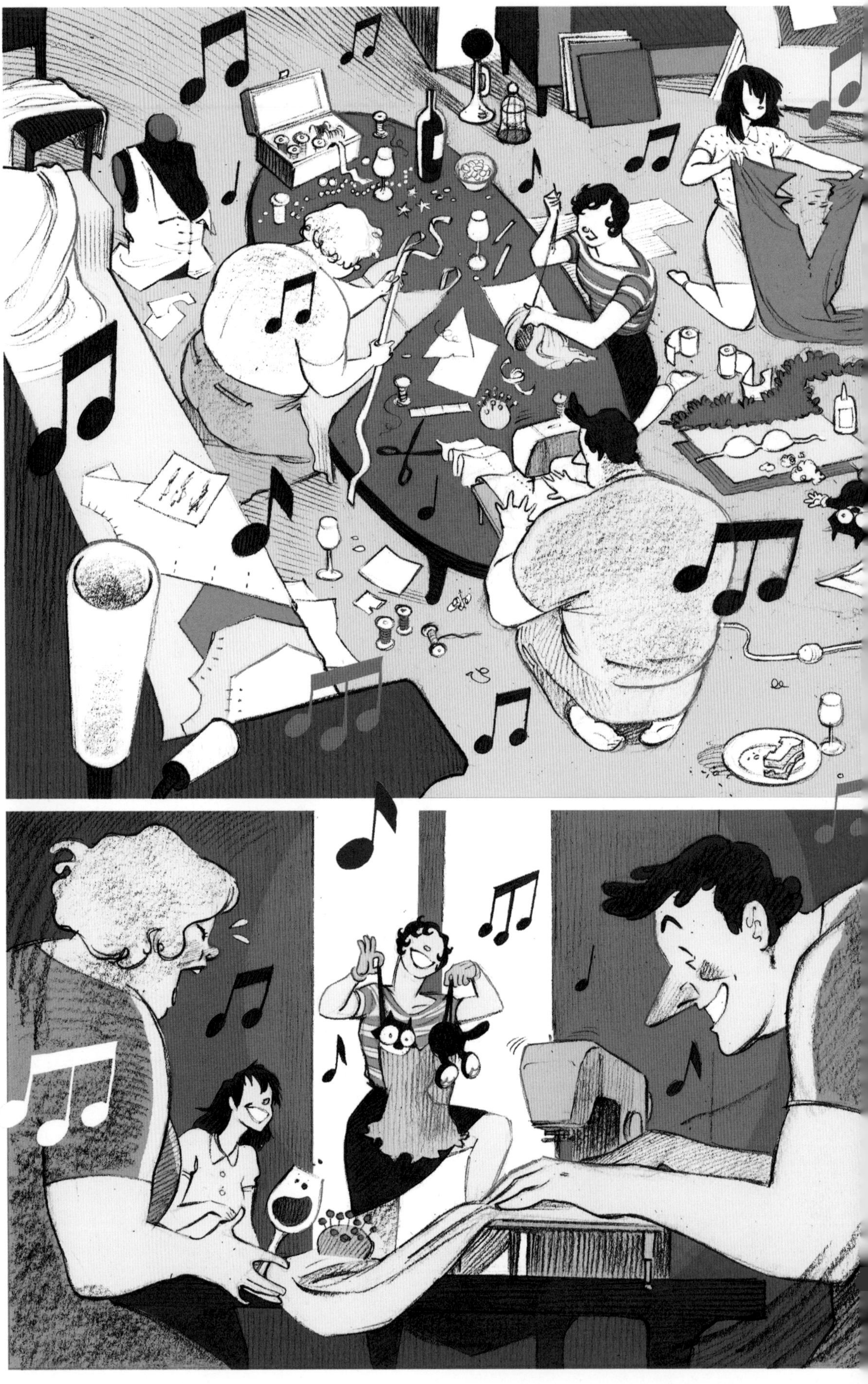

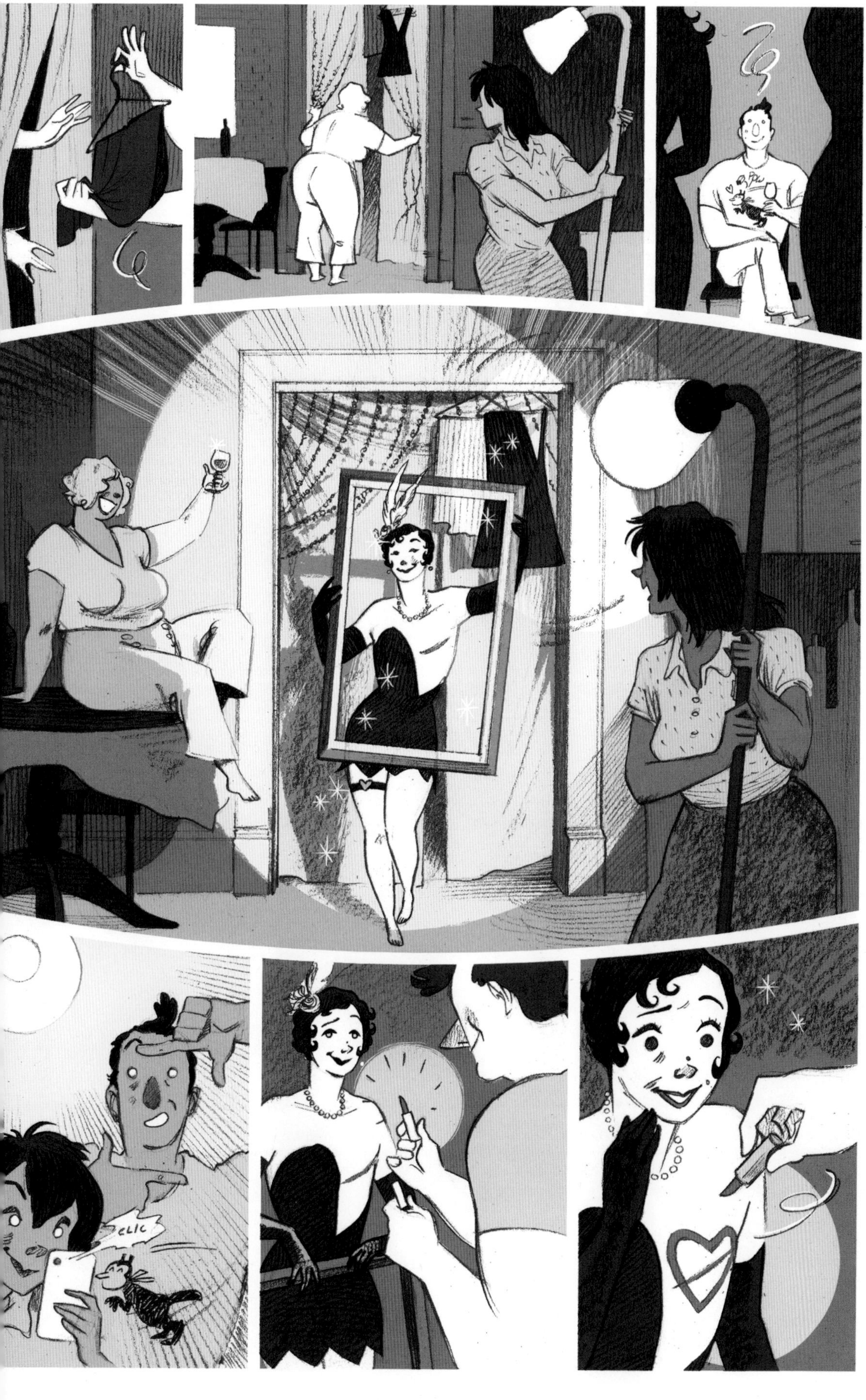
CLIC

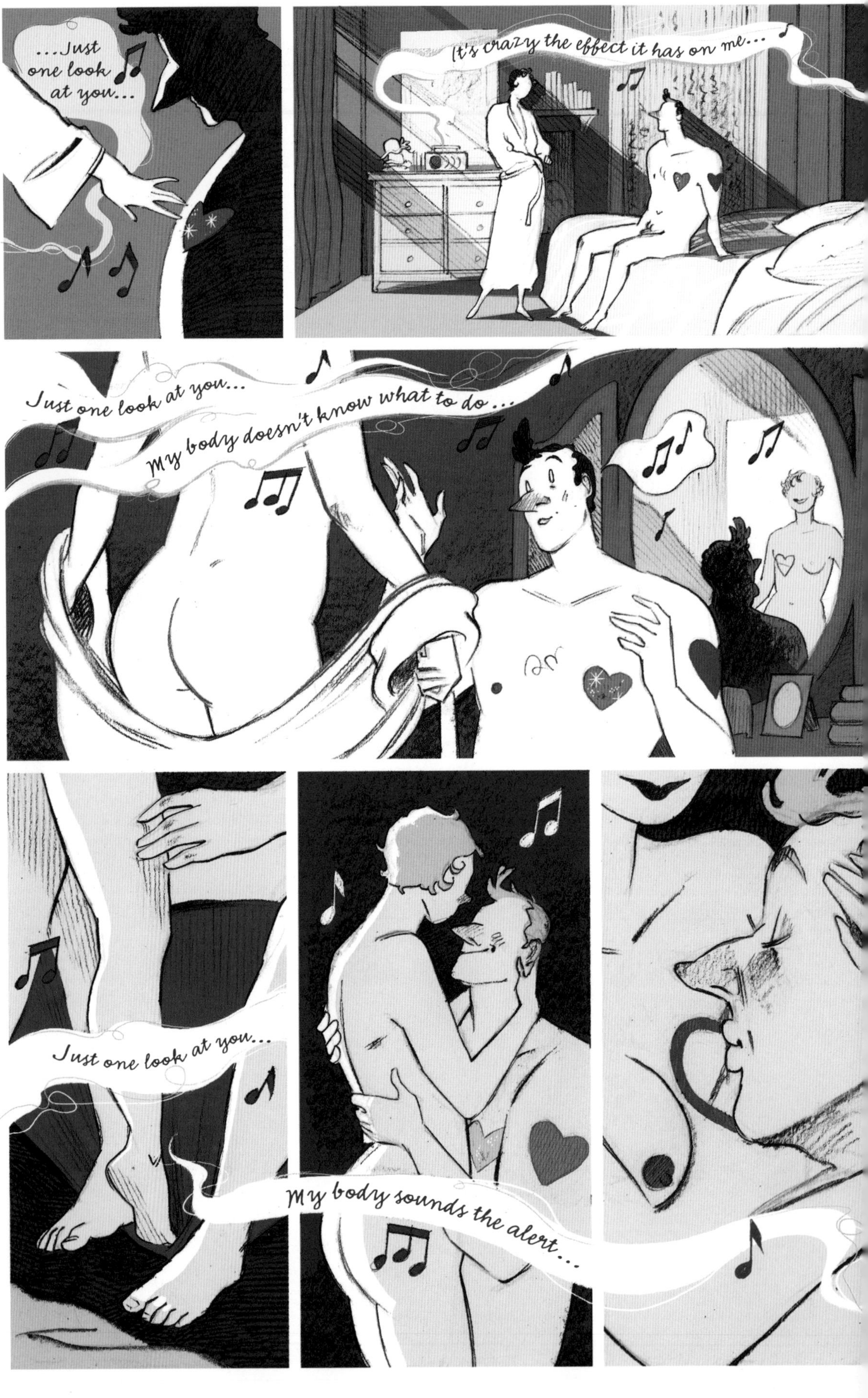
...Just one look at you...
It's crazy the effect it has on me...
Just one look at you...
My body doesn't know what to do...
Just one look at you...
My body sounds the alert...

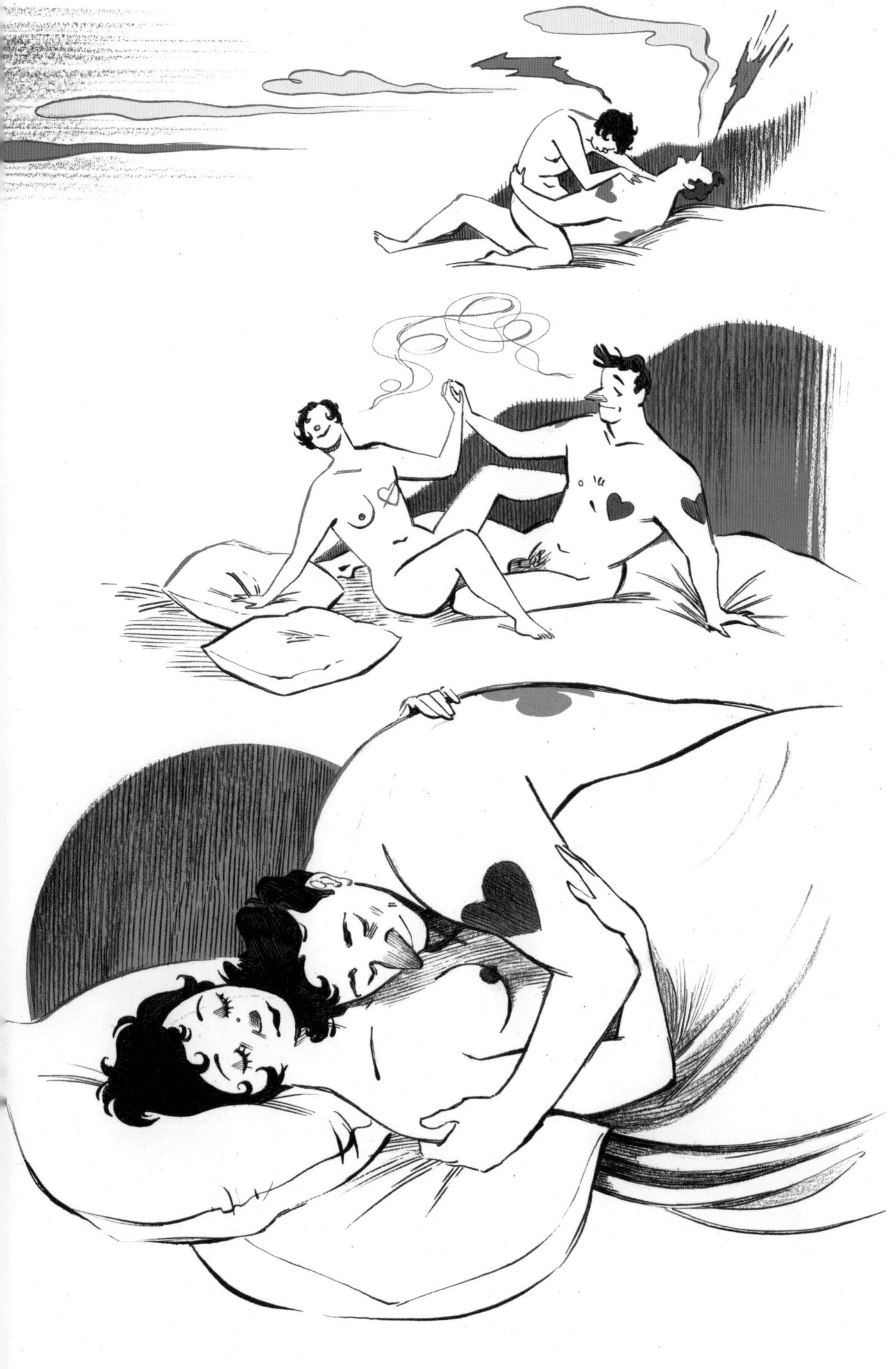

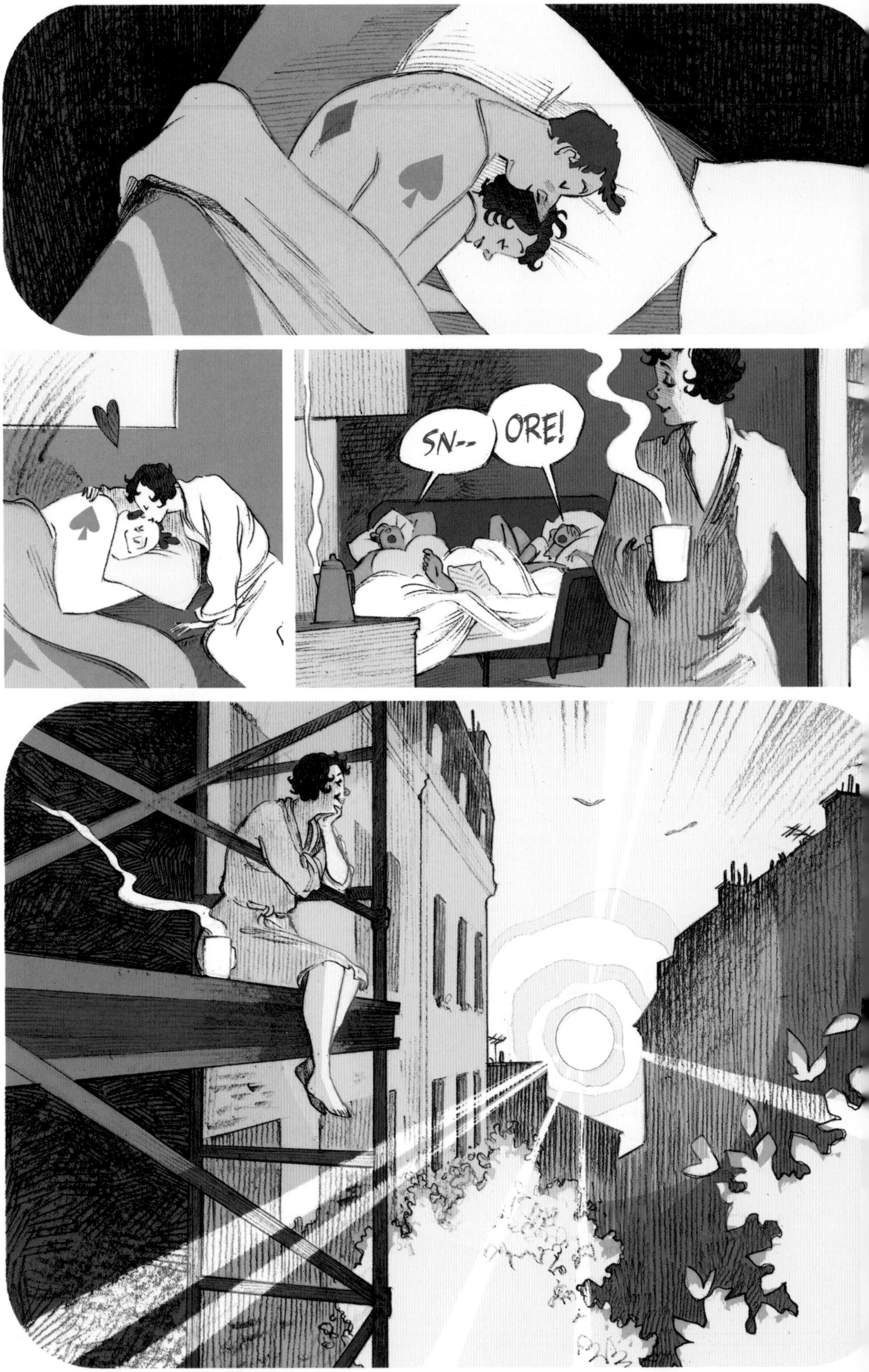
SN--
ORE!

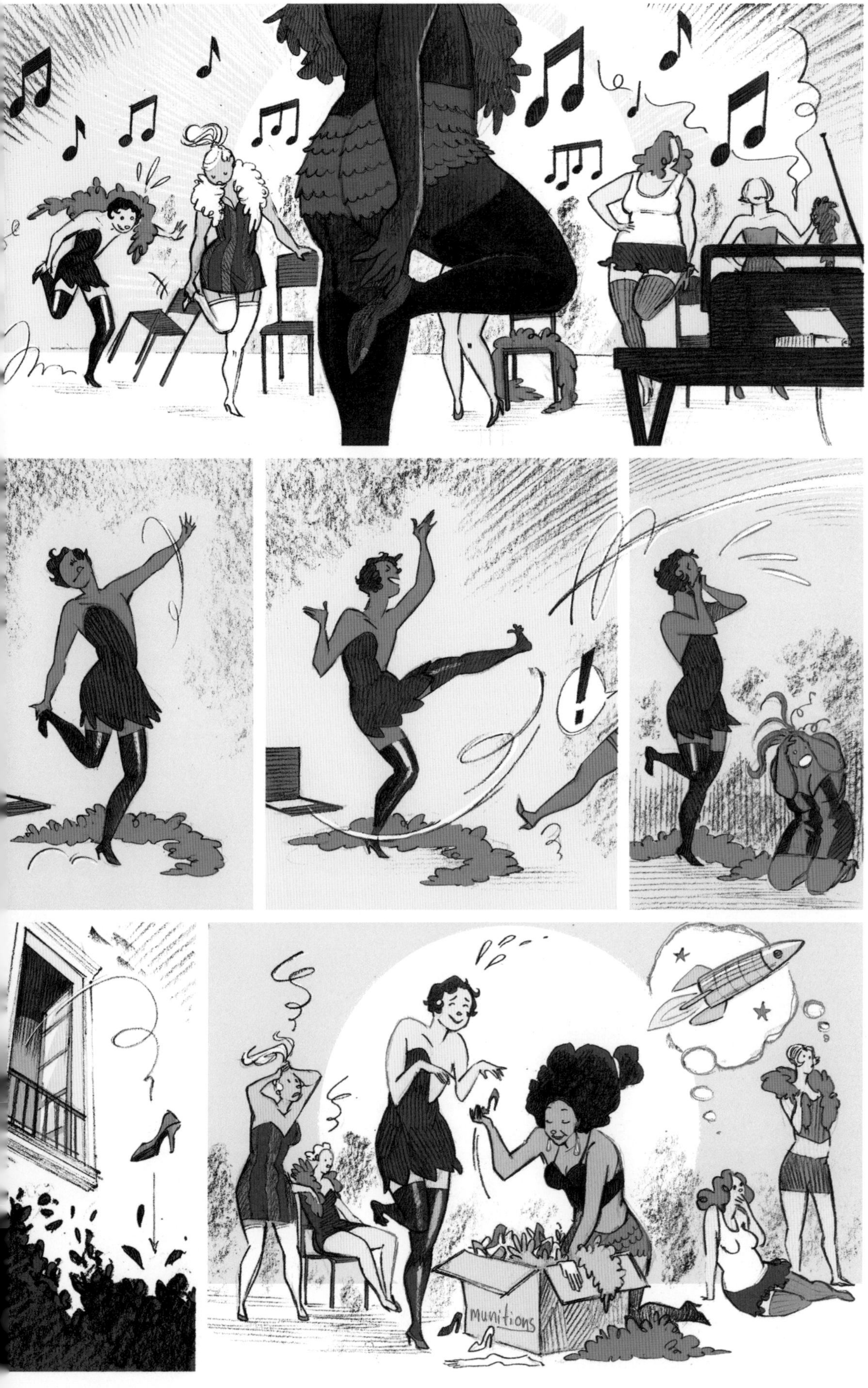
!
munitions

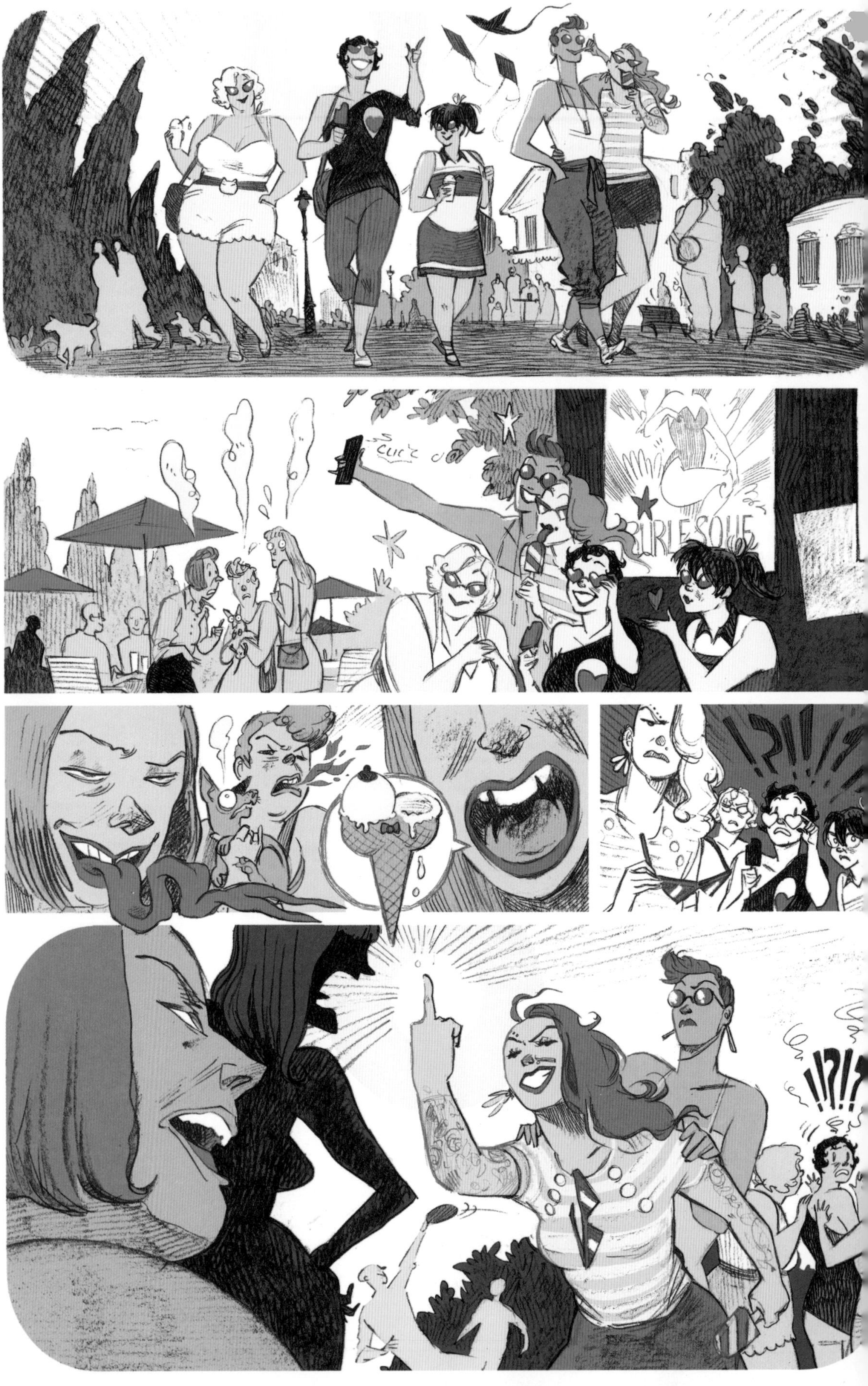
!?!!
!!?!!

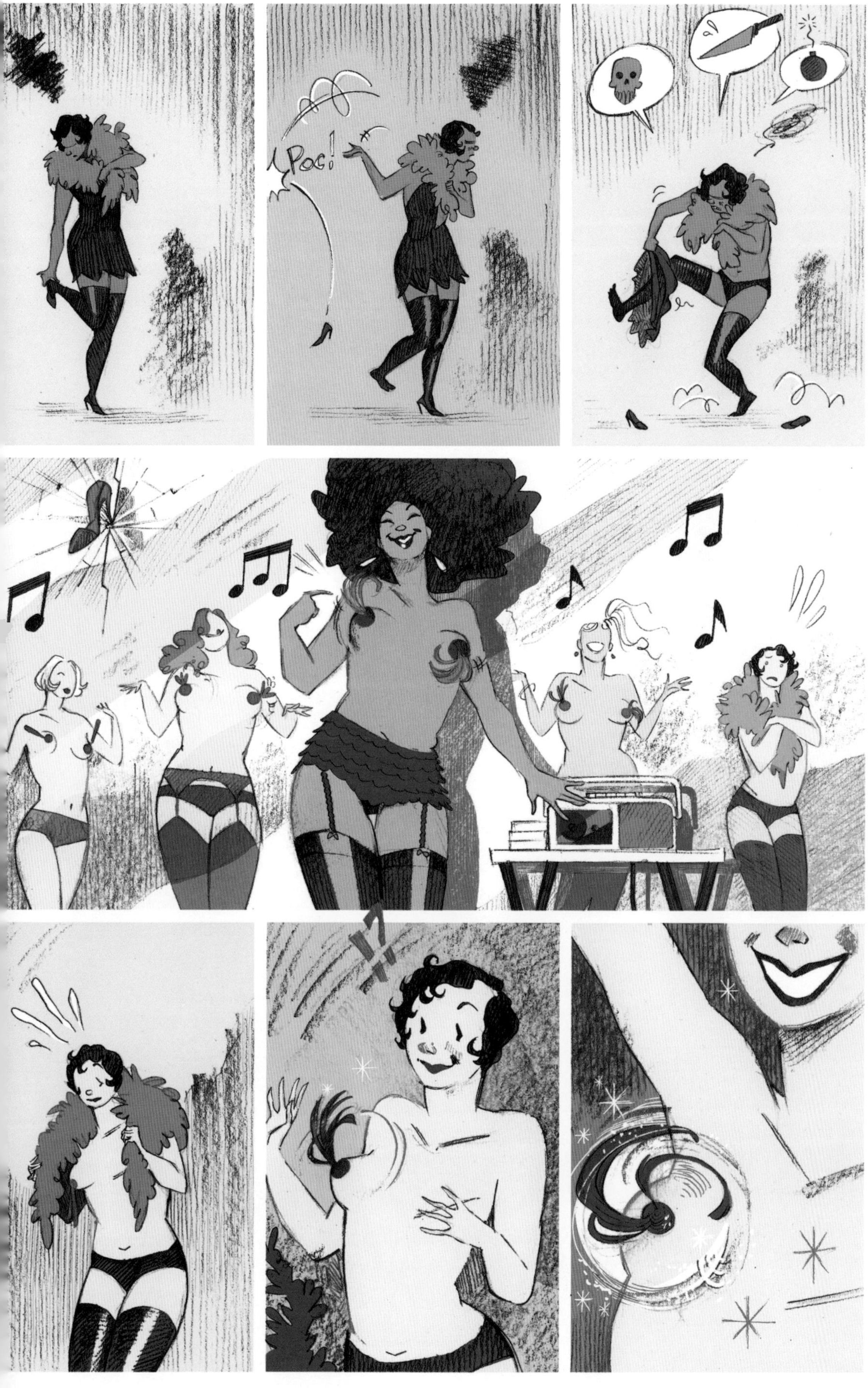
¡Poc!

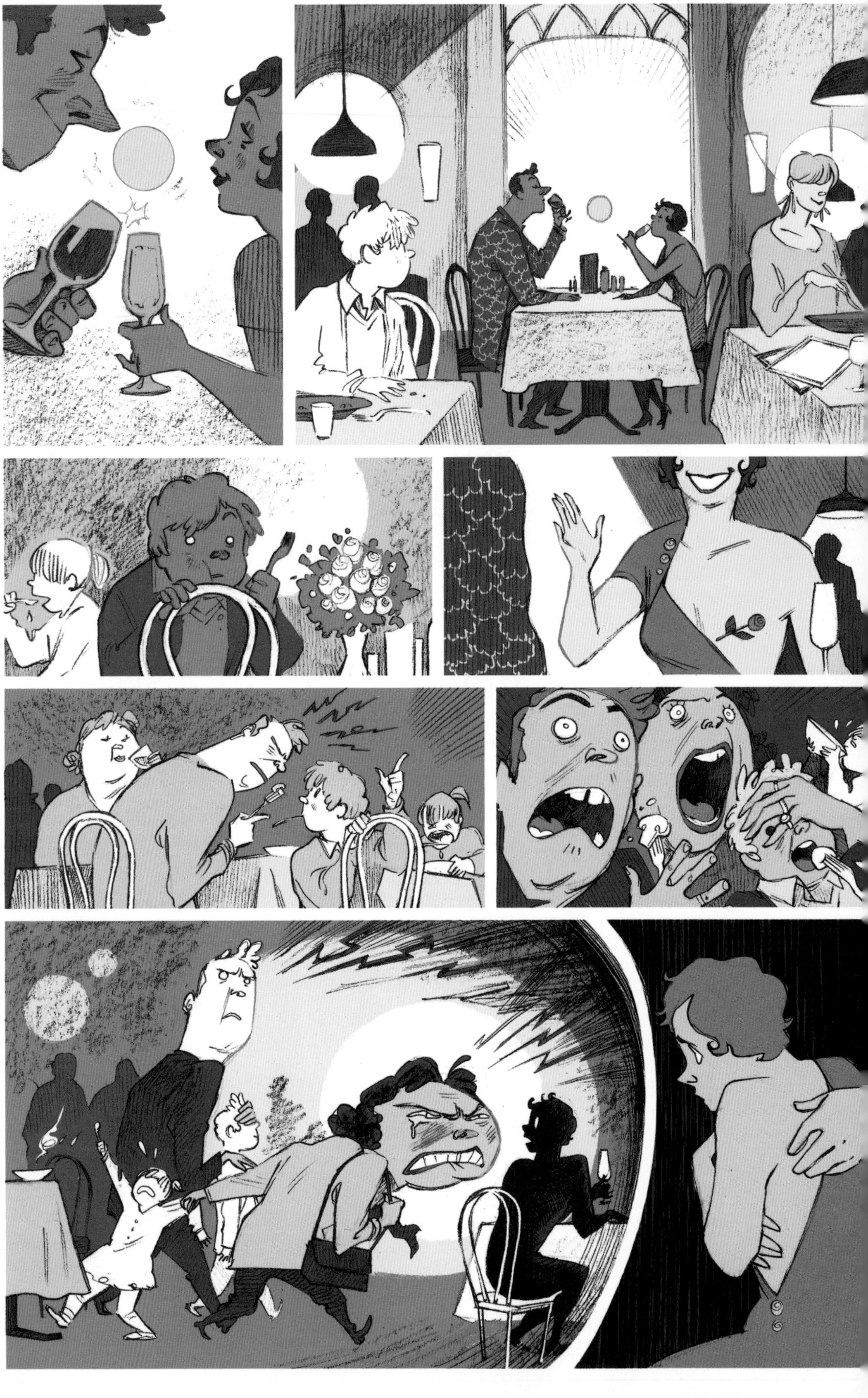

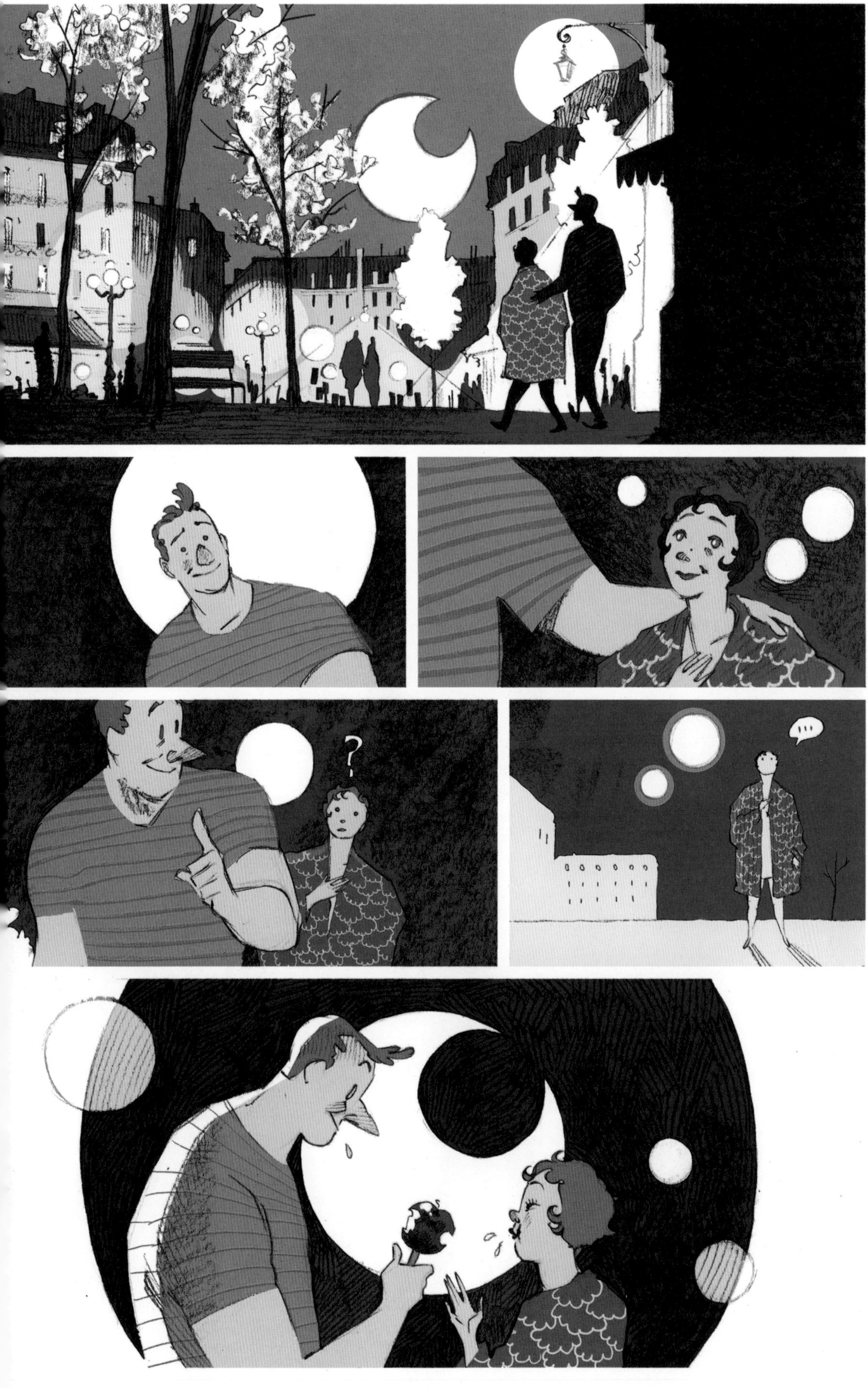
?
...

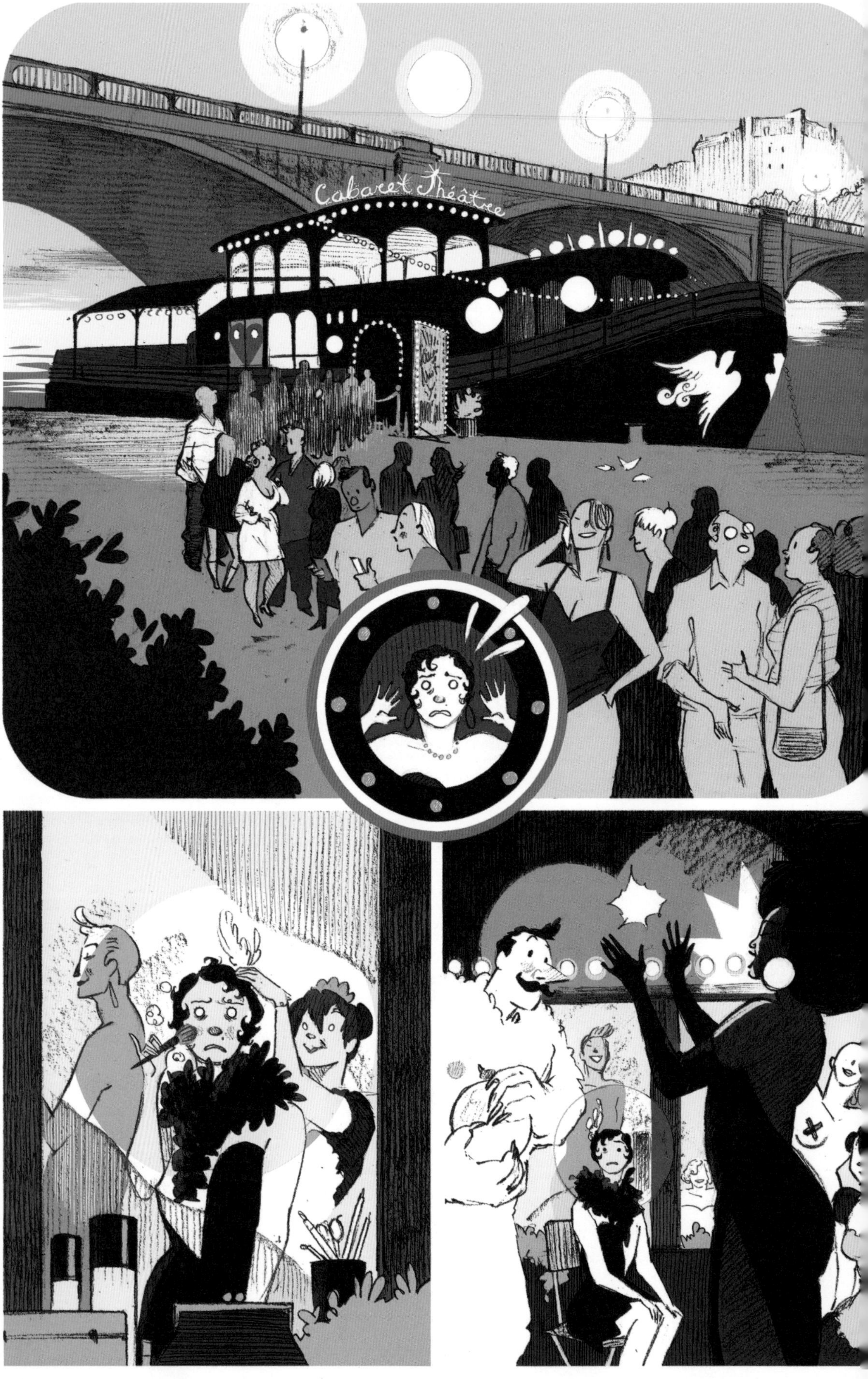
Cabaret Théâtre

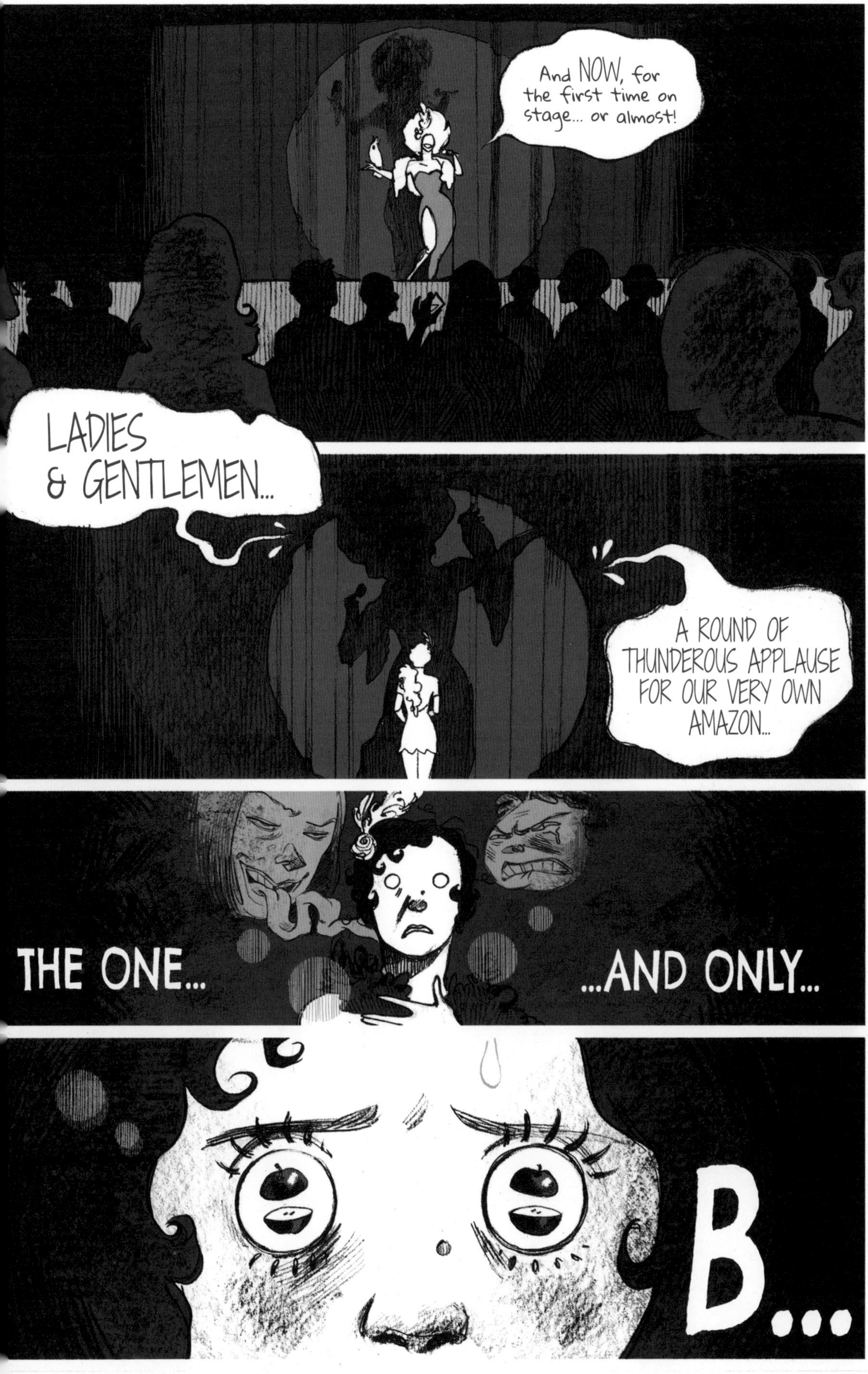

And NOW, for the first time on stage... or almost!
LADIES & GENTLEMEN...
A ROUND OF THUNDEROUS APPLAUSE FOR OUR VERY OWN AMAZON...
THE ONE...
...AND ONLY...
B...

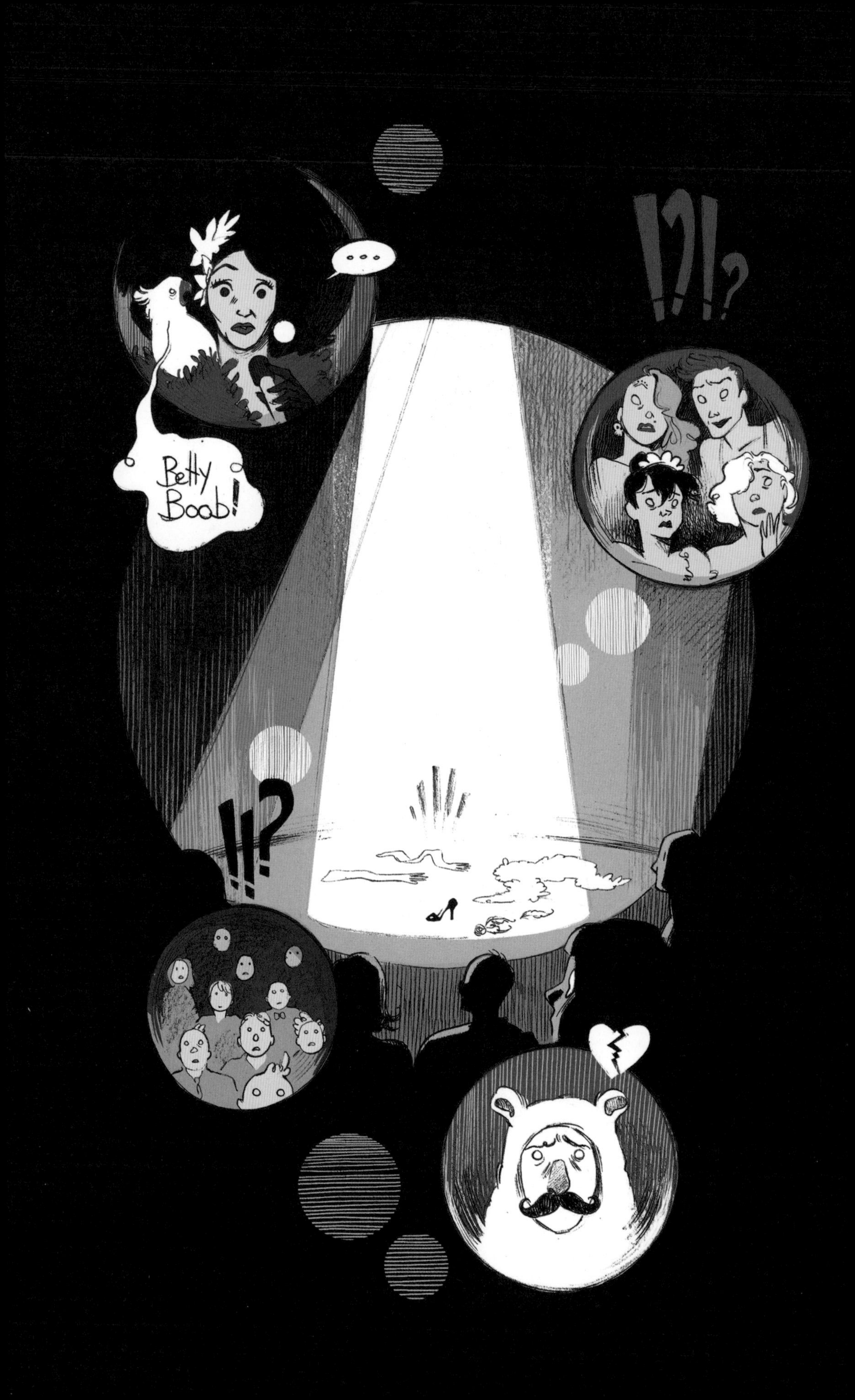
...
Betty Boob!
!?!?
!!?

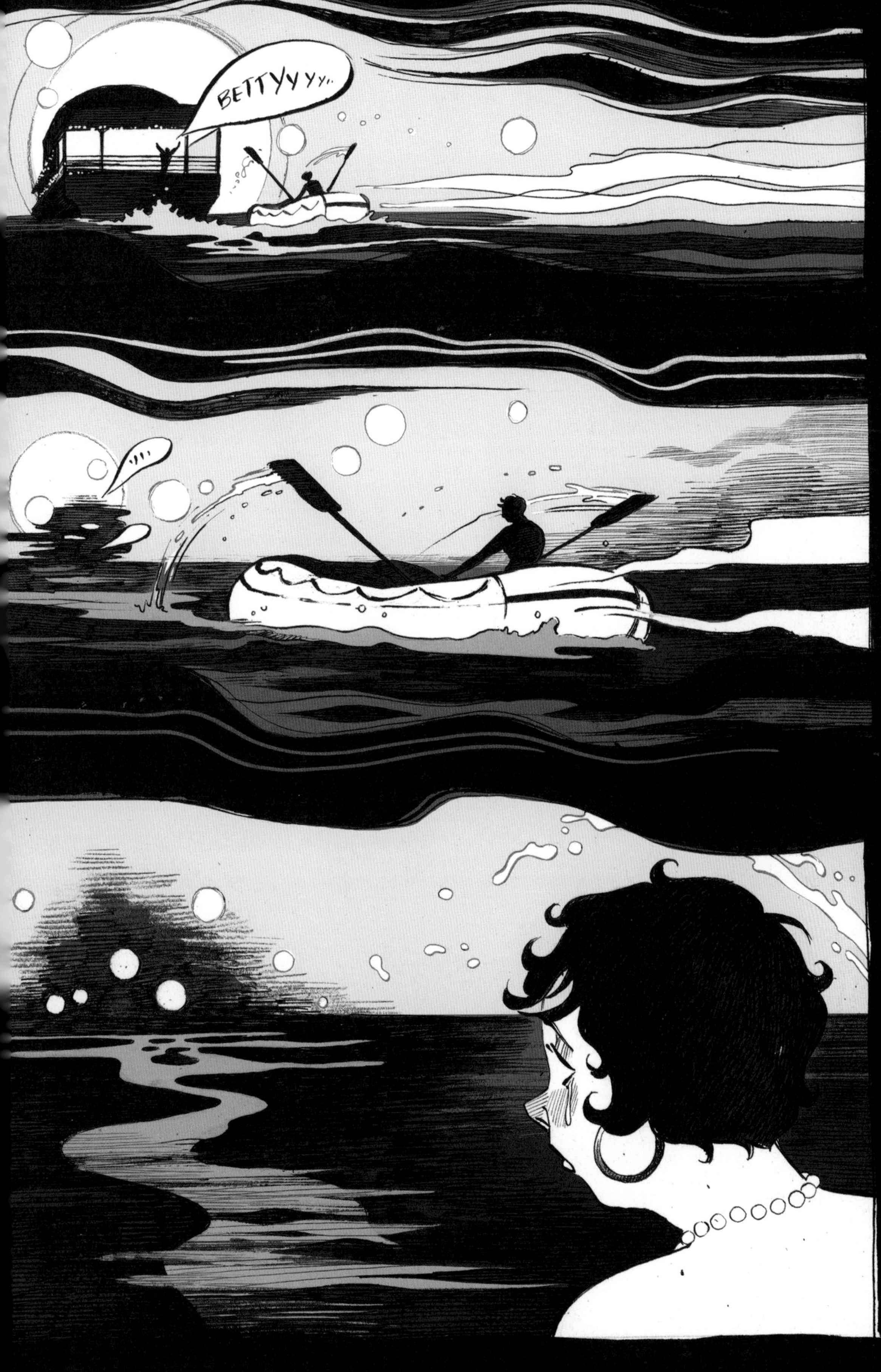
BETTYyyy..

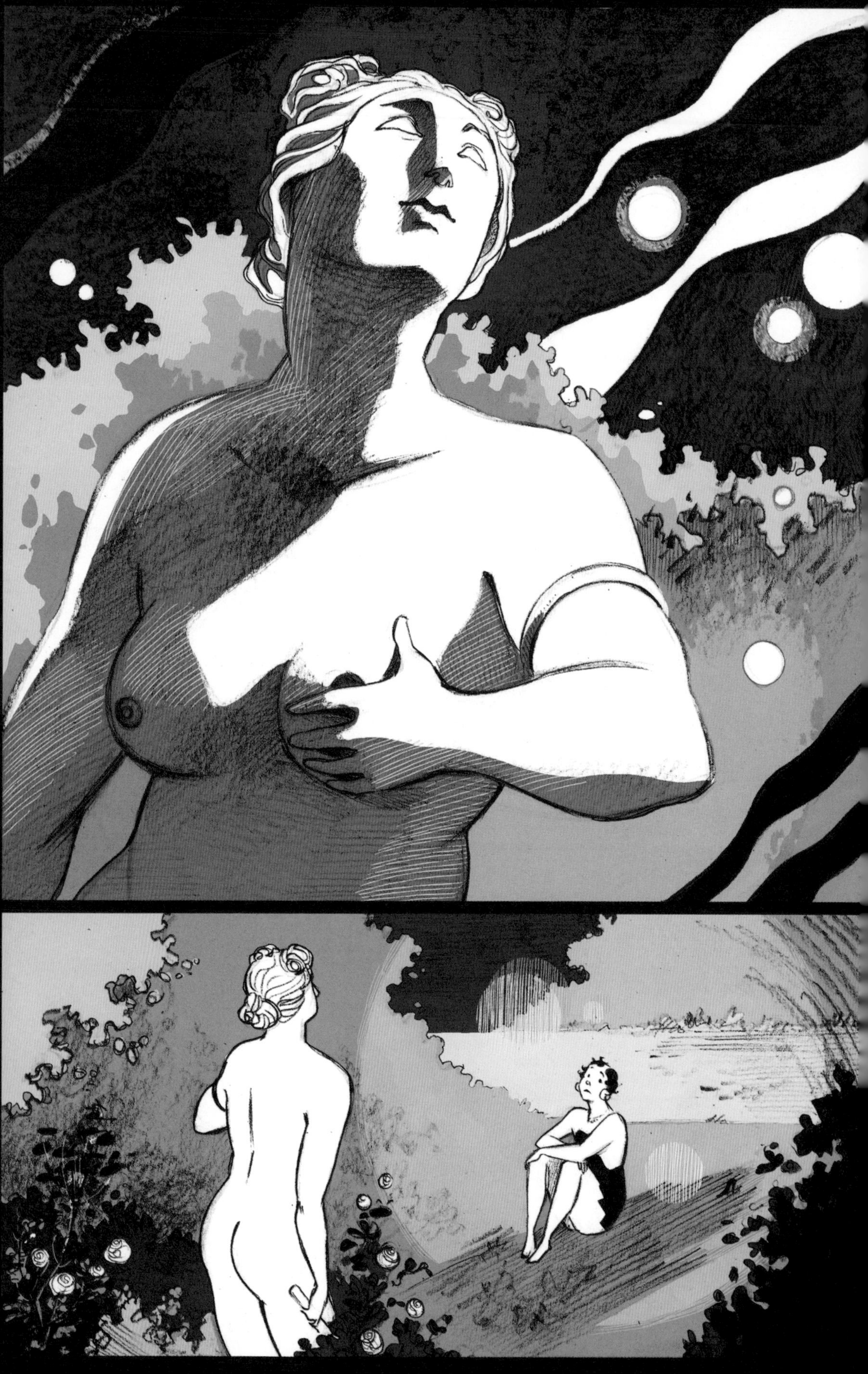

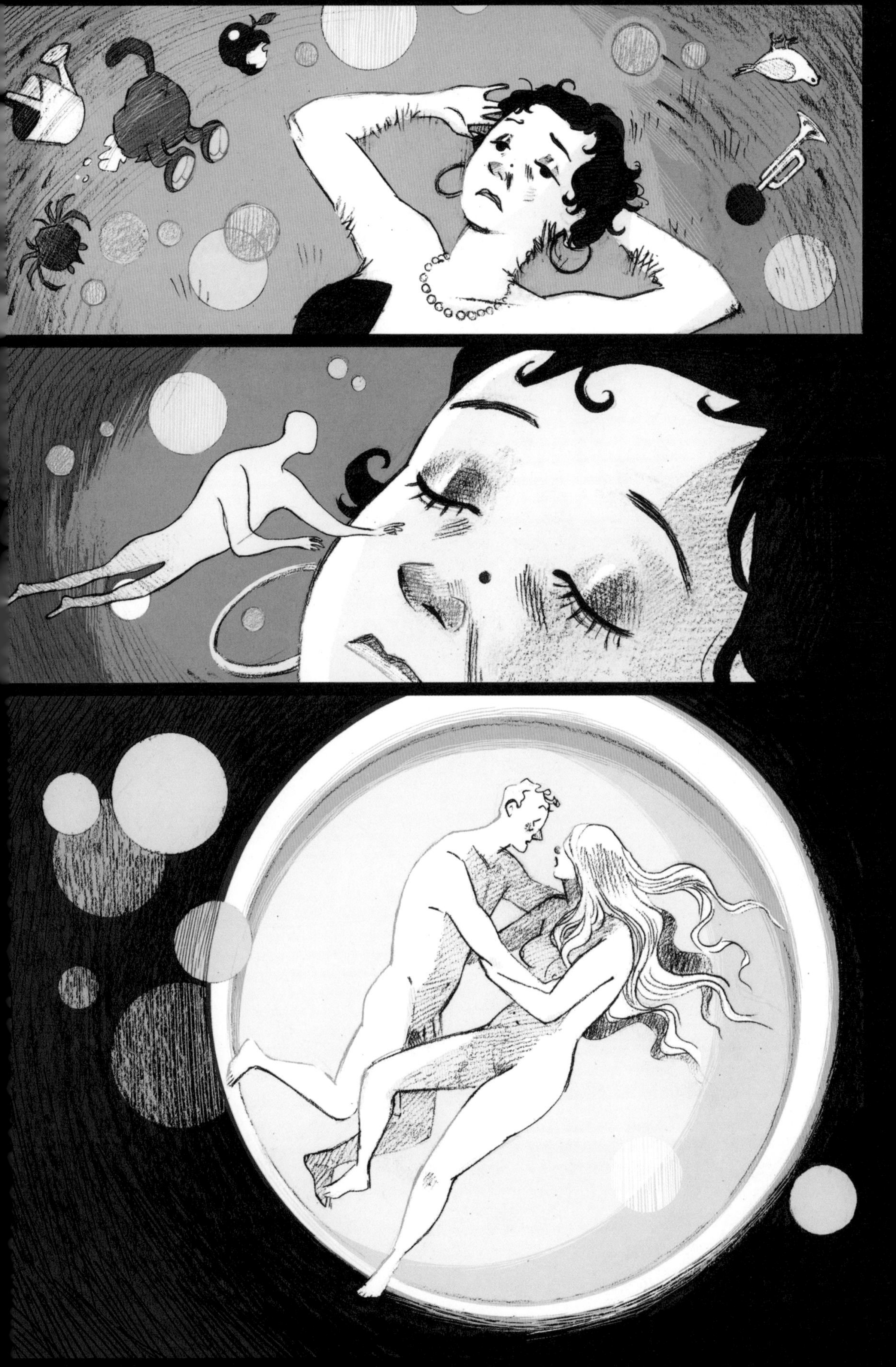

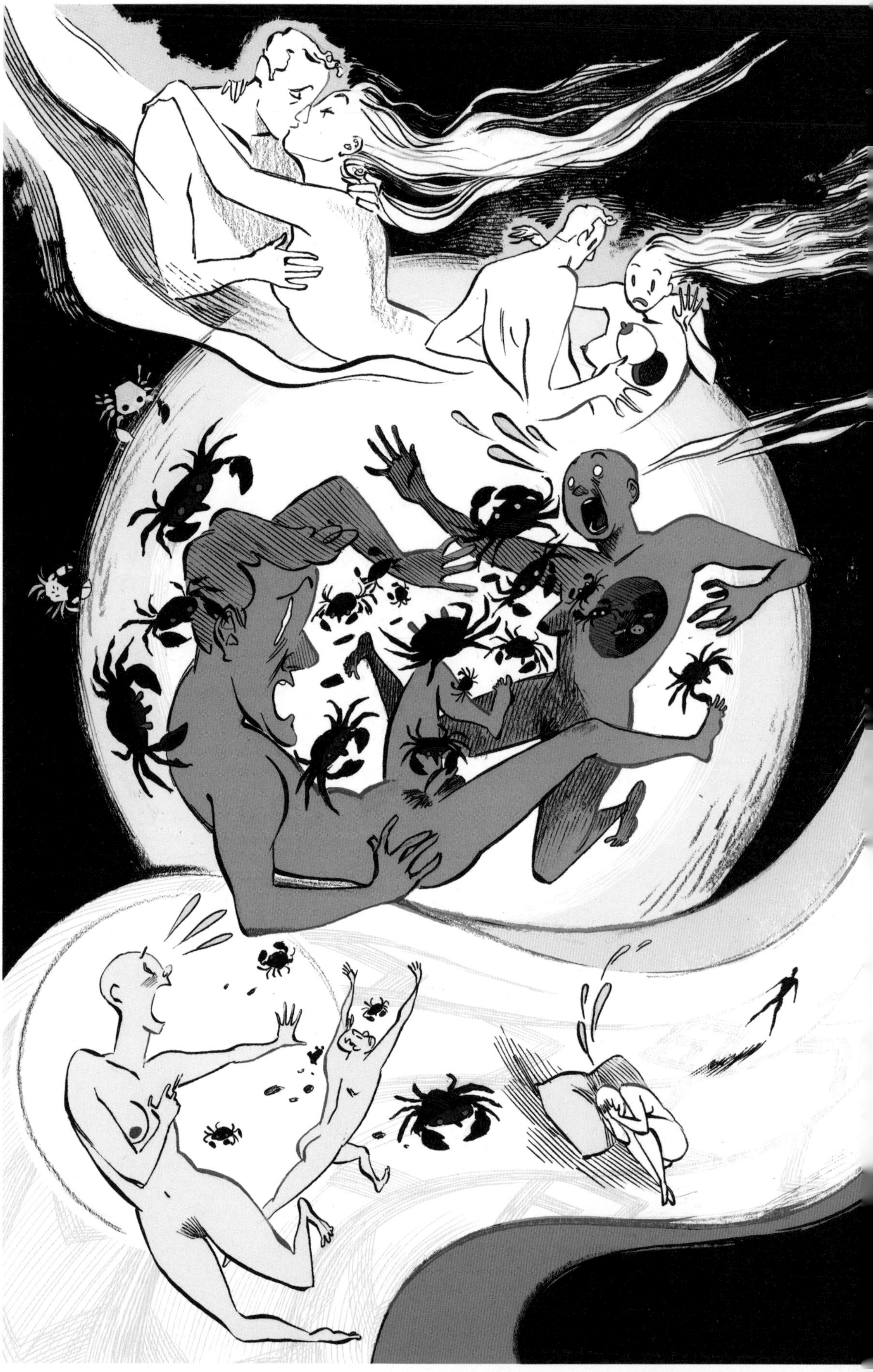

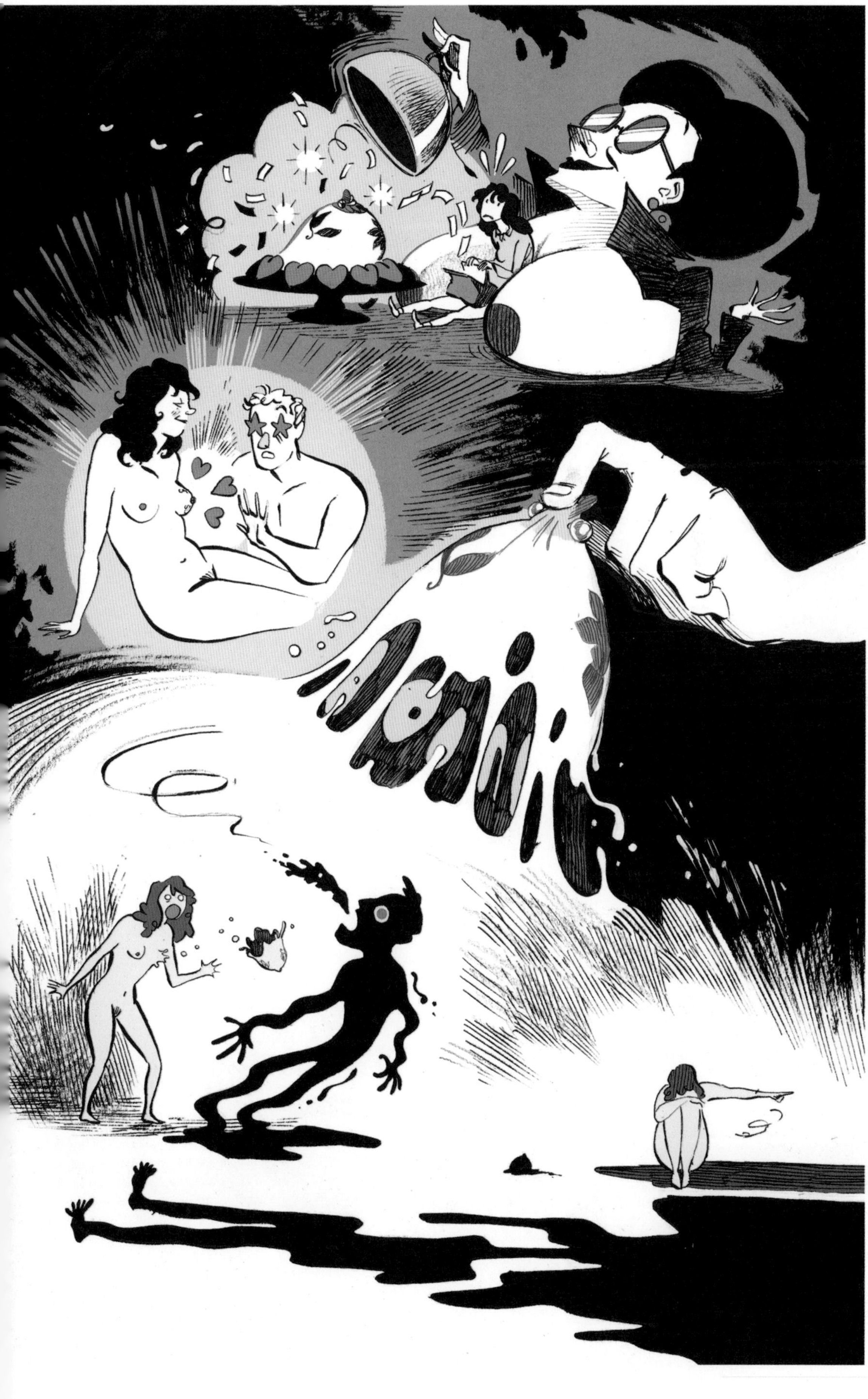

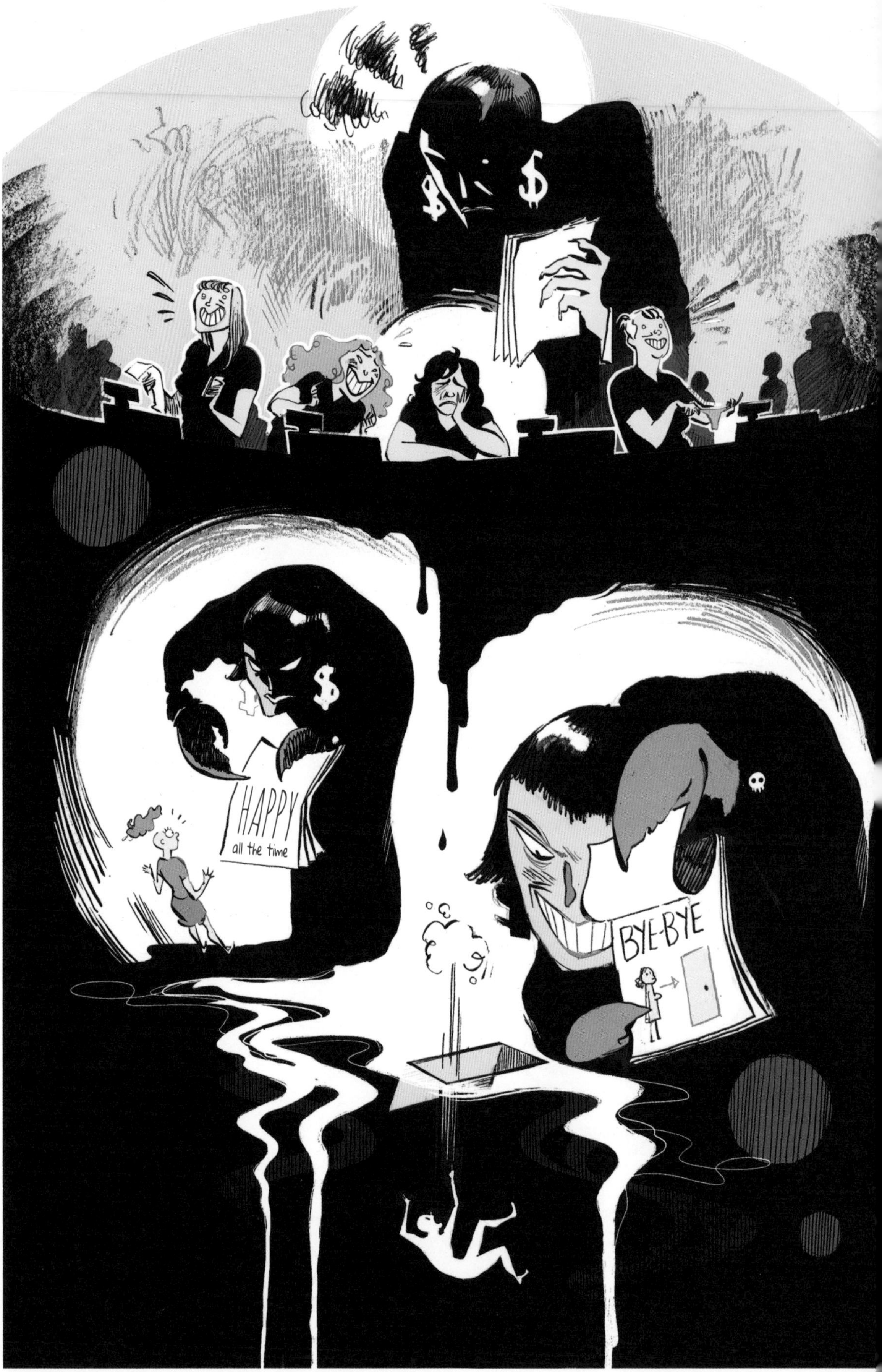
HAPPY
all the time
BYE-BYE

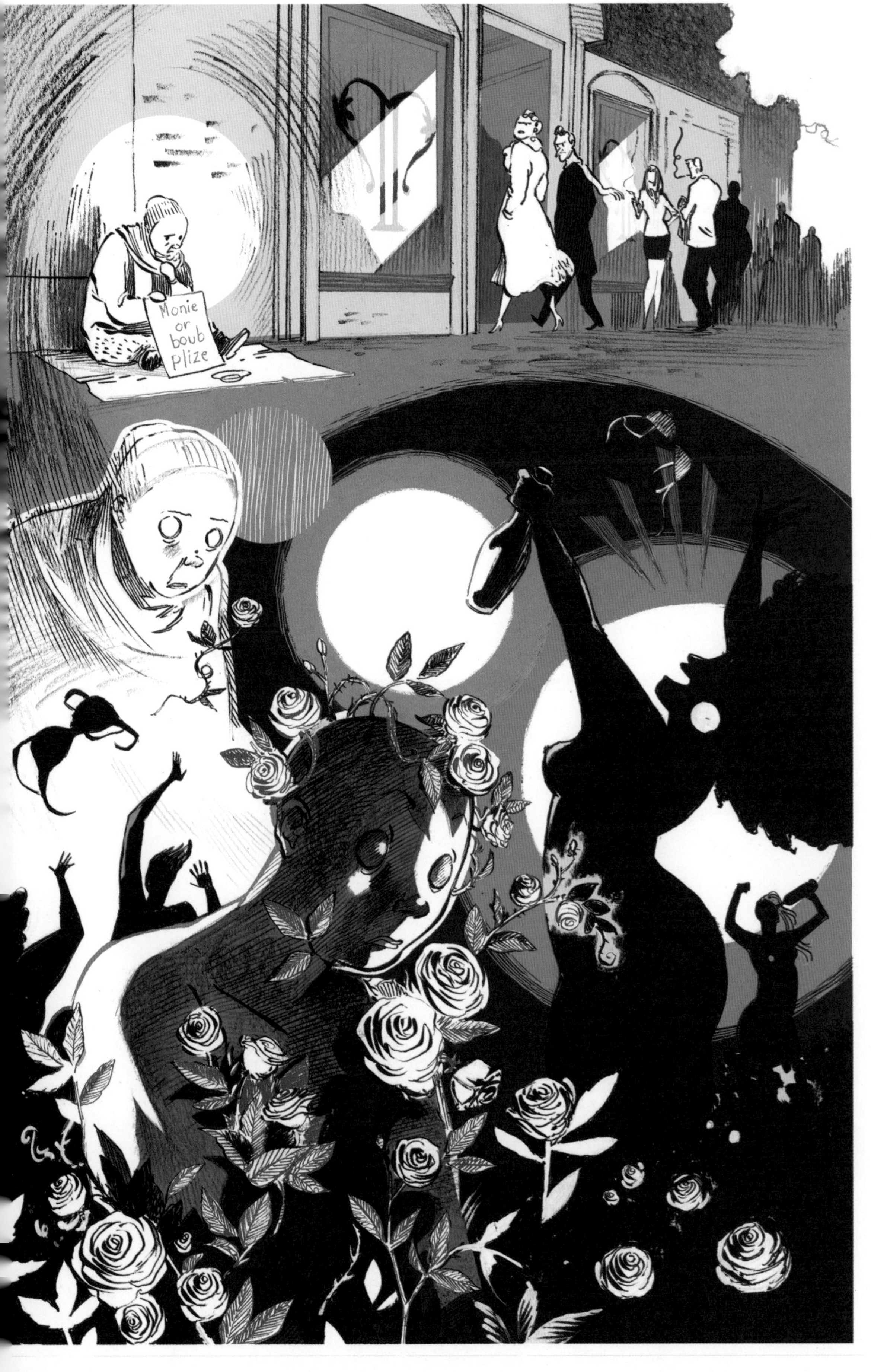
Monie or boub plize

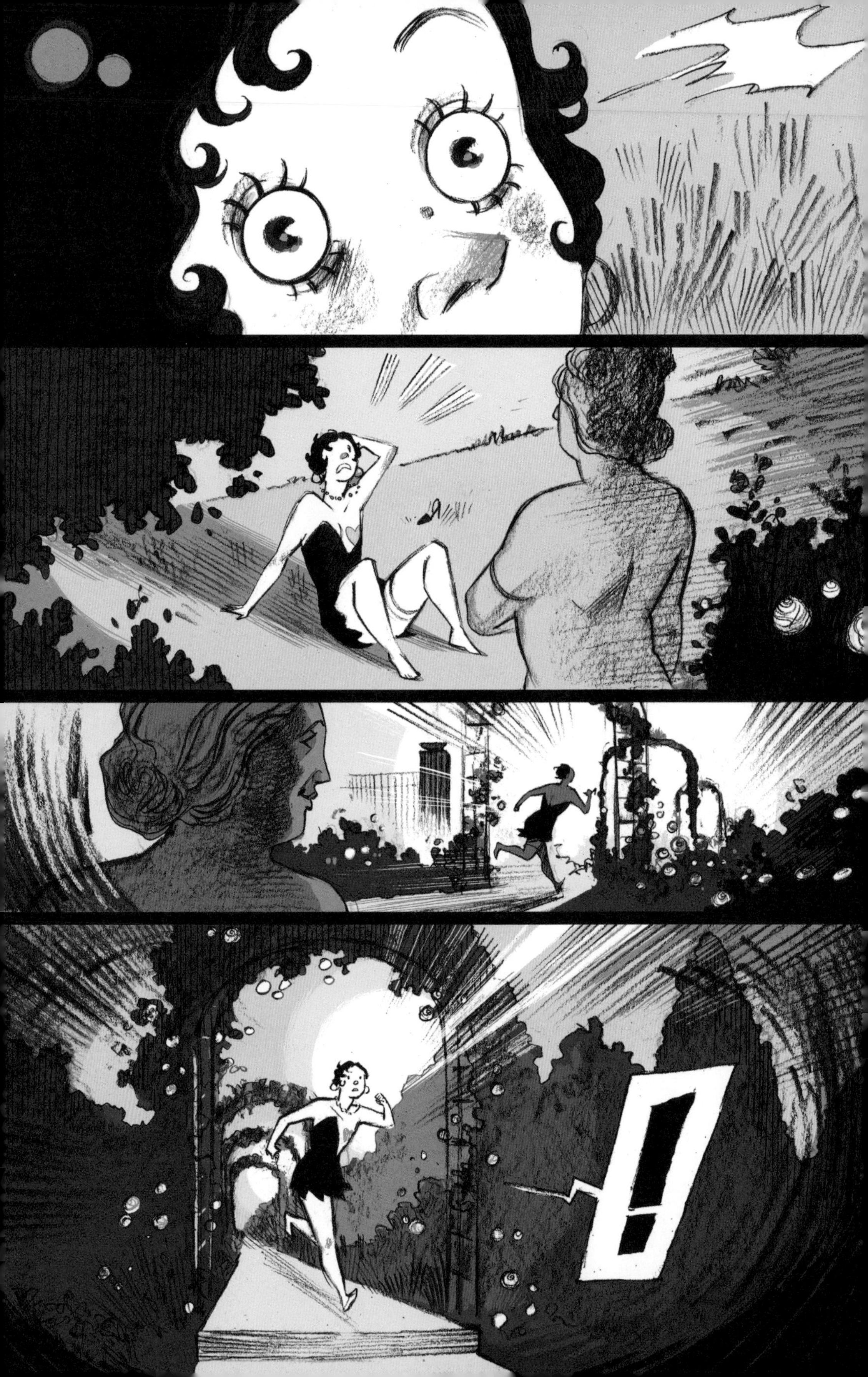
!

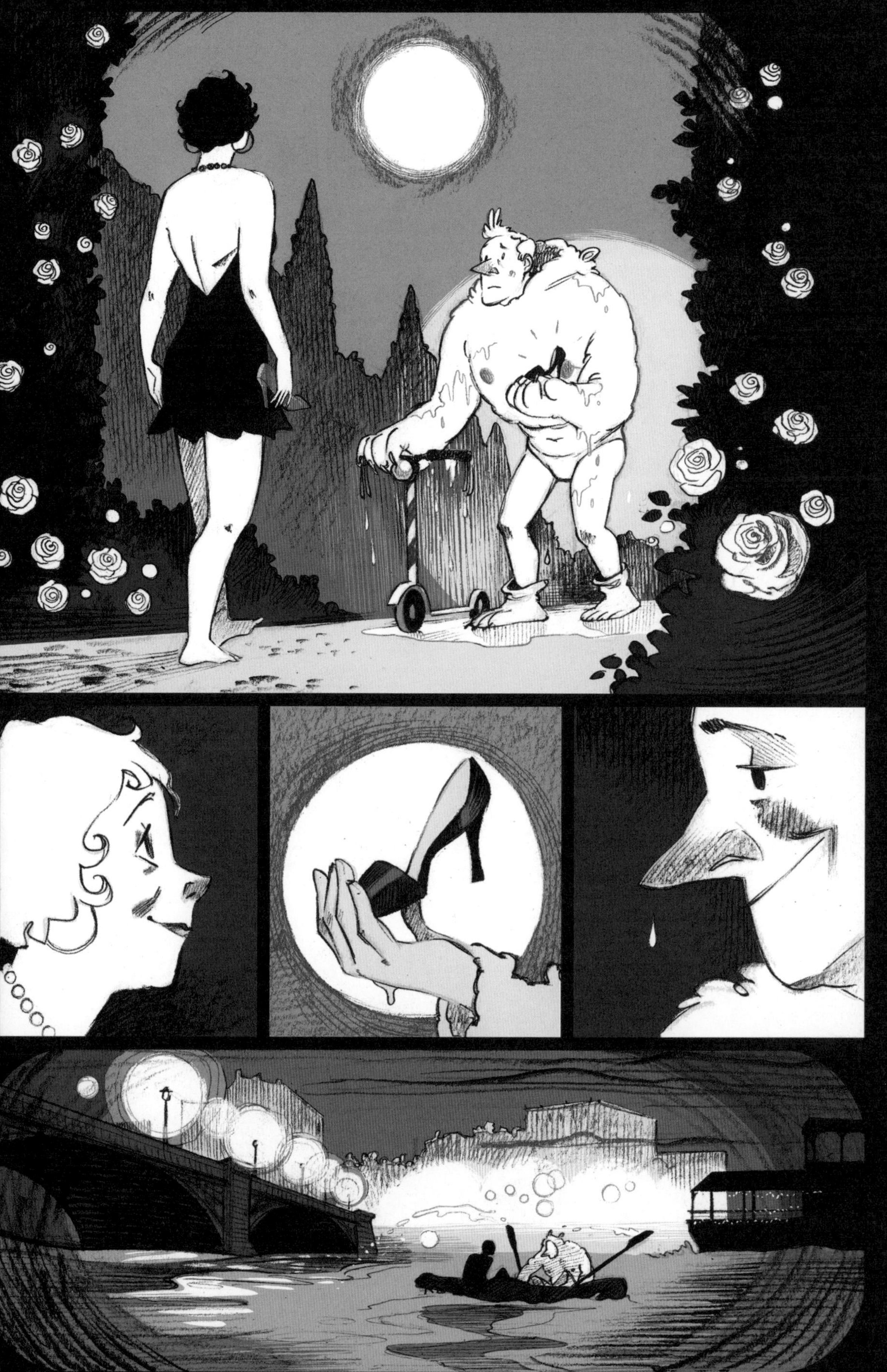

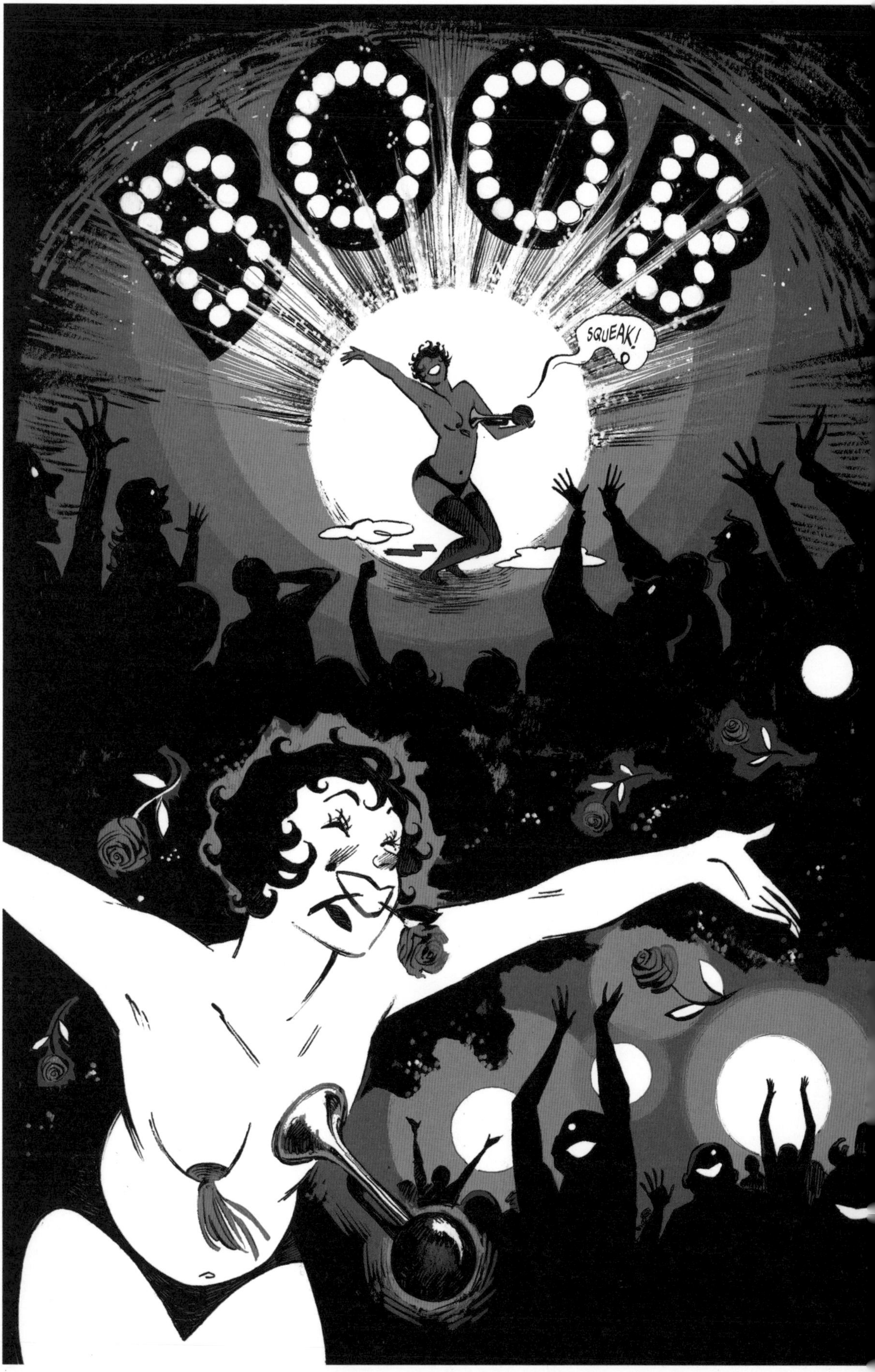
BOOB
SQUEAK!

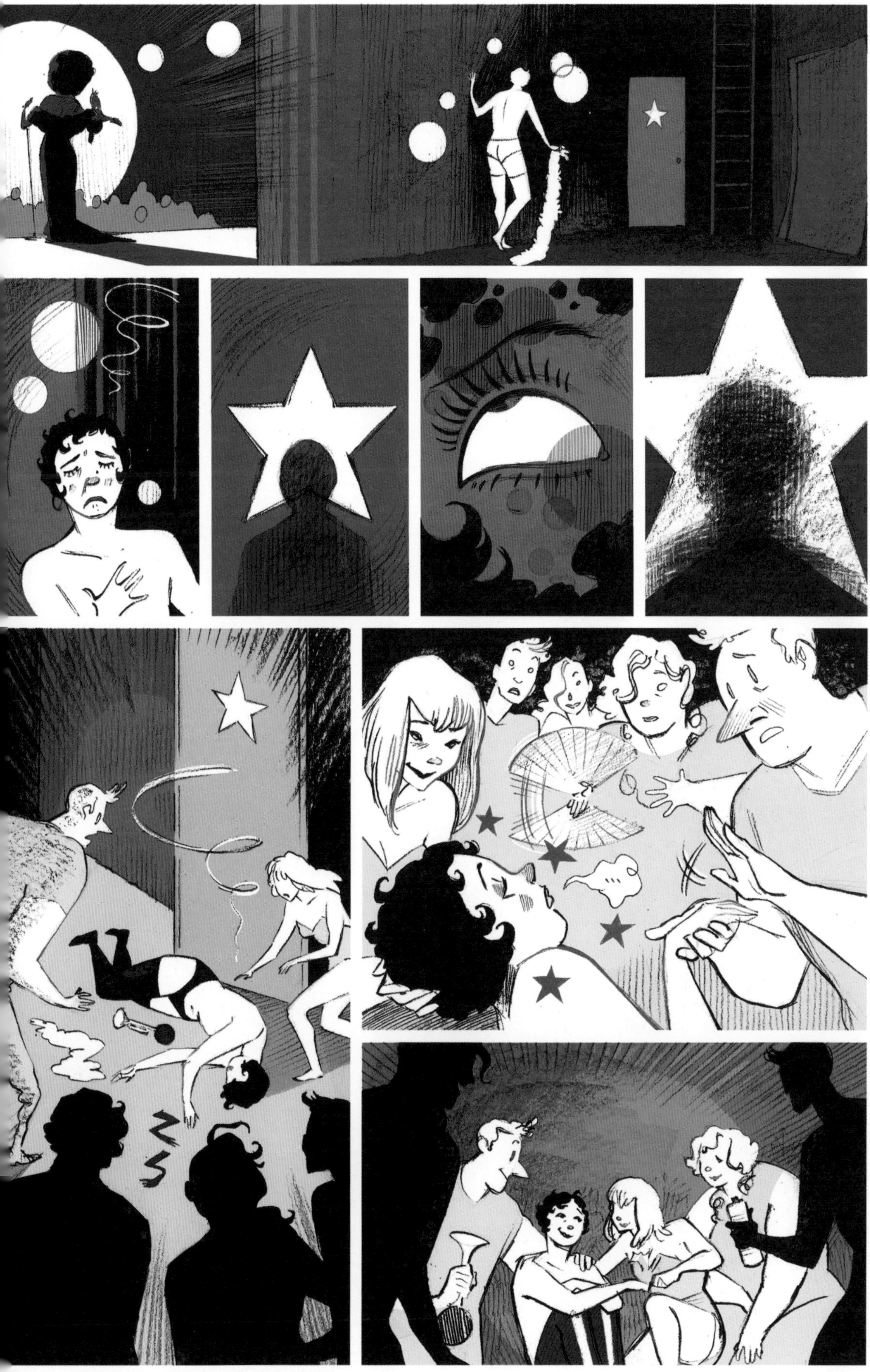

-What are you going to do now?
-Whatever I want.

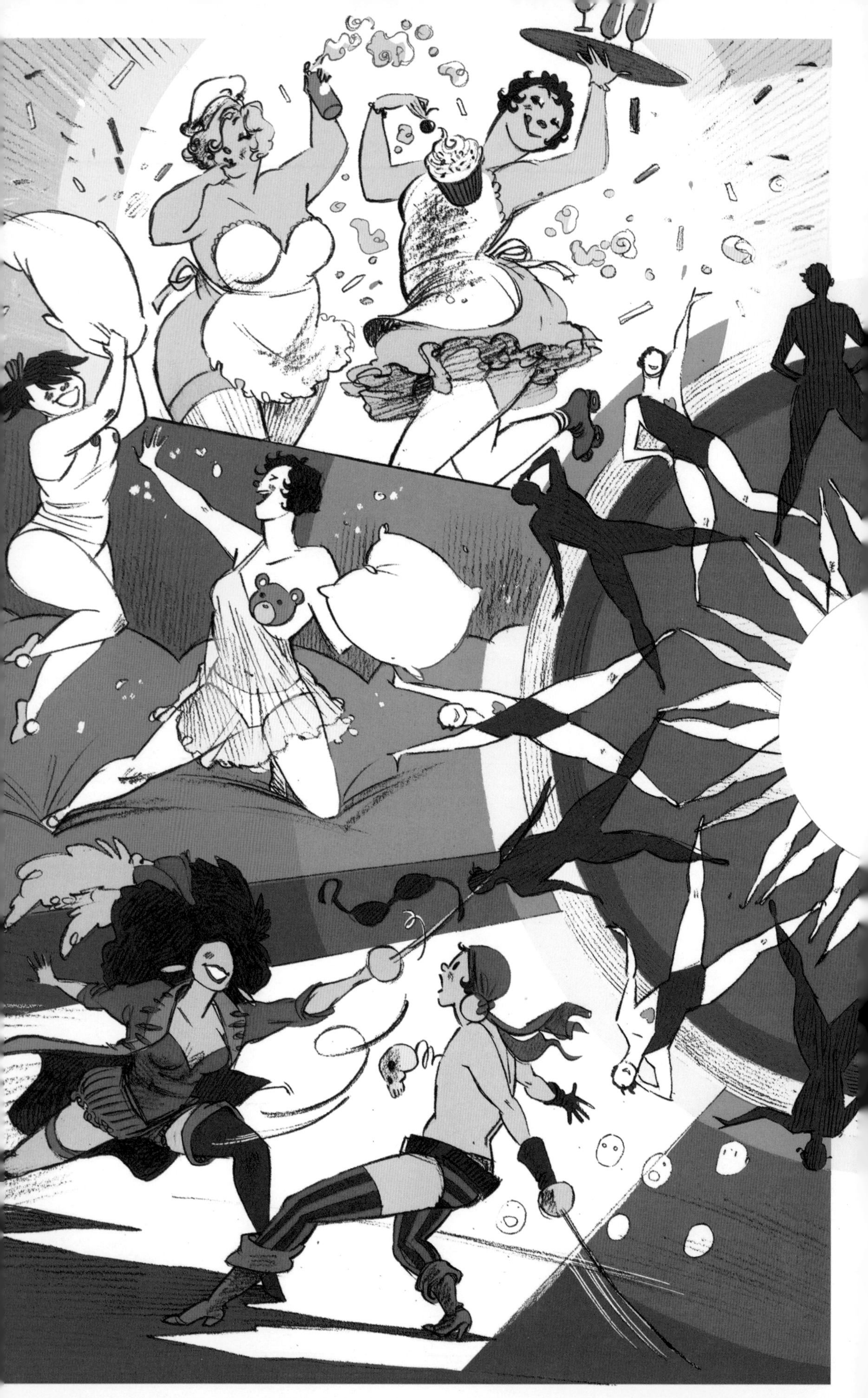

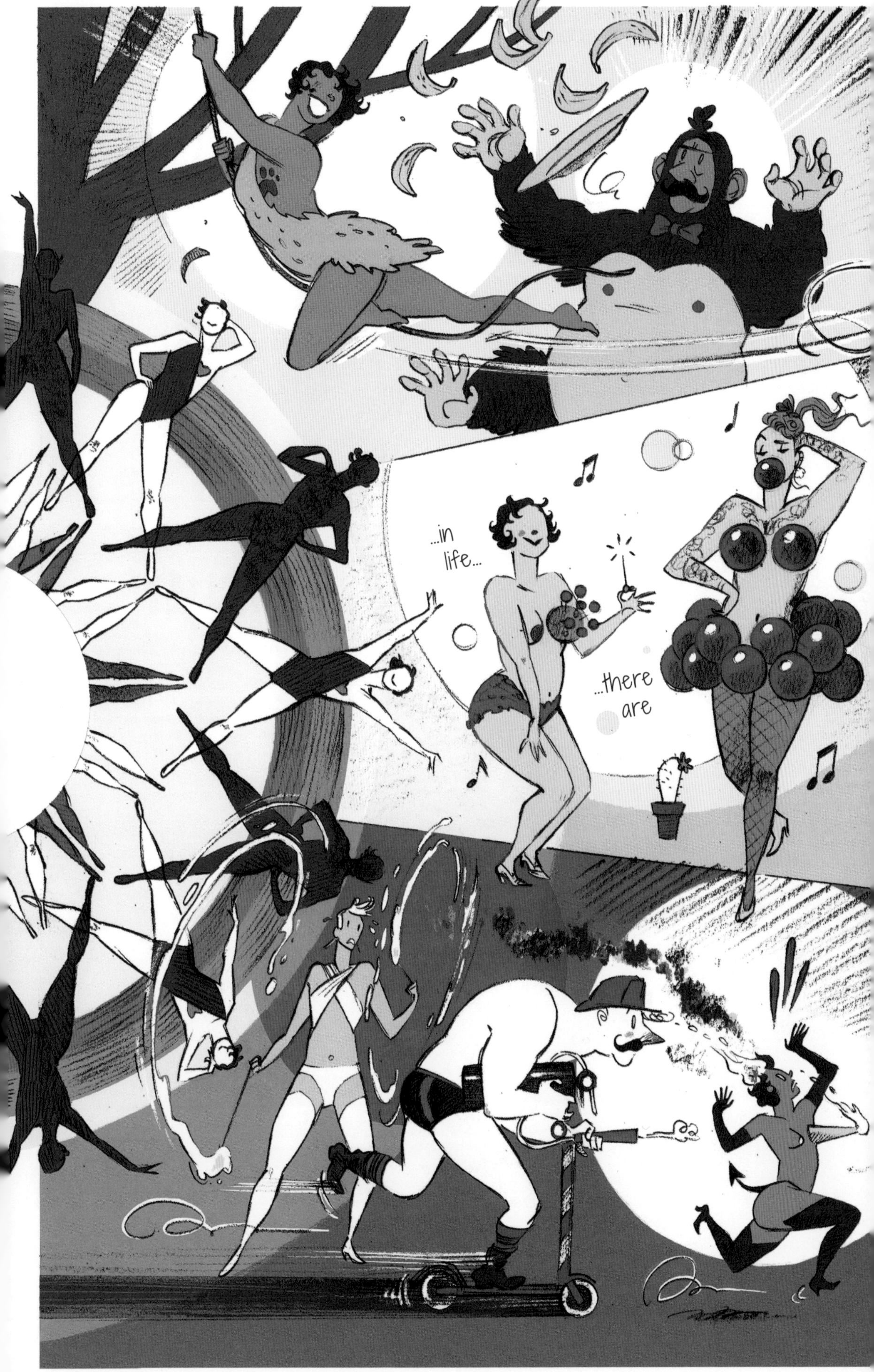
...in life...
...there are

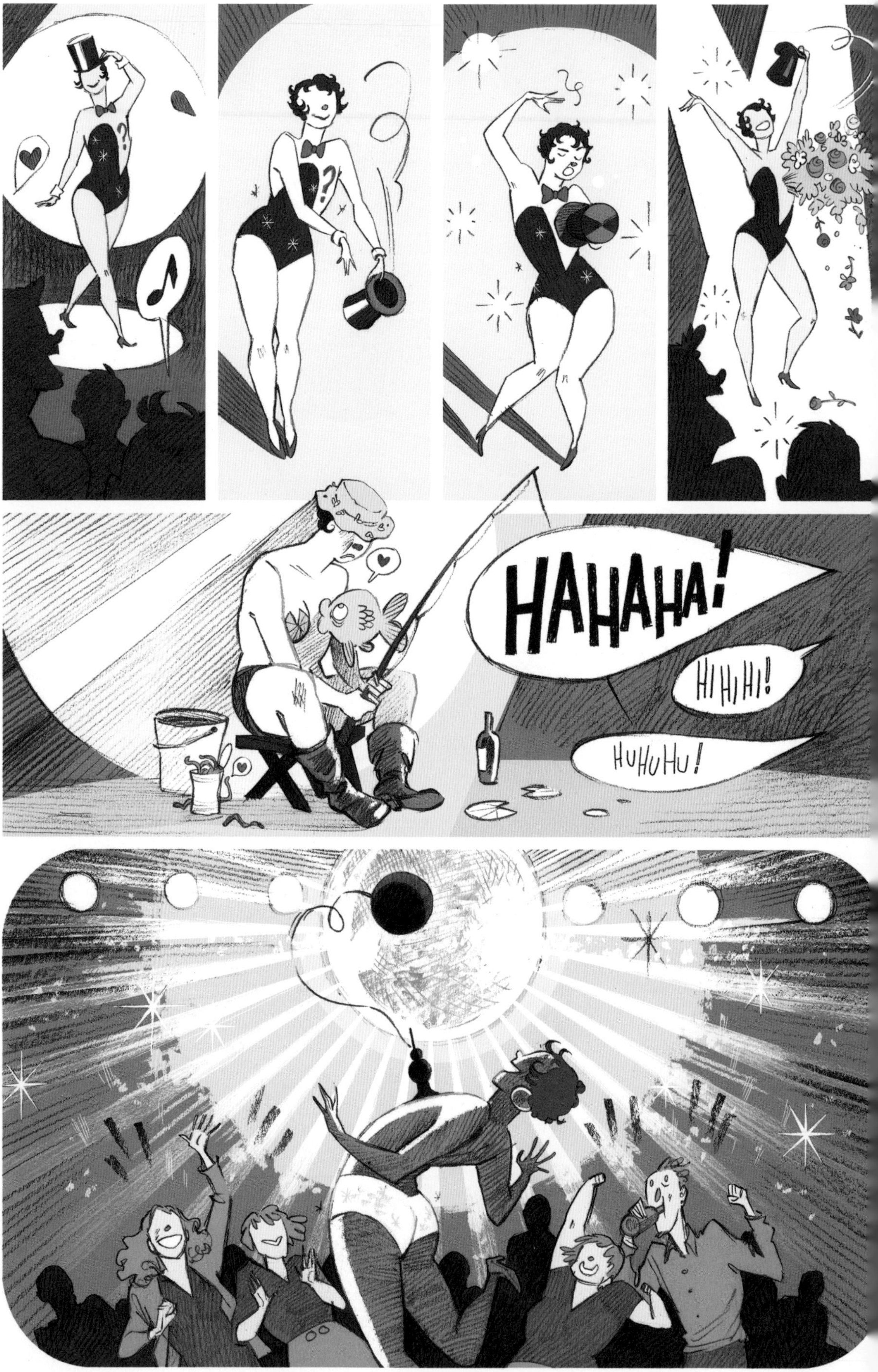
HAHAHA!
HIHIHI!
HUHUHU!

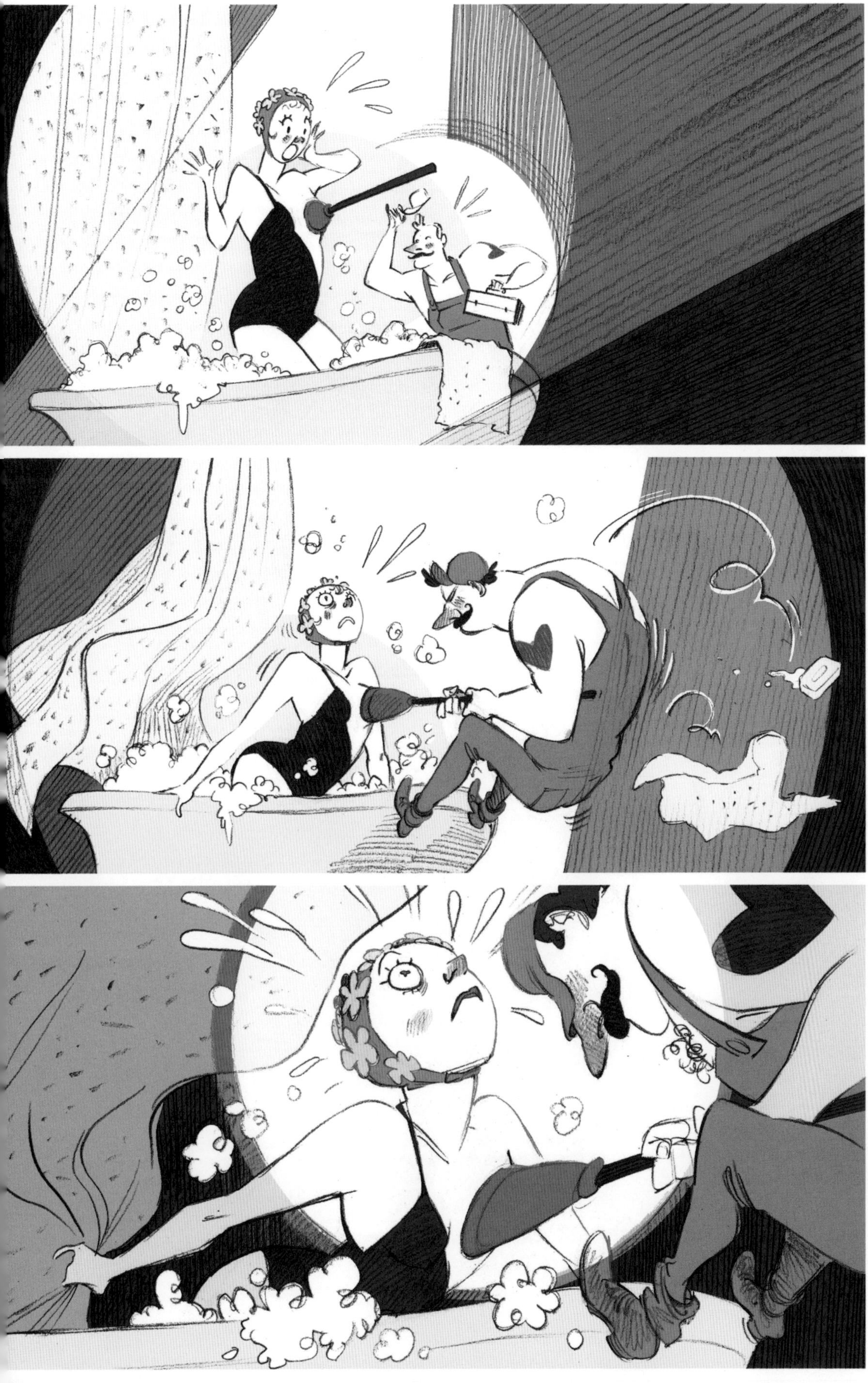

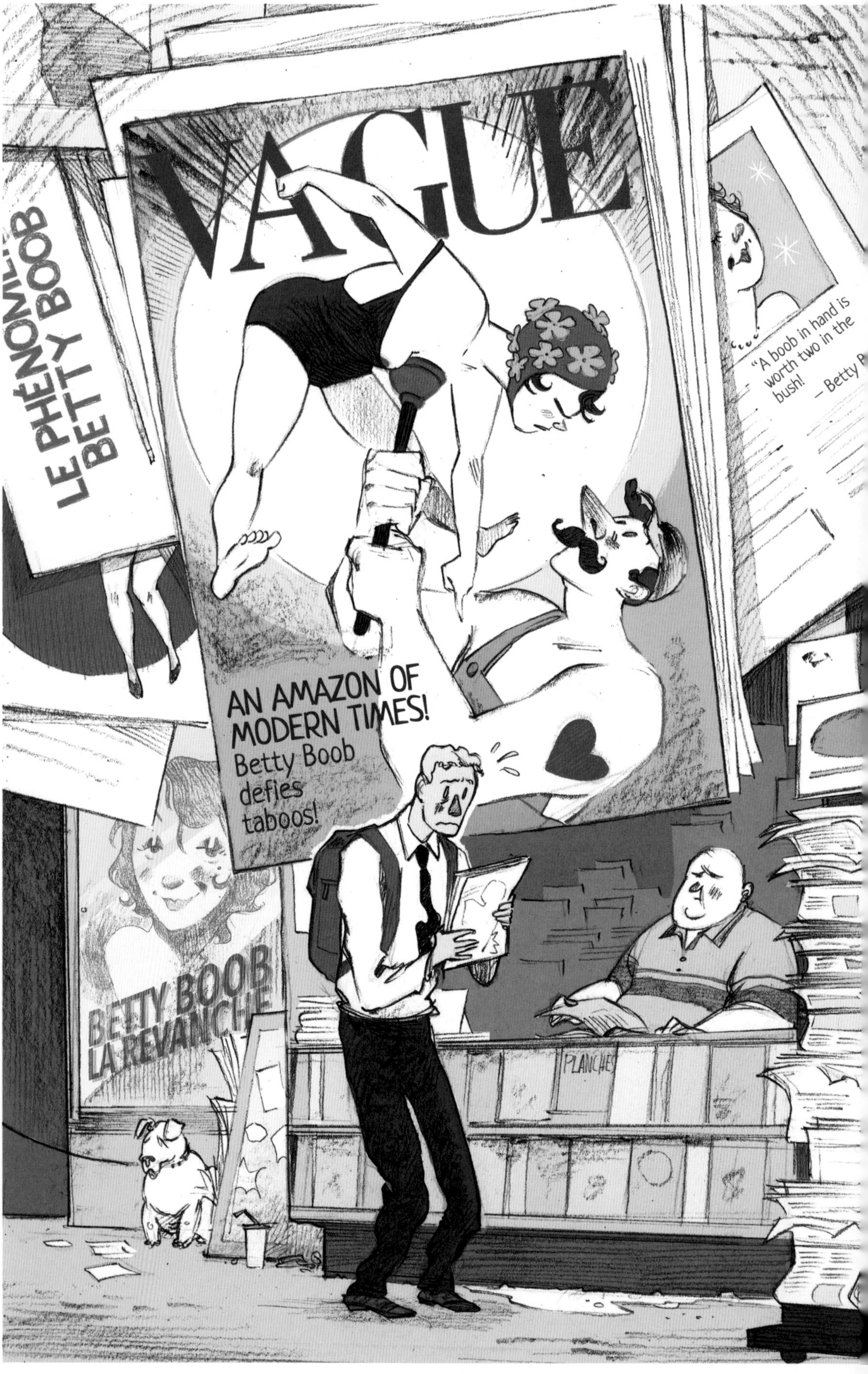
LE PHÉNOMÈNE BETTY BOOB
VAGUE
AN AMAZON OF MODERN TIMES! Betty Boob defies taboos!
"A boob in hand is worth two in the bush!
– Betty B
BETTY BOOB LA REVANCHE
PLANCHES

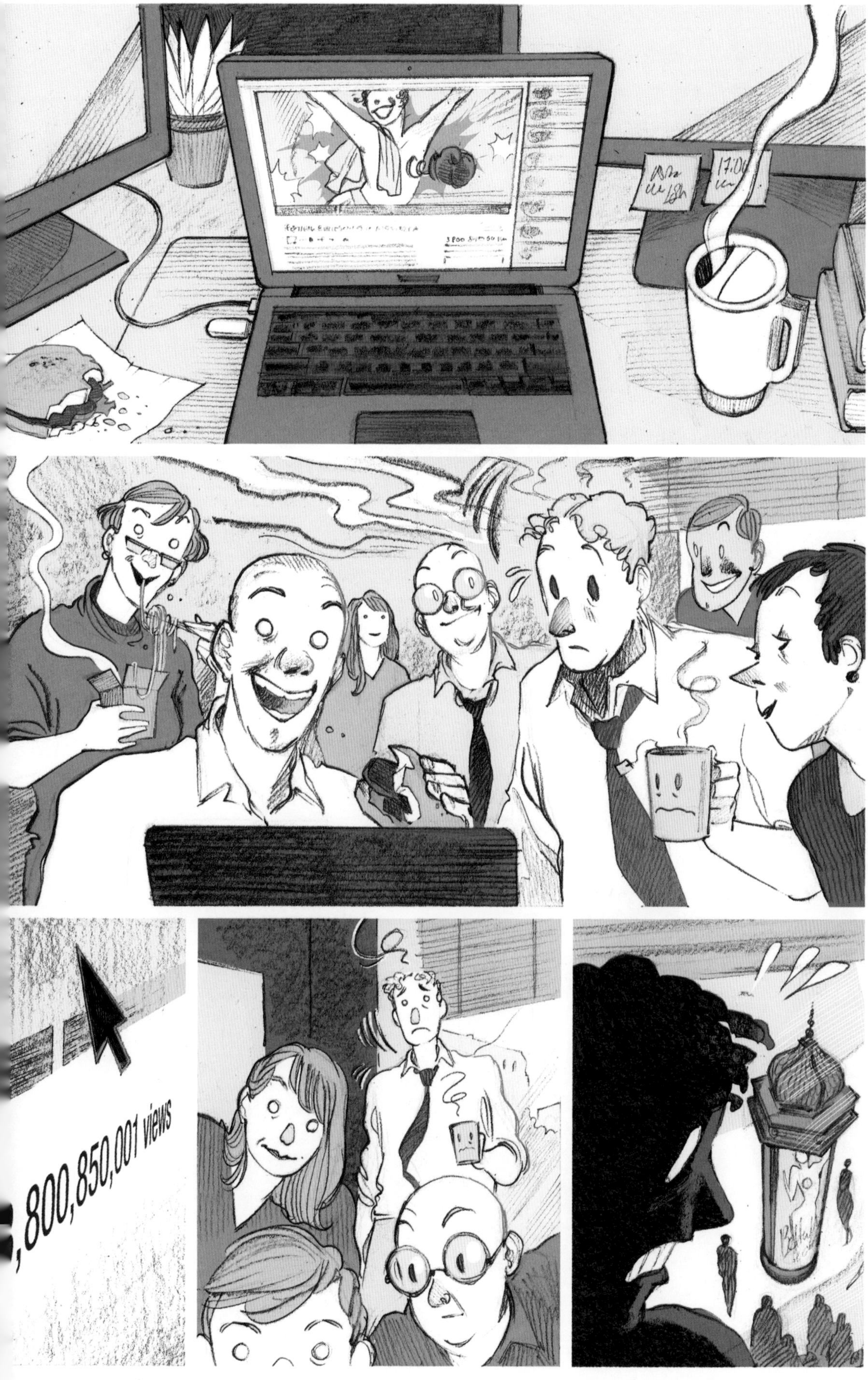
,800,850,001 views

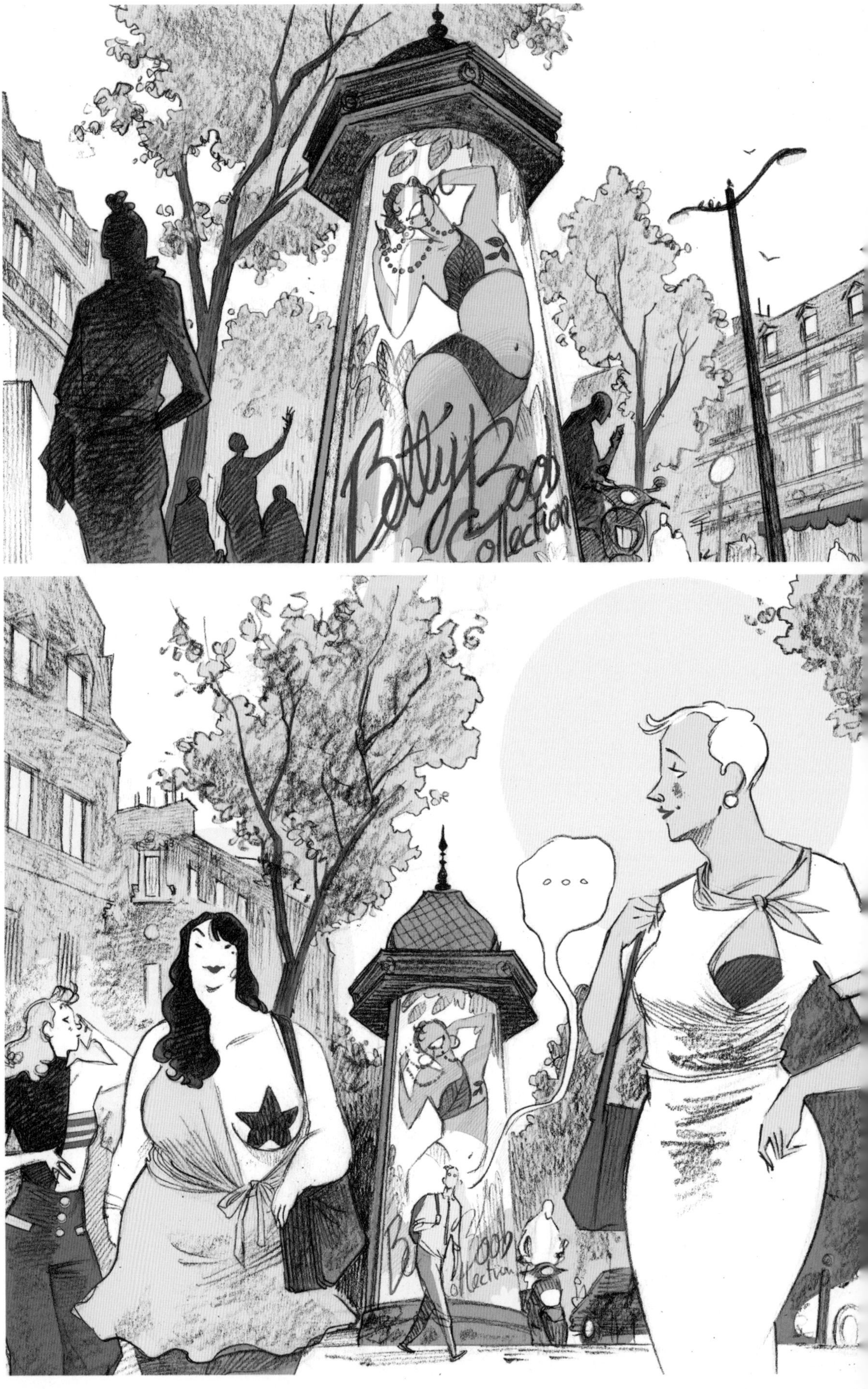
Betty Boob
Collection
...

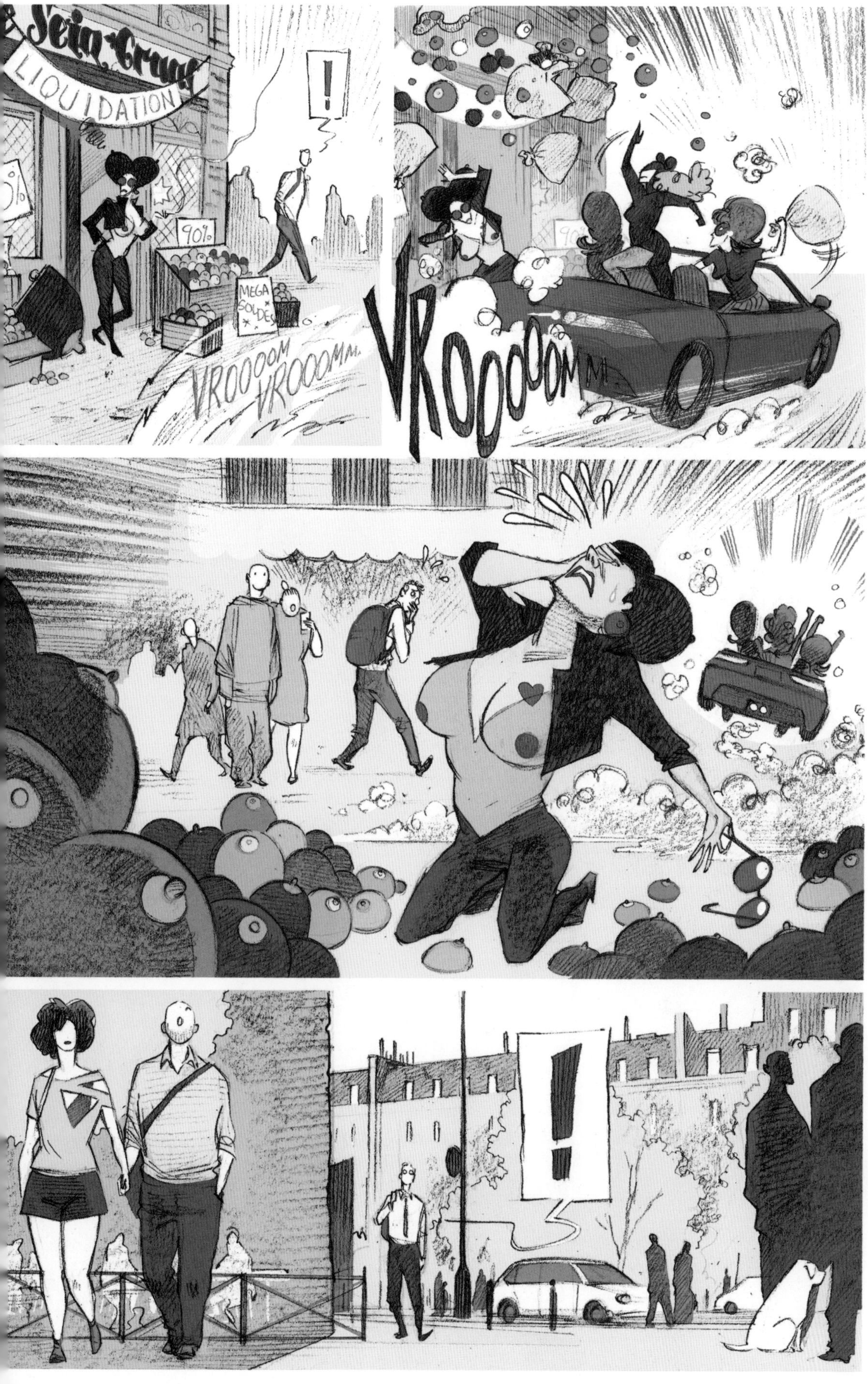
LIQUIDATION
90%
MEGA SOLDES
!
VROOOOOM VROOOMM..
VROOOOOMM!
!

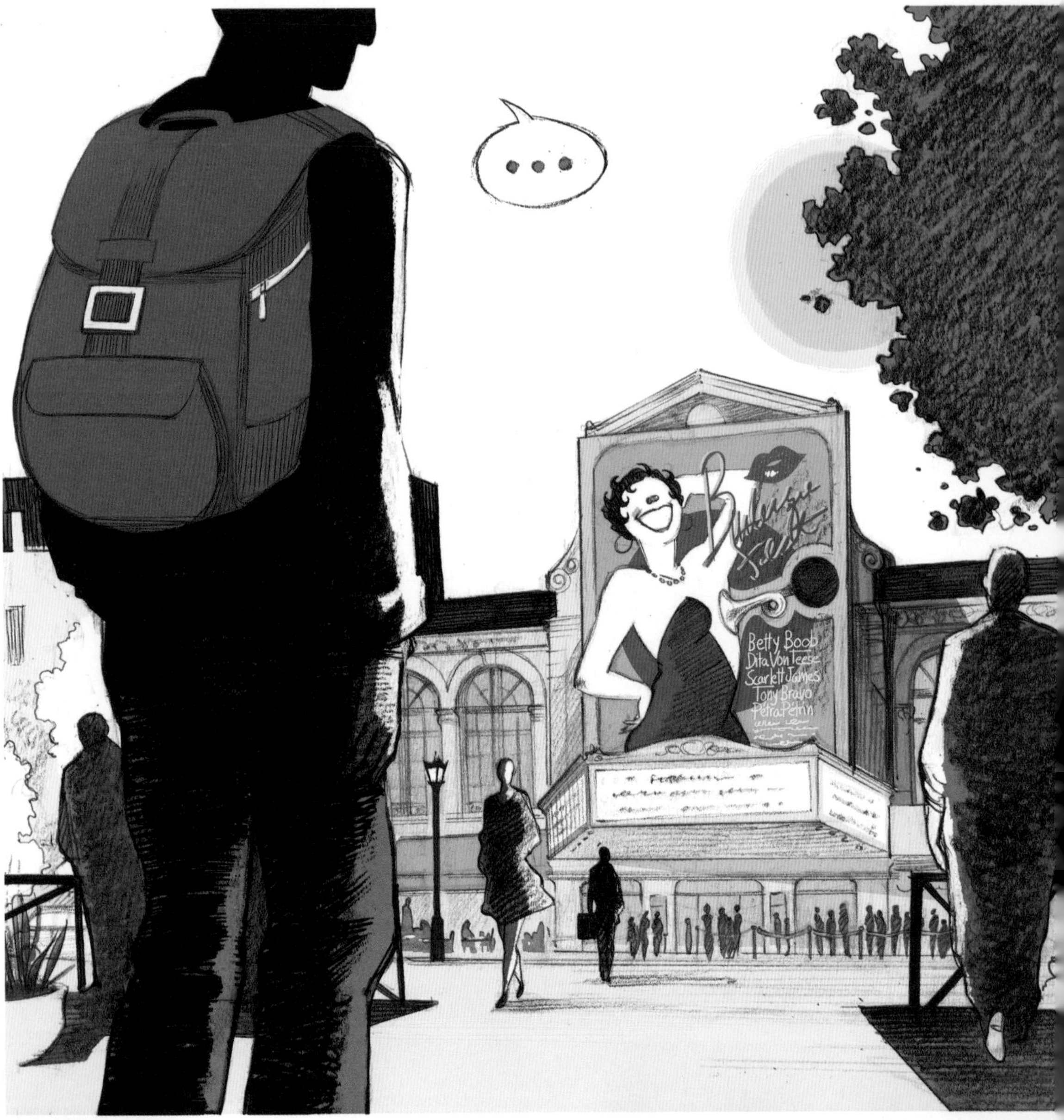
...
Betty Boob
Dita Von Teese
Scarlett James
Tony Bravo
Pétra Pétrin

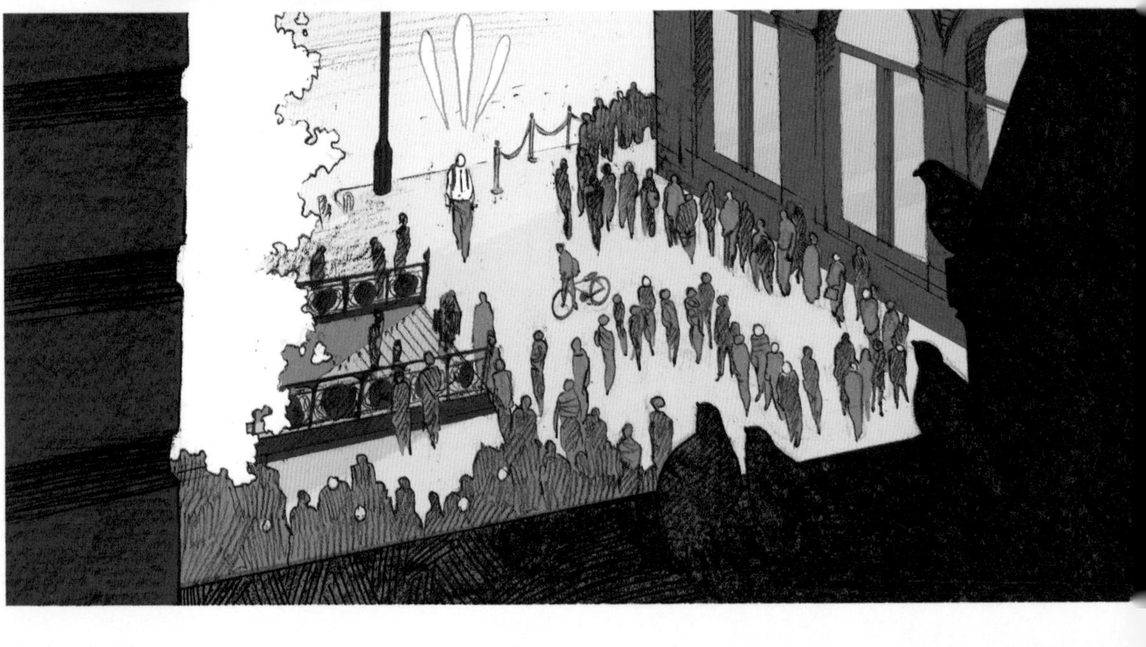

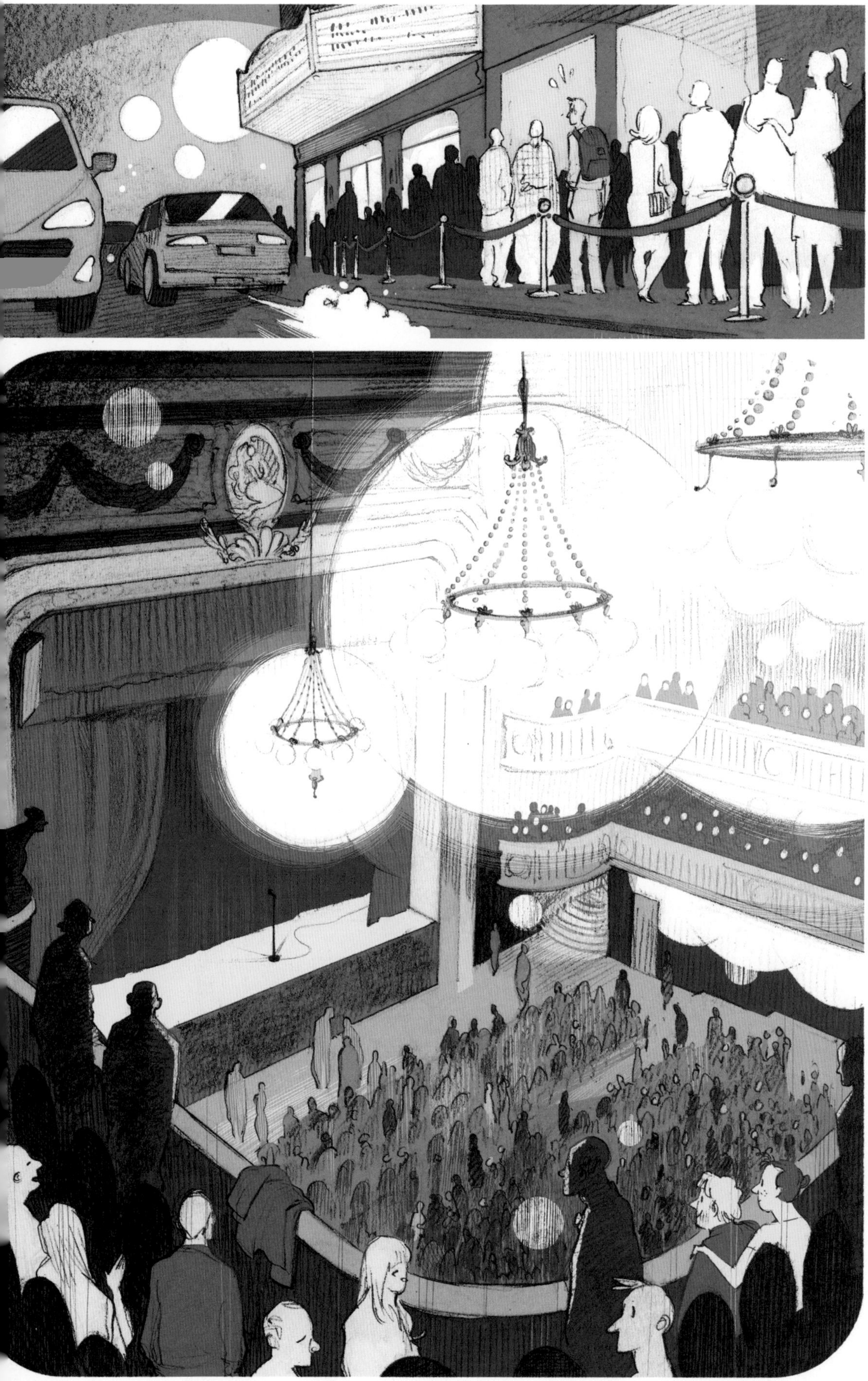

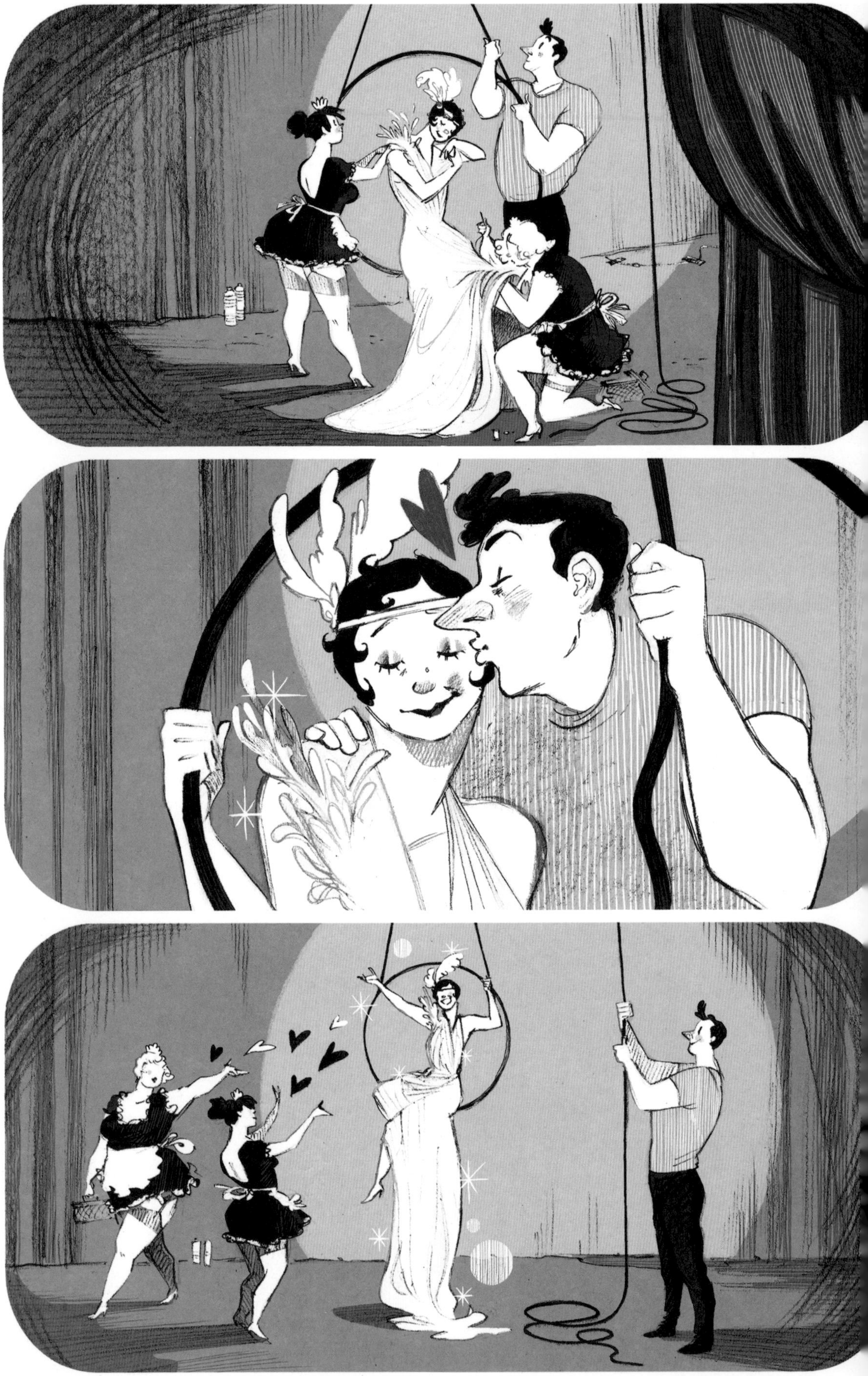

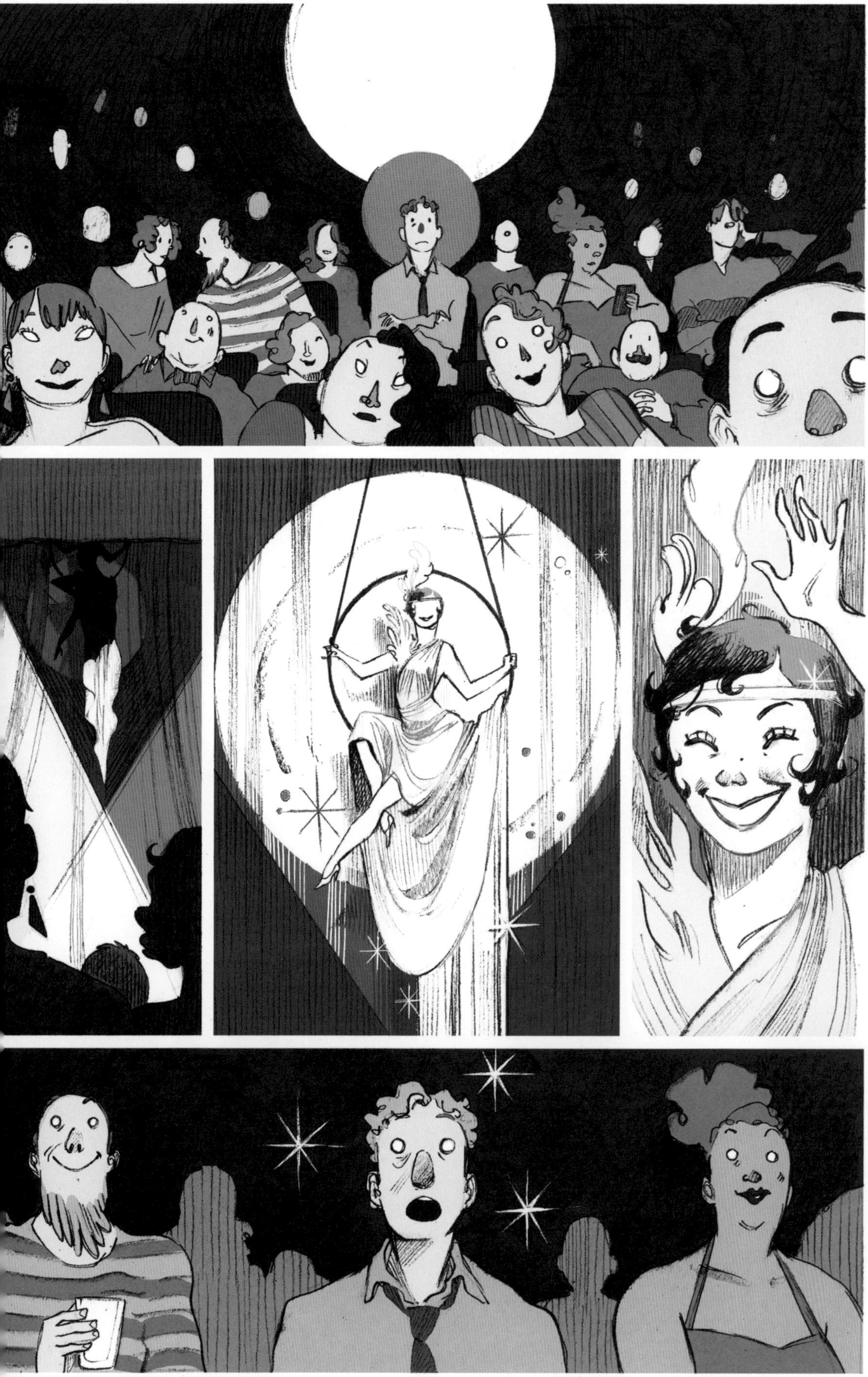

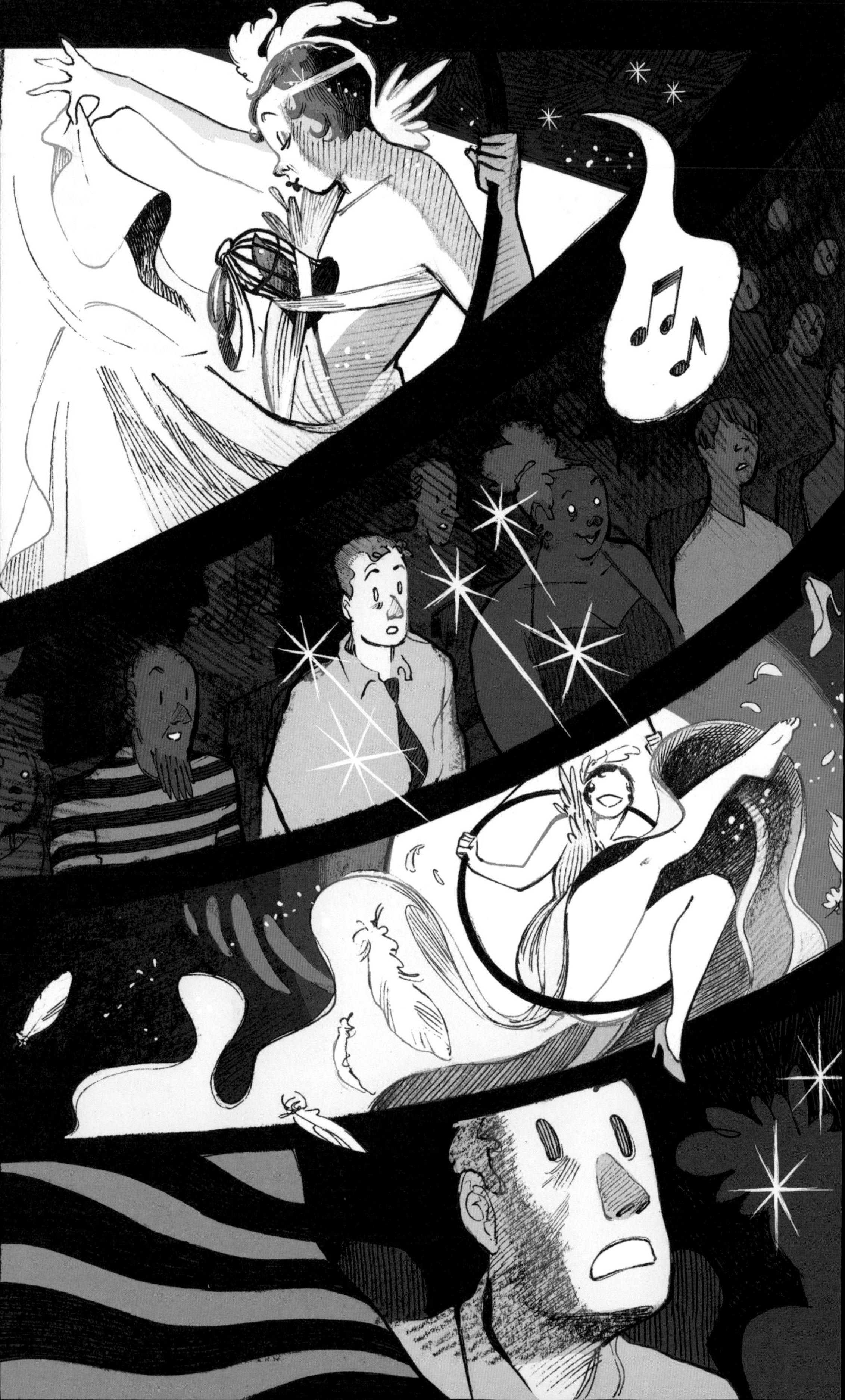

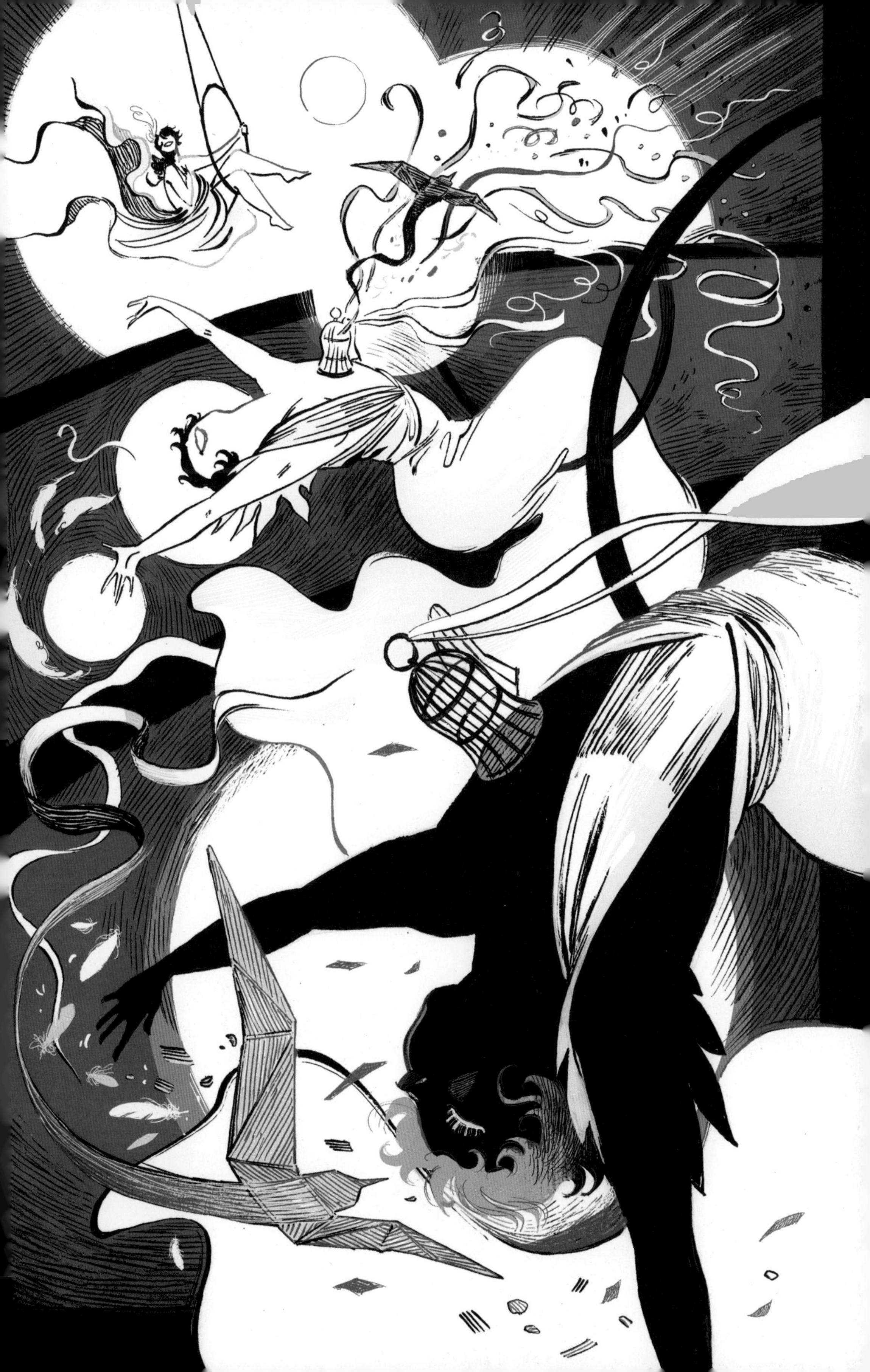

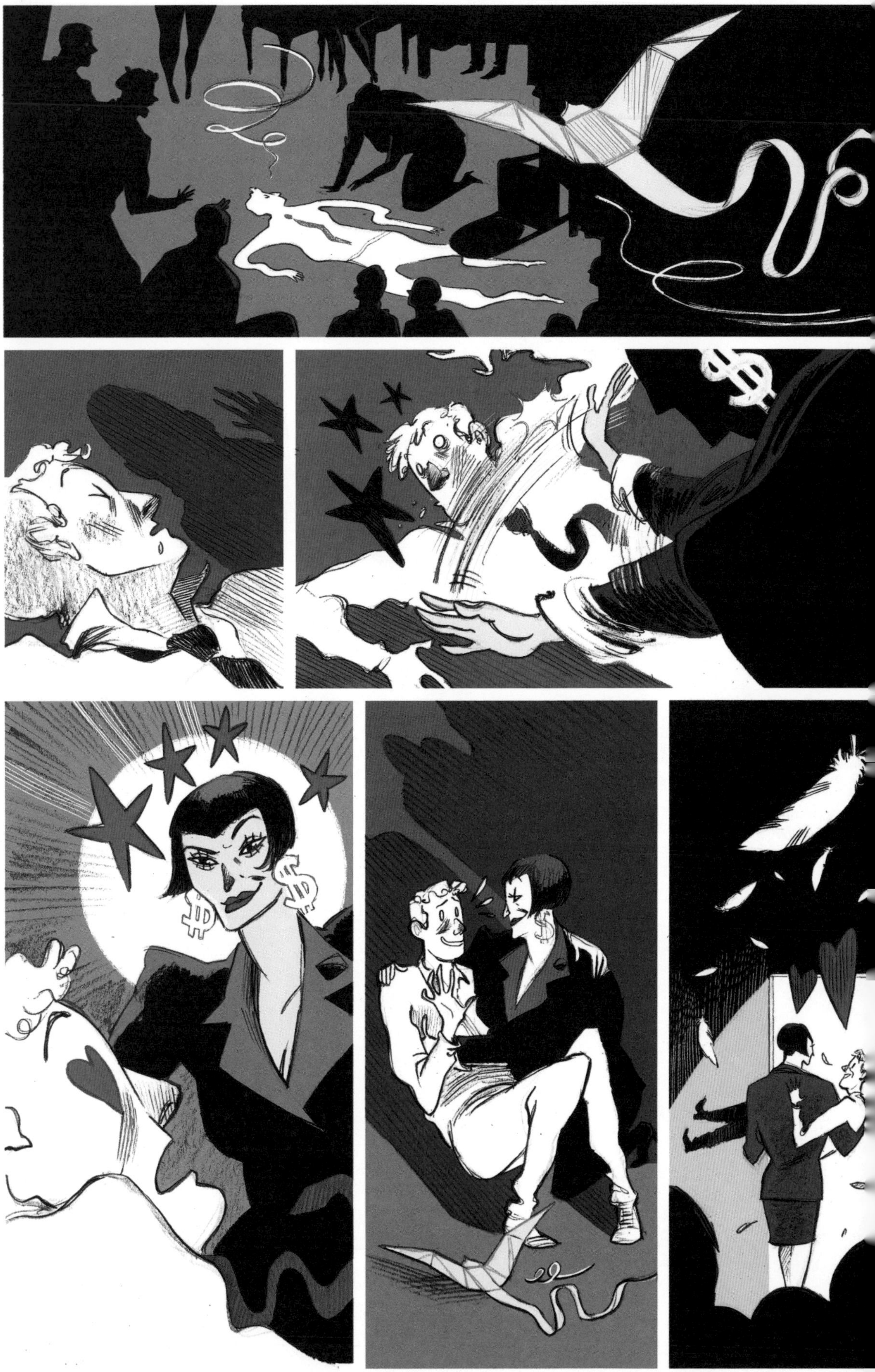

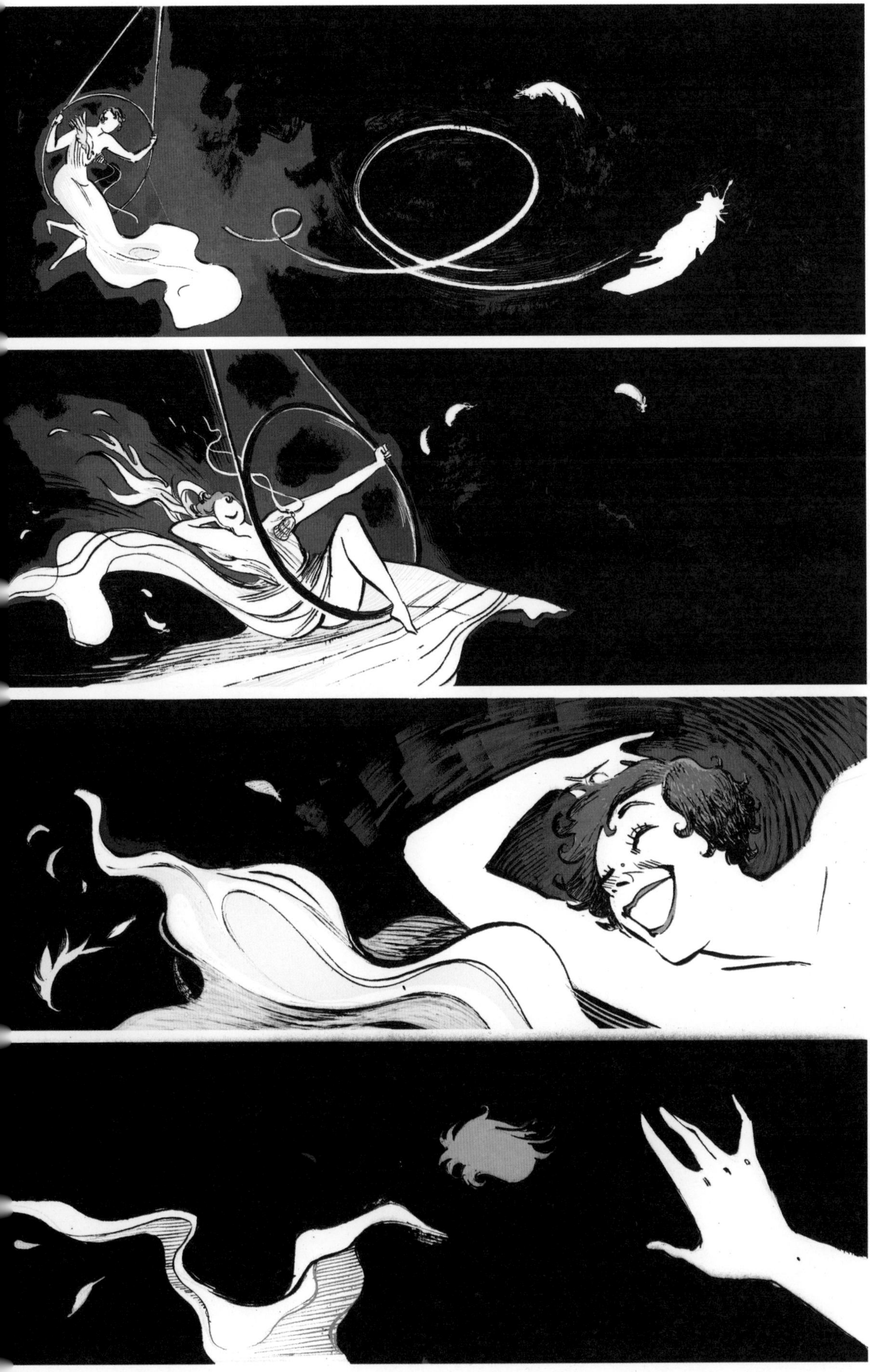

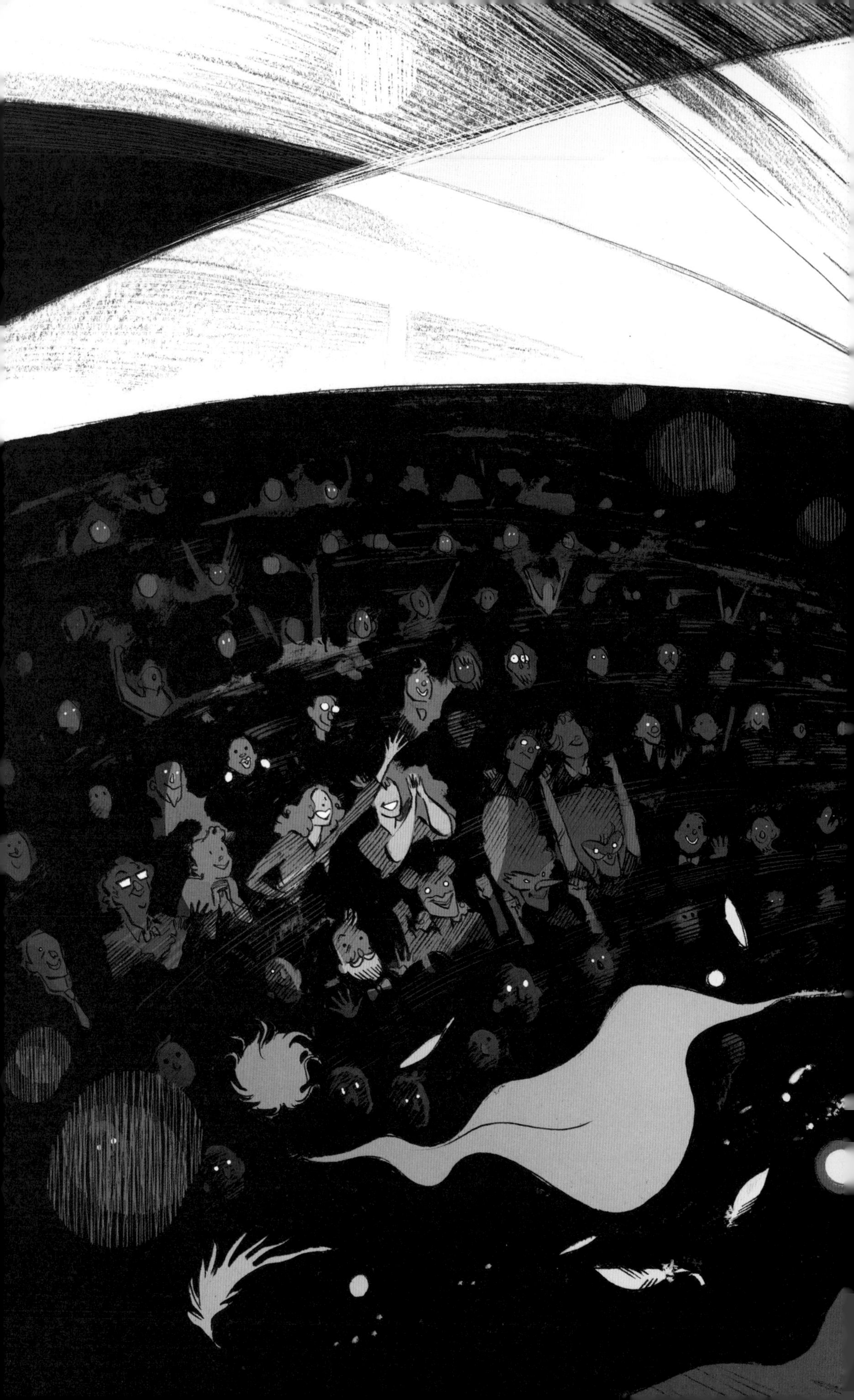

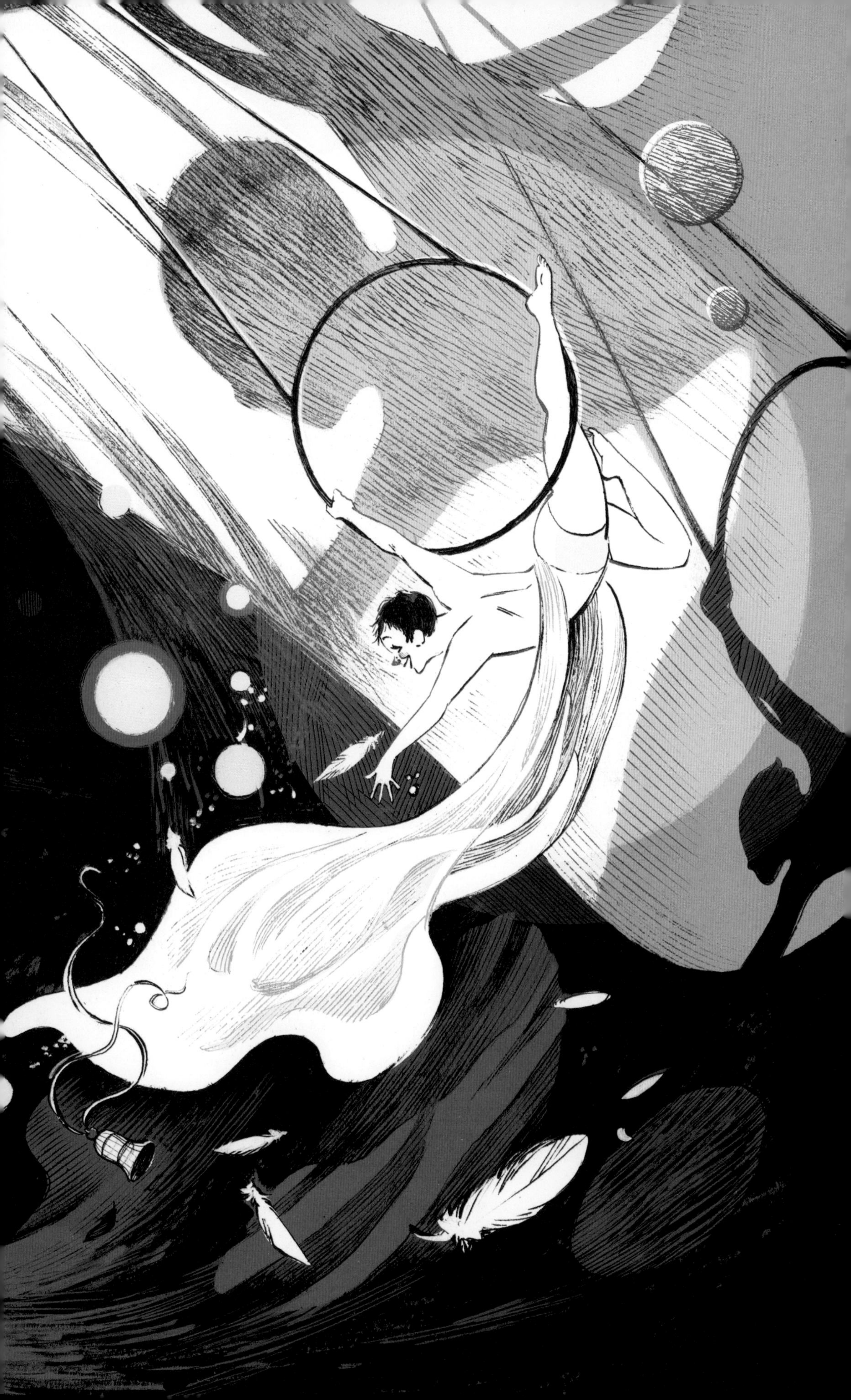

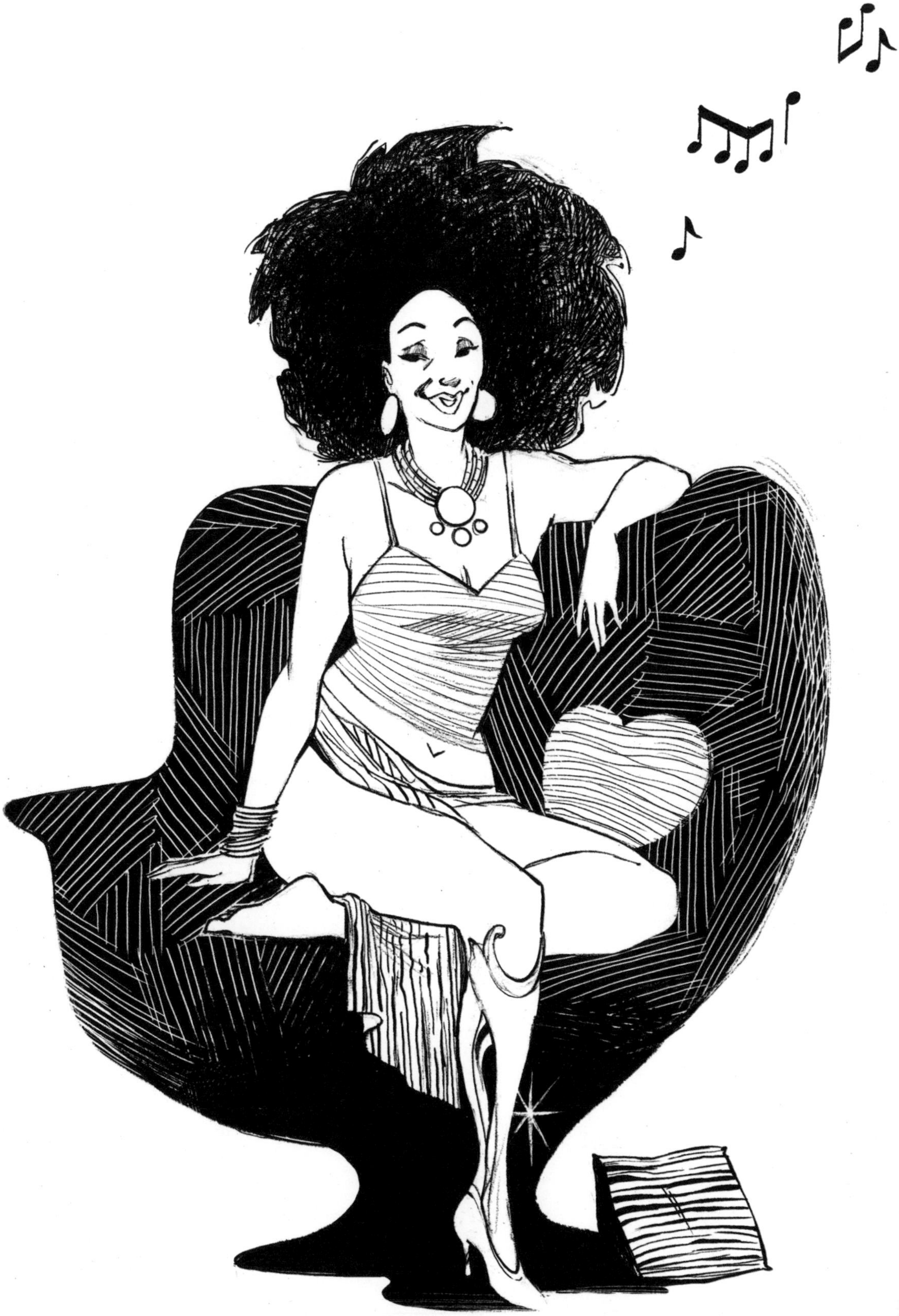

Long Jane's Song
In All My States

It's our very first date
And I'm in such a state
All your eyes on me, bright,
Your arms open tonight

Down my tongue runs a shiver
And my ears are aquiver
My gaze start to glisten
And my inner thighs, moisten

I've got hands that are naughty
And lips that are pouty
Oh, just one look at you
My body doesn't know what to do

My mouth starts to water
And my heart's all aflutter
A flush on my face
Thoughts all over the place

My lips gently part
And my nipples are pert
Just one look at you
My body sounds the alert

It's our very first date
And I'm in such a state
All your gazes on me, bright,
with your arms open tonight

My love button's poking
its head out for stroking
Got ants in my pants
and I'm antsy to dance

I'm open for business
From my head to my prosthesis
Ladybits fit to spout
Tip me o'er, pour me out

It's our very first date
And I'm in such a state
All your gazes on me, bright,
with your arms open tonight

Author: Vero Cazot
Composer: Mr. Meuble

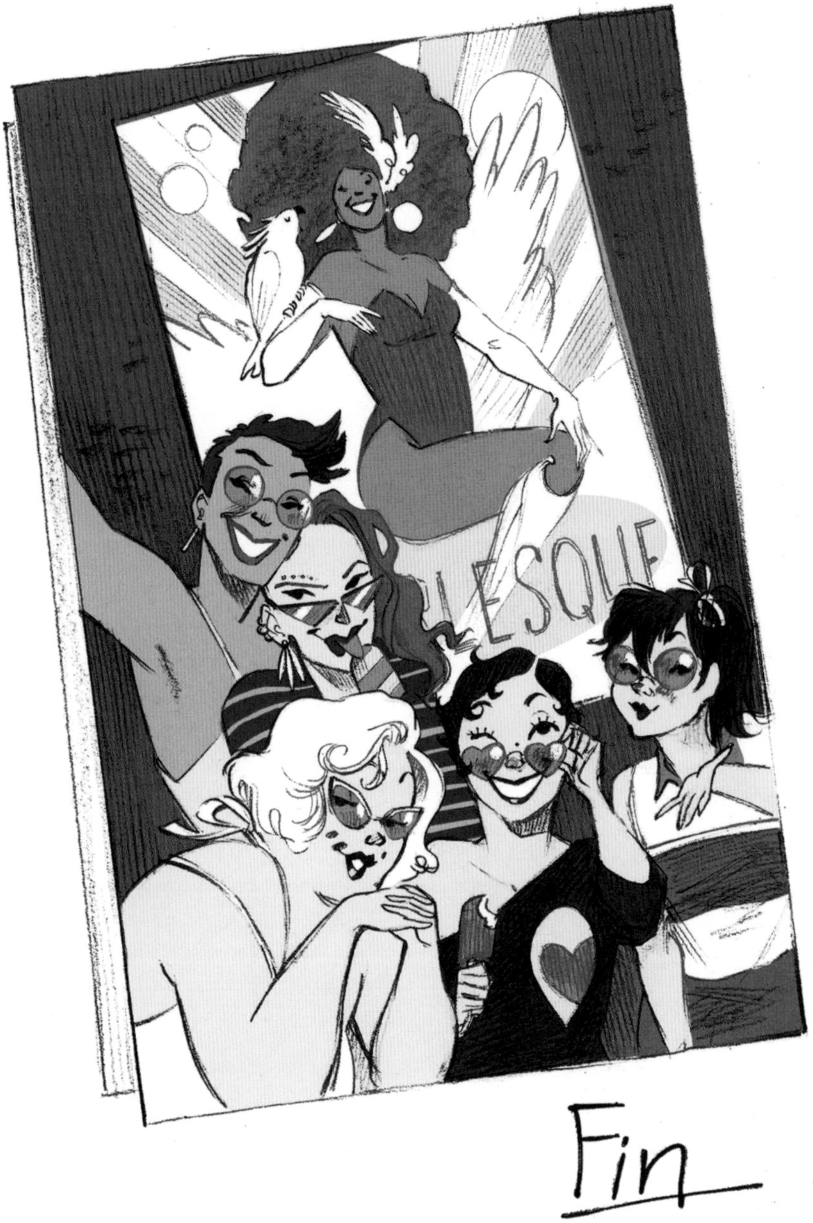
LESQUE

Fin

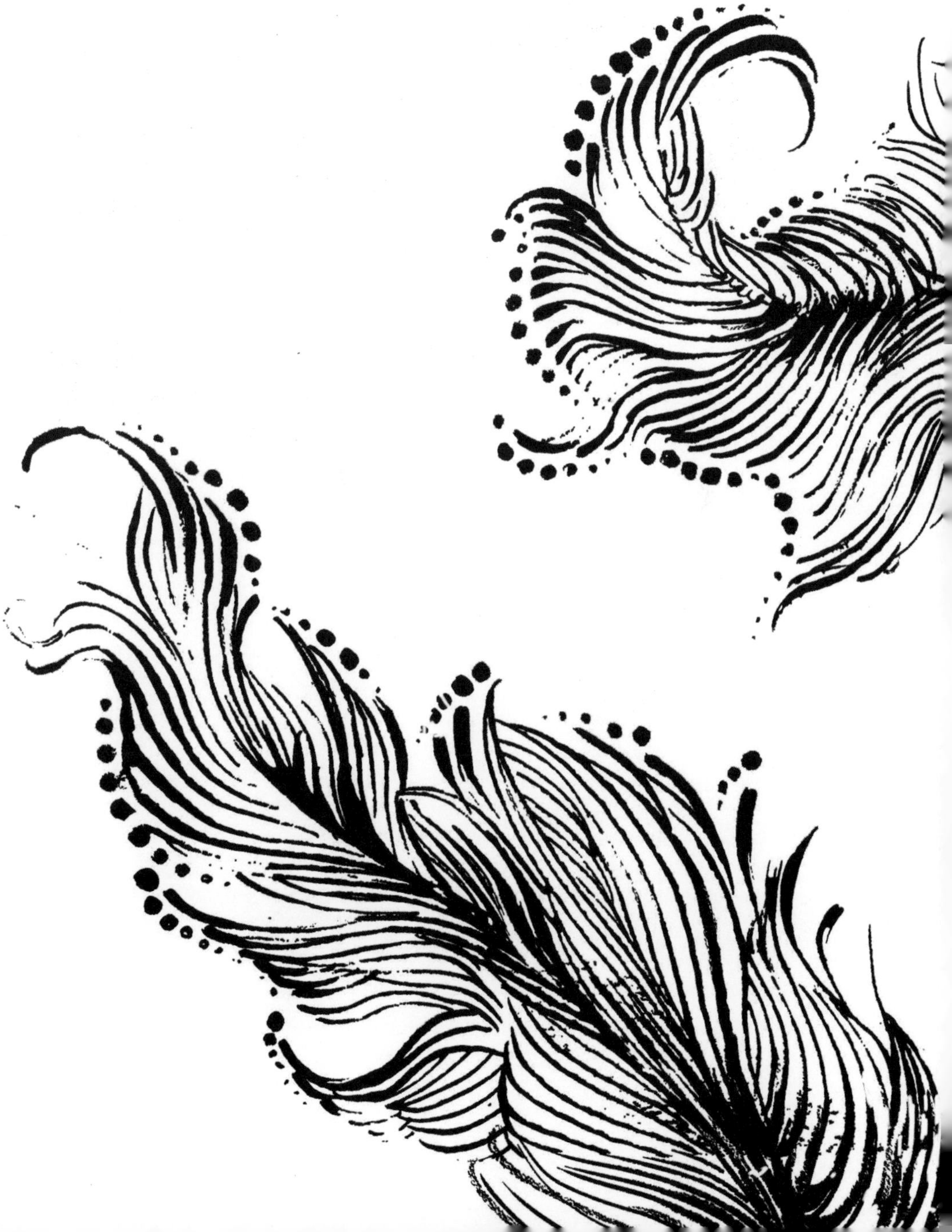

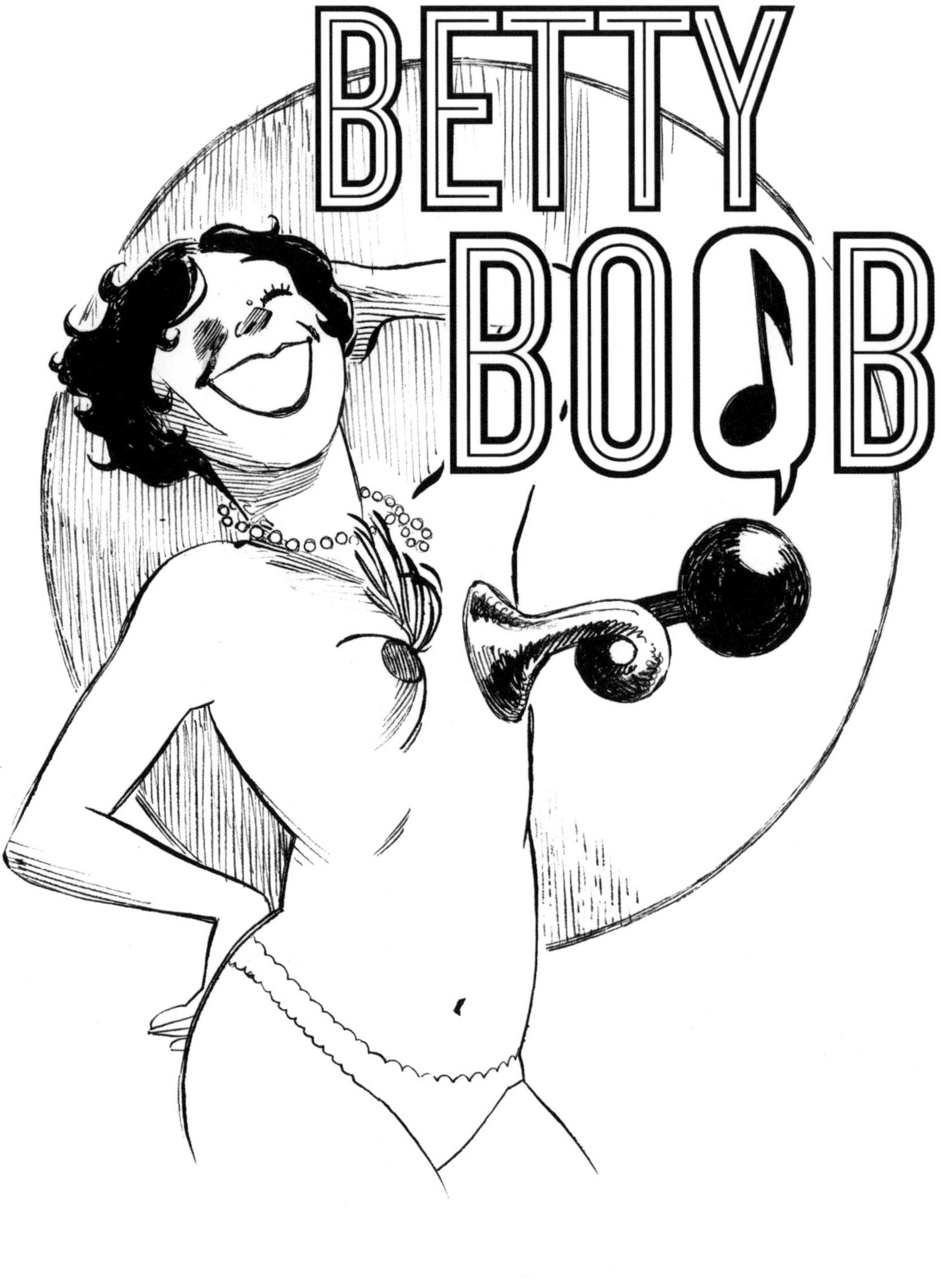
BETTY
BOOB

Not a strong conversationalist, **Vero Cazot** had to learn at an early age to use a pen, and then a keyboard, to write all types of things: love letters, cover letters, commercials, comedy sketches for a one-woman show, film, and television scripts. But now, she flourishes in comics writing. As the author of the humorous series *Et toi, quand est-ce que tu t'y mets? (So, When Will You Have a Baby?)* with artist Madeleine Martin, she continues her gift of combining humor and life with *About Betty's Boob,* created with illustrator Julie Rocheleau.

Montreal illustrator **Julie Rocheleau** took her first steps into comics in 2010 with *The Invisible Girl,* written by Émilie Villeneuve. The two storytellers went on to win a Bédais Causa from the Quebec Francophone Comics Festival. The same year, Julie received the Joe Shuster Award for Best Colorist, and was nominated for Best Designer. Along with *About Betty's Boob,* her comics adventures continue with the series *The Wrath of Fantômas* with Olivier Bocquet and *La Petite Patrie (The Little Homeland)* with Normand Grégoire.

DISCOVER
GROUNDBREAKING TITLES

ASAF HANUKA
THE
REALIST

LONG WALK TO VALHALLA
ADAM SMITH MATTHEW FOX

THE MARCH OF THE CRABS
THE CRABBY CONDITION
ARTHUR DE PINS

Jane
ALINE BROSH McKENNA
RAMÓN K. PÉREZ

ROYDEN LEPP
RUST
VOLUME ONE
VISITOR IN THE FIELD

MOUSE GUARD
THE BLACK AXE
DAVID PETERSEN

The Realist
Asaf Hanuka
ISBN: 978-1-60886-688-5 | $24.99 US

The Realist: Plug and Play
Asaf Hanuka
ISBN: 978-1-60886-953-4 | $24.99 US

Long Walk to Valhalla
Adam Smith, Matt Fox
ISBN: 978-1-60886-692-2 | $24.99 US

The March of The Crabs
Arthur De Pins
Volume 1: The Crabby Condition
ISBN: 978-1-60886-689-2 | $19.99 US
Volume 2: The Empire of the Crabs
ISBN: 978-1-68415-014-4 | $19.99 US

Jane
Aline Brosh McKenna, Ramón K. Pérez
ISBN: 978-1-60886-981-7 | $24.99 US

Rust
Royden Lepp
Volume 0: The Boy Soldier
ISBN: 978-1-60886-806-3 | $10.99 US
Volume 1: Visitor in the Field
ISBN: 978-1-60886-894-0 | $14.99 US
Volume 2: Secrets of the Cell
ISBN: 978-1-60886-895-7 | $14.99 US

Mouse Guard
David Petersen
Mouse Guard: Fall 1152
ISBN: 978-1-93238-657-8 | $24.95 US
Mouse Guard: Winter 1152
ISBN: 978-1-93238-674-5 | $24.95 US
Mouse Guard: The Black Axe
ISBN: 978-1-93639-306-0 | $24.95 US

The Cloud
K.I. Zachopoulos, Vincenzo Balzano
ISBN: 978-1-60886-725-7 | $24.99 US

Cursed Pirate Girl Coloring Book
Jeremy A. Bastian
ISBN: 978-1-60886-947-3 | $16.99 US

ARCHAIA™

AVAILABLE AT YOUR LOCAL COMICS SHOP AND BOOKSTORE
To find a comics shop in your area, call 1-888-266-4226
WWW.**BOOM-STUDIOS**.COM

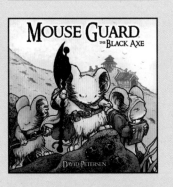